Democratic Criticism

POETICS OF INCITEMENT AND THE MUSLIM SACRED

Masood Ashraf Raja

LEVER
PRESS

Lever Press (leverpress.org) is a publisher of pathbreaking scholarship. Supported by a consortium of higher education institutions focused on, and renowned for, excellence in both research and teaching, our press is grounded on three essential commitments: to be a digitally native press, to be a peer-reviewed, open access press that charges no fees to either authors or their institutions, and to be a press aligned with the liberal arts ethos.

DOI: https://doi.org/10.3998/mpub.12682261
Print ISBN: 978-1-64315-045-1
Open access ISBN: 978-1-64315-046-8
Library of Congress Control Number: 2022947922

Published in the United States of America by Lever Press, in partnership with Michigan Publishing.

*For my parents, Raja Muhammad Ashraf
and Zain-ul-Arab Raja. May they rest in peace!*

Contents

Member Institution Acknowledgments

Lever Press is a joint venture. This work was made possible by the generous support of Lever Press member libraries from the following institutions:

Amherst College
Berea College
Bowdoin College
Carleton College
Central Washington University
Claremont Graduate
   University
Claremont McKenna College
Clark Atlanta University
College of Saint Benedict &
   Saint John's University
The College of Wooster
Davidson College
Denison University
DePauw University
Grinnell College
Hamilton College
Harvey Mudd College
Hollins University

Iowa State University
Keck Graduate Institute
Knox College
Lafayette College
Macalester College
Middlebury College
Morehouse College
Norwich University
Penn State University
Pitzer College
Pomona College
Randolph-Macon College
Rollins College
Santa Clara University
Scripps College
Skidmore College
Smith College
Spelman College
Susquehanna University

Swarthmore College
Trinity University
UCLA Library
Union College
University of Idaho
University of Northern
    Colorado
University of Puget Sound
University of San Francisco
University of Vermont

Ursinus College
Vassar College
Washington and Lee
    University
Whitman College
Whittier College
Whitworth University
Willamette University
Williams College

Acknowledgments

I owe a debt of gratitude to my parents for their love and for giving me a great start in my life through access to the best possible education. I must also thank all my teachers—Pakistani and American—who taught me to think critically and to write with compassion and love.

Thanks are also due to my brother, Naeem Raja, and my sister, Najma Tariq, for always believing in me.

This book, like all my other projects, would not have materialized without the constant love and support of my wife, Jenny Caneen-Raja. Many thanks to Jenny for always listening to my bizarre and often convoluted ideas about the world and for always believing in me.

Many thanks also to Andrew Smith and Andrew Tolle, my two dear friends, who helped in copyediting the manuscript.

Most of the ideas presented in this book were first discussed with my students in various classes and I, therefore, owe a great deal to my students for always asking me the most interesting questions and for being patient with the intellectual ramblings during my classes.

INTRODUCTION

I first read Salman Rushdie's *The Satanic Verses* while deployed at a military post in the northern areas of Pakistan. I was an infantry officer then, and though I was an avid reader, I was never really trained to read as a scholar of literature. My interest in the book was certainly piqued by the controversy that surrounded it immediately after its publication. I do not remember much of what I thought of the book or what I understood from my reading, but what I do remember clearly is that the content of the book and some specific representations of early Islam and the figure of the Prophet were deeply troubling and hurtful to me as a practicing Muslim. Of course, I had no training in critical reading and no capacity to read the novel from a Western liberal perspective—all I had were the very givens of the specific meaning-making processes that guided my reading, my understanding, and my experiencing of the text. This book, therefore, is a long overdue journey back into my own development as a reader of literary texts and also a sort of exhortation to my American students and colleagues and my Muslim brothers and sisters to develop modes of reading that go beyond the very givens of our lives. My hope is to develop a mode of reading and understanding that does not rely on a binary structure and that does not privilege only one mode of receiving and writing about literary texts, especially those texts that are transgressive and push against the normalized boundaries of culture and religion.

Thus, the so-called Rushdie Affair is a sort of a beginning point for my project, even though my discussion will go far beyond that and will also sometimes delve into the texts that preceded the arrival of a novel called *The Satanic Verses*.

"Why write this book?" This is the question that Fanon asks in the beginning of his first book, *Black Skin, White Masks*. And since, in terms of my personal growth as a scholar, I owe so much to Fanon's vision, I dare cite him here. Fanon always gives me a space to speak from and a voice to emulate, and he sometimes puts me in touch with a positive rage against those who have already bought and sold our dreams and turned this world into one of nightmare and anguish. They don't read such books. Yes, those masters of the universe who, in Ngugi wa Thiong'o's words, "build Hell for the people on earth" (13). So, yes, to Fanon:

> Why write this book? No one has asked me for it.
> Especially those to whom it is directed.
> Well, well, I reply quite calmly that there are too many idiots in this world.
> And having said it, I have the burden of proving it. (7)

Thus, in a truly Fanonian sense, this book is for all of us who read and teach literature, which is, I admit, a sort of a quixotic pursuit within the instrumental logic of neoliberal capital. As for the "idiots," they don't read such books. But let us just say that some of us do teach literature for a living and read it for pleasure or for learning. If you read literature, this book is meant for you. As far as the "idiots" are concerned, this book will have no effect on them.

I always return to early Fanon, still capable of imagining a path "toward a new humanism" (7), a Fanon who could conclude his book with a hopeful whisper: "I want the world to recognize, with me, the open door of every consciousness" (232). This Fanon, or should I say *my Fanon*, attempts to go beyond the pulls and pressures of a reductive, binaristic world of victims and oppressors, colonizers and colonized, Black and white—that is, *beyond the paradigmatic hierarchy of signification toward the syntagmatic democracy of the semiotic chain.* But many of us know that while we attempt to democratize the sign across a linear plane, the hierarchy of its differences with other signs—stabilized through binaries—is unavoidable, for other signs keep inserting themselves into the neat linearity of our expressions. We must account for these hybrid, intrusive, menacing presences that we keep at bay to create our neat and convincing readings of literary texts. In other words, we must practice *democratic criticism.*

What do I mean by *democratic criticism*? The term comes from Edward Said. Briefly stated, when I invoke the term *democratic criticism*, I do so to refer to a sort of criticism that carries the trace of Others in our reading practices. This is not a very revolutionary idea. It is for that reason that I must, first, pay tribute to those who have theorized and discussed this so-called revolutionary idea long before me. How else can I speak meaningfully if I do not account for those who have spoken before me, often more eloquently? Indeed, can there be anything more eloquent than Fanon's last whisper, his expression of a wish, a hope at the end of his first book?

So, an account of my predecessors first, for without them I would not have this space, this platform to stand on, to erect my edifice of self and to structure my authorial practice. They are the props that enable me to stand upright and speak. My account, however, cannot be exhaustive and all-inclusive; I will be selective, then, and the selection, of course, is guided by my own prejudices. I start with Edward Said.

From the beginning of his career, Said was deeply concerned with the question of the Other and always advocated for a complex form of reading, a reading that incorporated the Other without effacing difference. "Contrapuntal reading" is Said's term for this. In a contrapuntal mode of reading, Said argues, "we look back at the cultural archive" and read it "with a simultaneous awareness both of the metropolitan history . . . and of those other histories against which . . . the dominant discourse acts" (*Culture* 51). What Said had hoped, then, was that modes of critical reading in the metropole will become more complex and construct a reader capable of looking at a narrative not just with a more complex and inclusive historical knowledge but with the possibility of inhabiting different subjectivities. The idea, as far as I understand it, was not just to develop a diverse repertoire of critical strategies but to overload dominant Western modes of reading with a knowledge, an understanding, and maybe some sympathy for "resistance and . . . native nationalism" (51). In other words, Said urges us to read a novel, or any other narrative, not just with the worldview and tools of the metropolitan[1] but with the tools of the colonized native as well, if that is at all possible. An impossible project, perhaps, for it is a challenge to localized immanence and relies quite heavily on a hope for a transcendent mode of criticism. But Said, throughout his career, never abandons this emphasis on inserting the silenced histories and cultural traces that shape and stabilize Western self-perception and self-presentation.

In Said's posthumously published *Humanism and Democratic Criticism*, his final word from beyond, he returns to his beginnings as a humanist philologist. In another way, this book also presents to readers a Said who looks back at his own legacy and with whom early Frantz Fanon would have been very comfortable. What does Said mean by democratic criticism? A good question to start: more importantly, how does it enable, augment, or enhance the project of this book? In the introduction to the book, Said provides a brief explanation of what he means by "humanism"—a problematic term itself—as well as its efficacy for critics: "What concerns me is humanism as a useable praxis for intellectuals and academics who want to know what they are doing, what they are committed to as scholars, and who also want to connect these principles to the world in which they live as citizens" (*Humanism* 6).

Said's humanistic critics, therefore, must inhabit a layered subjectivity and see humanism and humanistic pursuits as a matter of praxis and not just as detached academic exercises; they must also be self-reflexive of their own positions, and, most importantly, they must also understand the value and impact of their critical stances on the world in which they are "citizens." The practice of humanism is not related to being *human* but instead a practice for becoming a *citizen of the world.* A humanist must therefore at least attempt to inhabit the subjectivity of a world citizen and not necessarily a citizen of one or another nation-state. Humanism, in such a scenario, is a cosmopolitan practice beyond the pushes and pulls of any particular nation-state and, if I may add, the dictates of one's primary culture. Such a criticism would thus become democratic by attempting to defy immanence and hope to write itself from a place of transcendence.

Of course, *transcendence*, just like humanism, is also a problematic term; is it at all possible to transcend the very givens of one's life and culture? Within the American context, some stalwarts of theories of justice and cosmopolitanism have decidedly opposed any such possibilities of transcendence. Even John Rawls, according to Kok-Chor Tan, "expressed a reluctance to endorse the cosmopolitan approach in his . . . writings on international justice" (9) and thus confined his thought only to subjects of a nation and their obligations to each other. Building on Rawls's emphasis concerning the question of justice within a national space, Richard Rorty provides an important and interesting discussion about the nature of justice and transcendence. Positing justice and loyalty as two competing registers, Rorty offers a rereading of Rawls through the concept of cosmopolitanism in a book chapter entitled "Justice as a Larger Loyalty." The crux of Rorty's argument, at least in the beginning of the chapter, is that the way we view justice and our responsibility to others is relative to our own existential conditions. Thus, within such a logic, "sharing food with impoverished people down the street is natural and right in normal circumstances, but perhaps not in a famine, when doing so amounts to disloyalty to one's family" (45). This idea of justice and lateral solidarity is suited only for the best of times and under the best of conditions, and only to share one's spare change, so to speak. There is no humanistic or Christian drive behind it. In other words, this logic can also very conveniently be employed to underwrite our own privilege by assuming that all we can be responsible for is ourselves and if, like the self-maximizers of neoliberalism, every individual took care of their own, the world would not need any lateral solidarities. In discussing Rawls's emphasis on justice, Rorty uses Rawls's instructive term "reasonable people" (51). According to Rorty, Rawls suggests that for inclusion into the larger project of Western liberalism as equals, various societies must possess certain attributes that qualify them as "reasonable people." Unsurprisingly, Rorty's entire argument becomes, toward the end of the chapter, yet another argument for Western superiority. He asserts that this "superiority" should be claimed in a consequentialist argument rather than as a matter of a priori truths. Here is what he asserts about how to convince "irrational peoples" into becoming more like their "superior" Western counterparts:

> It would be better to say: "Here is what we in the West look like as a result of ceasing to hold slaves, beginning to educate women, separating church and state, and so on. Here is what happened after we started treating certain distinctions between people as arbitrary rather than fraught with moral significance. If you try treating them that way, you might like the results." (56)

So, the basic supposition remains the same. The West certainly has a lot to teach the non-Western world; only the didactics of paternalistic teaching must now be fine-tuned. In the end, then, the top-down didactic role of the West remains undisputed, and only the efficacy of *how* to teach these lessons is worthy of questioning so that the West can "approach the non-West in the role of someone with an instructive story to tell" (56). Needless to say, in this discussion of the rights of the people, the non-West is automatically offered as the abode of the categorically irrational who require instruction. Sadly, Western literary critics quite easily internalize this approach. The nonrationality of Islamic metaphysics in terms of experiencing texts thus automatically falls into the realm of the irrational, retrievable only through the purifying panacea of Western reason. This is where this book intends to intervene: to attempt to open this space and show Western literary critics that there can and should be more than one way of reading texts, ways beyond predominantly Western modes of reading. This book also aims to reveal to Western critics the ways to understand Muslim responses to Western representations of their culture. For such understanding to occur, the modes of reading must first be invoked, discussed, taught, and incorporated in our repertoire of theory.

Rorty's approach can also be articulated as "the aerial global view" (Robbins 4) that permits metropolitan scholars to "see" their global Others only through a vision enabled and underwritten by their unconscious investment in the absolute superiority of their primary cultures. In such an approach, the non-West can only find a respectable place within the metropolitan space through its degree of Western-ness: the more Western, the more respectable. The purpose of my inquiry is to force this issue to a point where Western intellectuals cannot judge their non-Western counterparts from the safety of their own "living room" (4) without sounding, at the least, ill-informed. While Rorty deals with the Other as an abstract non-West and places the West in a hierarchical, pedagogical position, the polemical strain of writing in the United States chooses political Islam as its target and offers Western remedies for Islam as apodictic truths. For example, writing in the wake of the Rushdie Affair, Daniel Pipes suggests, "Only if Muslims [living in the West] accept secularism can they fully integrate into society" (247). And while Pipes does acknowledge that Muslims living in the West do have a right to practice their religion, he also asserts that the only way Muslims can be accepted in the West is if they cohere to the general consensus about "civilized" life in the West.

Thus, overall, Muslims living in the West are perpetually suspect, and now, post-9/11, a constant threat. In all these pronouncements about Muslims and Islam, neoconservatives offer no nuanced discussion of any of the aspects of neoliberal capital and US adventurism in the Muslim world as complicit in the advent of Islamic fundamentalism.

In fact, post-9/11 writings originating from the American right have become increasingly self-righteous and unsophisticated.[2] Anti-Muslim sentiments can now be openly expressed in mainstream political speeches, and works by conservative scholars usually contain obvious biases against all things Muslim and Islamic.

The transcendent mode of reading, as impossible as it might sound, is not only desirable but also necessary in today's world, where many are returning to the tropes of culture and national identity that had previously been put to rest: hypernationalism, various ethnic nationalisms, sectarian and religious identities, and the rise of racially defined political groups. The perceptions of Islam in the West and of the West in the Islamic world have reached new lows. According to a recent survey by Zogby Analytics:

> 42 percent of Americans believe law enforcement is justified in using profiling tactics against Muslim-Americans and Arab-Americans. The survey also shows American attitudes toward Arab-Americans and Muslim-Americans have turned for the worse since the Arab American Institute first began polling on the subject in 2010. The new poll found favorability toward Arab-Americans at 36 percent, down from 43 percent in 2010. For Muslim-Americans, favorability was just 27 percent, compared with 36 percent in 2010. (Siddiqui)

On the other side of the divide, "Pew polls find that less than half the populations in five Middle Eastern Countries have a favorable opinion of the United States" (Shannon 2). Thus, on both sides of the global division of labor, distrust of the Other is reciprocal.

Reading literary texts about Islam and the Islamic world is, therefore, a test case in how to use literature as a tool for understanding rather than a mechanism for perpetuating stereotypes. This will be my main focus throughout the rest of the book, and I will deal also with what I term the *poetics of incitement*.

POETICS OF INCITEMENT

By *poetics of incitement*, I refer to a specific kind of textual production. Generally speaking, texts employing poetics of incitement are centered on certain core concepts of Islam and attempt to rewrite them according to a purely Eurocentric, secular mode of representation. These texts are usually produced either by diasporic authors with Muslim heritage or by Western authors interested in eliciting an immediate counter-response from the Islamic world. Furthermore, such texts are produced under the general rubric of an author's right to an absolute form of free speech. Such a poetics, by its very intent, is transgressive and attempts to challenge Muslim history, religious beliefs, and the very idea of the Muslim sacred. As a result, the (sometimes violent) Muslim responses to such texts, both material and semiotic, are used by the West as evidence of so-called Muslim intolerance and the general atavistic nature of the Muslim world. These texts, then, being openly opportunistic, help highlight, solidify, and normalize public prejudices about Islam that already permeate the very fiber of metropolitan societies.

There is a certain *secular fundamentalist* criticism in vogue concerning texts about Islam. With the seemingly oxymoronic term *secular fundamentalism*, I do not refer to its usage by the American conservatives who challenge the secular assumptions of the US political and educational systems as forms of secular fundamentalism. I am rather using it as a descriptive term. Thus, I will first explain the two terms[3] separately and then provide my rationale for combining them as one overarching signifier. The Oxford

English Dictionary (OED) defines secularism as "[t]he doctrine that morality should be based solely on regard to the well-being of mankind in the present life, to the exclusion of all consideration drawn from belief in God or in a future state." On the other hand, the OED explains fundamentalism as "[a] religious movement, which orig. became active among various Protestant bodies in the United States after the war of 1914–1918, based on strict adherence to certain tenets (e.g. the literal inerrancy of Scripture) held to be fundamental to the Christian faith." Secular fundamentalism could then be defined as a combination of an extreme interpretation of the two terms: *an absolute denial of any metaphysical sacred* (secular) and an *inerrant faith in the writer's right to represent* (fundamentalism). In such a poetics, the affective value of the text is elided and the reader's right to read and interpret the text according to their own particular meaning-making practices is severely curtailed while authorial intent is overly privileged. There is, thus, a need for a different kind of critical consciousness.

Here, I believe, a brief discussion of Said's explanation of critical consciousness will be useful. While elaborating upon what he means by critical consciousness, Said provides the following insight about the critic's place in the world:

> My position . . . is that the contemporary critical consciousness stands between the temptations represented by two formidable and related powers engaging critical attention. One is the culture to which critics are bound filiatively (by birth, nationality, profession); the other is a method or system acquired affiliatively (by social and political conviction, economic and historical circumstances, voluntary effort and willed deliberation). (*World* 25)

The role of one's filiative and affiliative identity is crucial for the production of any given kind of critical work. Thus, in Said's conception, filiation is *inherently primordial*[4] while affiliation is generated through *learned experience*. For literary critics, affiliation could mean associating one's critical practice with a certain school of thought or critical method. Said also asserts in the same work that at times the critic is so heavily invested in their affiliative practices that their critical work becomes a sort of filiation. Secular criticism, for Said, therefore implies an attempt to transcend the limiting confines of a rigid affiliation with any particular method. Thus, for Said, "the inevitable trajectory of critical consciousness is to arrive at some acute sense of what political, social, and human values are entailed in the reading, production, and transmission of every text" (*World* 26). It is obvious from this brief detour into Said's work that a critical consciousness unwilling to transcend and question its own limitations and that forecloses the lived realities of writing and reading results in the production of a secular fundamentalism diametrically opposed to the idea of secular criticism. Secular fundamentalist criticism is therefore a complete denial of the recognition of the Other, even when the works being interpreted appropriate the Other for artistic representation.

These texts, Said also suggests, "have ways of existing that even in their most rarefied form are always enmeshed in circumstance, time, place, and society—in short, they are in the world, and hence worldly" (35). The privileging of a writer's right to represent over the reader's right to respond according to their own "worldliness" is therefore, at the least, problematic.

Paul Ricoeur, who Said quotes in the above-cited work, deals with the text-reader problematic as follows:

> A written text is addressed to an unknown reader and potentially to whoever knows how to read. . . . Of course this universality is only potential, a book is addressed to only a section of the public and reaches its appropriate readers through media that are themselves submitted to social rules of exclusion and admission. In other words, reading is a social phenomenon and therefore suffers from specific limitations. Nevertheless, the proposition which says that a text is potentially addressed to whoever knows how to read

must be retained as a limit on any sociology of reading. A work also creates its public. . . . To that extent, the recognition of the work by the audience created by the work is an unpredictable event. (31)

The poetics of incitement serves a two-pronged function. First, it addresses itself to a primarily secular, metropolitan audience and expects the text to be read within the normative structure of a largely secular culture. Second, it also exceeds its limits by reaching out to an audience beyond the limits of Western secular modes of reading. It is this larger audience, those in the Islamic world, with its own specific modes of reading and responding to texts, whose voices are silenced in metropolitan debates about texts of incitement. Thus, if "the right of the reader and the right of the text converge in an important struggle that generates the whole dynamic of interpretation" (Ricoeur 32) of texts, then a poetics that silences the interpretive voice of Muslim readers becomes a sort of secular fundamentalism. Any exclusion of the metaphysical explanation of reality central to the meaning-making process of an average Muslim reader is, therefore, openly paternalistic and imperialistic. A sound "sociology of reading" must, therefore, be aware of this problematic.

Thanks to the rise of reception theory and the academic significance of reader-response criticism, the role of the reader in "actualizing" the text is no longer viewed as unimportant. In fact, Said putatively explains the importance of the reader-text nexus through his impressive discussion of worldliness. While responding to Ricoeur's explanation of the process of actualization of the text by the reader,[5] Said amplifies Ricoeur's assertion as follows:

My contention is that worldliness does not come and go; nor is it here and there in the apologetic and soupy way by which we often designate history, a euphemism in such cases for the impossibly vague notion that all things take place in time. Moreover, critics are not merely the alchemical translators of texts into circumstantial reality or worldliness; for they too are subject to and producers of circumstances, which are felt regardless of whatever objectivity the critic's method possesses. (*World* 35)

Said's intervention into Ricoeur's explanation of the critical process, in which the critic actualizes the text into circumstantial reality, grounds both the text and the reader-critic in their worldliness, a sort of reality that constitutes them and which they themselves also constitute. I find it necessary here to revisit Ricoeur, as his intervention into the theory of interpretation is extremely crucial to my overall argument. In his celebrated work *Interpretation Theory: Discourse and the Surplus of Meaning*, Ricoeur provides an extensive discussion of his privileged method of interpretation. Responding critically to structuralist and semiotic assumptions about textual interpretation, Ricoeur grounds his discussion on the other end of syntactic polarity; namely, the predicate instead of the subject of a sentence. While alluding to classical discussions of the problem of truth, Ricoeur retrieves the following working definition of discourse as informed by the "mature works of Plato" (1) and Aristotle's intervention into the debates about the nature of truth: "A noun has a meaning and a verb has, in addition to its meaning, an indication of time. Only their conjunction brings forth a predicative link, which can be called logos, discourse" (2). From here Ricoeur moves on to a brief discussion of the structuralist method and then offers his insightful intervention into the langue versus parole debates of the early structuralist movement by way of differentiating between semiotics and semantics. In Ricoeur's view, while semiotics deals with the "sign" semantics is the science of the "sentence" (7). This implies, as Ricoeur discusses further, that the sentence might be "made up of signs, but is not itself a sign" (7). In other words, Ricoeur suggests, a sentence is "made up of words, but it is not a derivative function of its words" (7). A sentence must, therefore, be read with a higher degree of complexity than just treating it as a simple semiological chain comprised of a syntagmatic series of signs. The emphasis thus must shift to the semantic pole of the divide instead of being placed on the semiotic end of the speech act.

In such a scenario, the text, instead of masquerading as an object without a reference, comes to the reader as already constituted in the world and is read by a reader within the material realities of their own material existence. Thus, if the process of interpretation is grounded in the worldliness of the text and the reader, the mode of interpretation cannot be completely detached from the reader and the reader wrests the right to read the text within the material realities of their own existential, material, and circumstantial realities. The lived experience of the reader, therefore, is essential to the actualization of the text, which forces one to account for the very worldliness of the Muslim reader in the process of interacting with the poetics of incitement. Thus, if a metaphysical explanation of reality is an important part of the critical repertoire of a given reader, then it must find at least an acceptable place, if not a privileged place, in our modes of reading texts—especially texts imbued with the poetics of incitement.

The Muslim response to the poetics of incitement is not just a question of individual readings but rather an act of reading informed by a collective consciousness of the Muslim sacred, a practice that can be safely explained through Stanley Fish's concept of interpretive communities:

> Interpretive communities are made up of those who share interpretive strategies not for reading (in the conventional sense) but for writing texts, for constituting properties and assigning their intentions. In other words these strategies exist prior to the act of reading and therefore determine the shape of what is read rather than, as is usually assumed, the other way around. (182)

What is crucial in this explanation of interpretive communities is an understanding that the modes of reading adopted by a certain community are already shaped, and it is these predetermined modes of interpretation that eventually determine how a text is read. Thus, in further discussion of the concept, Fish can account for the possibility of varied readings. According to Fish, the existence of different interpretive communities explains "the stability of interpretation among different readers (they belong to the same community)" (182), and the differences in interpretation are due to the interpreter belonging to a different interpretive community. In the same essay, Fish also suggests that competing reading communities, while reading texts according to their own interpretive strategies, "boast [of] a repertoire" (182) of these strategies and blame the opposing reading community for being "reductive" or "superficial" (182). Implicit in this explanation of separate reading communities, then, is at least a rudimentary awareness of the practices of the Other, for only such knowledge can bolster one reading community's claims against the reading practices of the Other. In the case of Muslim responses to the poetics of incitement, however, no such knowledge is deemed necessary by metropolitan critics: their experience of such texts is simply foreclosed as atavistic, uncivilized, and irrational, negated by the "superiority" of Western modes of interpretation. Therefore, the question of Muslim responses to the poetics of incitement is also a question of power: the members of secular, metropolitan reading communities expect Muslims to somehow transcend the limitations of their own particular interpretive communities and read texts of incitement immanently from the point of view of their metropolitan counterparts. This, I must assert, is a one-way conversation, for metropolitan critics and writers do not feel the same need to transcend their own interpretive communities and read the texts produced from the point of view of their Muslim audiences. There is an obvious need to focus on the meaning-making process of Muslim audiences of the poetics of incitement.[6] There is, then, a need to develop a more inclusive and democratic critical consciousness.

It is also important to note that the reader interacts with texts on two important, not necessarily mutually exclusive, planes: reason and aesthetics. There is a tendency in metropolitan critical practice to privilege the former over the latter. There is, however, a need to also focus on how texts *make us feel* besides articulating, in our critical practices, what texts *make us think*.

In the ensuing pages, my inquiry will follow a specific trajectory. In chapter 1, I offer a theorization of the democratic reader, especially as to what I mean by and why it is necessary to theorize and construct this democratic reader. Chapter 2, "A Genealogy of the Muslim Sacred," provides a brief overview of what constitutes a generalized Muslim sacred. I attempt to introduce the reader to the basic tenets of Islam, with a certain degree of temporal and spatial specificity, and then elaborate on how the Muslim sacred interacts with modernity and its place in the current regime of neoliberal capital. Chapter 3, "Incitements: Salman Rushdie and the Quixotics of Reforming Islam," provides a discussion of *The Satanic Verses* and its reception and also goes on to explain and discuss Rushdie's published self-justification for the work. I also discuss the nature and process of offering challenges to the Muslim sacred and discuss works that have done so successfully from within the Islamic tradition. Chapter 4, "Other Incitements: Islam and the Metropolitan Opportunists," provides a detailed account of how other authors, artists, and journalists have used the poetics of incitement as a new form of cashing in on the possible controversy that might arise with the publication of their work. This chapter will also explain and discuss the popularization of the poetics of incitement in metropolitan culture through an analysis of the controversy of the Danish cartoons and the publication of Sherry Jones's *The Jewel of Medina*. My main claim in this chapter will be that the poetics of incitement has now become an accepted, mainstream, and profitable genre of textual production in itself. Chapter 5, "Toward a Cosmopolitan Practice of Reading," offers a form of critical practice that would, at least, attempt to take into account the specific modes of reading and practice of experiencing literary texts as informed by an Islamic metaphysics. Chapter 6, "Reading Differently: The Case of the Taliban," offers an example of the complex mode of reading suggested by the book in analyzing one of the most problematic groups belonging to the fundamentalist strain of Islam. In chapter 7, "Reading and the Problem of Recognition and Redistribution," I discuss the need for paying attention to the acts of reading and questions of identity in opposition to simply focusing on the material understanding of reality. Chapter 8, "Iqbal and Mawdudi: The Need for Critical Reading and Thinking," attempts to open up a space within Muslim tradition(s) to perform different modes of reading.

I acknowledge, in advance, that this is by no means a perfect book, but I do sincerely hope that at least some aspect of it will be useful to students and teachers of literature and to the general public both within metropolitan cultures as well as within the Islamic world. If nothing else, I sincerely hope that this book will, at least, launch a rigorous debate both in metropolitan cultures as well as in its global periphery. If my attempt is only partially successful, I will consider it an outcome worthy of my labors.

CHAPTER 1

THE DEMOCRATIC READER

Most of what I am proposing in this book relates to the reader in two specific ways. First, I expect readers to be able to read texts about Islam or texts that invoke Islamic tropes in a way that allows them to read and receive them with their own cultural assumptions while also understanding how and in what way a general Muslim reader would receive the same texts. Second, I hope to encourage the construction of a reader who can, under varied circumstances, transcend the basic assumptions of their own culture in order to read and receive such texts more expansively. In both scenarios, the reader will have to come to the act of reading with an enhanced, complex, and nuanced consciousness. In this chapter, relying on some major debates regarding the practice of reading, I attempt to theorize this democratic reader.

READER AS AN ACTIVE PARTICIPANT

The moment I invoke the word *reader*, it becomes evident that in my understanding of critical engagement with the texts, the reader is always an active participant and not just a passive recipient of authorial intention. Louise Rosenblatt makes this exchange between the reader and the text more eloquently than any of the reception theorists I will invoke in this book. Explaining the transactional nature of the reading process, Rosenblatt provides the following explanation of the act of reading itself:

> The reader approaches the text with a certain purpose, certain expectation or hypotheses that guide his choices from the residue of past experiences. Meaning emerges as the reader carries a give-and-take with the signs on the page. . . . For the experienced reader, much of this may go on subconsciously, but the two-way reciprocal relation explains why meaning is not "in" the text or 'in" the reader. Both reader and text are essential to the transactional process of making meaning. (26–27)

If reading is a transaction between the text and the reader, and I strongly believe it is, then knowing what forms the historical and cultural meaning-making matrix of a reader is important, for that will decide what a text can mean to the reader. This insight is crucial to my argument because the kind of reader I would like to encourage, especially while dealing with the Muslim texts, is the reader who has the capacity to read these texts not simply based in their cultural assumptions but from the point of view of their Muslim global Others. This leads us to the problem of transcendence.

I have already invoked the problem of transcendence in the introduction by challenging Rorty's assumptions about the givens of one's culture and the (im)possibility of transcendence. Here, I first introduce some brief discussions of readerly practices and then theorize the kind of reader I hope to become myself, but also the kind of reader it would take to effectively read across cultures, especially across cultural divides. I address in this chapter both the Western reader and the Muslim reader, but my focus is primarily on the Western reader, as I teach, work, and write in the West. As stated at various places in this text, I use these generalized terms—the Western reader and the Muslim reader under erasure, or "sous-rature" in Derridean terms—and am in no way suggesting that these generalized terms can actually name these constituencies exhaustively or precisely.

While discussing the mechanics of literary reception, Terry Eagleton explains Roman Ingarden's insights about reading as follows:

> The literary work itself exists merely as what Polish theorist Roman Ingarden calls a set of "schemata" or general directions, which the reader must actualize. To do this, the reader will bring to the work certain "pre-understandings", a dim context of beliefs and expectations within which the work's various features will be accessed. (*Literary* 67)

One could argue that in order to really understand why and how readers receive certain texts, one must clearly understand the "preunderstandings" that readers bring to a text. These preunderstandings, preferences, and prejudices form an inherent and imperceptible part of the reading process. The reader performs a categorical mistake when they apply, uncritically, their own preunderstandings to a text, such as texts about the Islamic world, that rely on the raw materials from another culture, history, or society, for the reader would then simply reduce the complexities of such texts using the dominant prejudices of their own culture.

About the practice and acts of reading, Peter Rabinowitz provides some brilliant insights about the construction of the reader as elaborated in his groundbreaking book *Before Reading*. In defining his conceptual term "authorial reading," Rabinowitz argues for the usefulness of his concept as follows:

> The notion of the authorial audience is clearly tied to authorial intention, but it gets around some of the problems that have traditionally hampered the discussion of intention by treating it as a matter of social convention rather than of individual psychology.

In other words, my perspective [authorial reading] allows us to treat the reader's attempt to read as the author intended, not as a search for the author's private psyche, but rather as the joining of a particular social/interpretive community; that is, the acceptance of the author's invitation to read in a particular socially constituted way that is shared by the author and their expected readers. (22)

If we unpack some of Rabinowitz's insights, we can abstract some of the following core assumptions about the practice of reading: (1) The reader ought to seek and read the likely intention of the author in a text. (2) This "sought" authorial intention is not private but rather socially constructed. And (3) the process of meaning-making relies heavily on the shared assumptions of the author and the reader about the form and content of the text.

An ideal reader, under such conditions, would be the reader who understands authorial intention by carefully understanding the sociopolitical context that shapes it and then, in order to understand the text properly, also learns those sociopolitical assumptions in order to construe the intended meaning of the text. In such a practice, if the reader were to approach the text purely on their own situated assumptions about the act of reading, the reading performed would absolutely misread the authorial intention. Furthermore, if we extrapolate further from authorial reading, we could also argue that if the reader is not privy to the historical, cultural, or philosophical raw materials employed in a work of literature—Islamic history, for example—then the reader would reduce the text according to the confines of their own "pre-understanding" of the text.

From this we could argue that Muslim responses to the poetics of incitement, perhaps, are partially constructed through this category mistake: readers are reading the text without a clear understanding of authorial intention, and the fact that they bring to the text their own socially produced expectations, and since those expectations do not match the authorial intention, they end up reading the text differently or "wrongly." One could also argue that if the text is the arrived intention of the author then this intention can only be unpacked and read if the reader is privy to the meaning-making processes and preunderstandings that can guide such readings. In fact, Rushdie and his supporters during the Rushdie Affair constantly insisted on this restricted mode of reading authorial intention: if Muslim readers could have, somehow, been trained in this method of receiving the text, then certainly they would have had no problem with the novel. But to them the very intention of the text, and hence of the author, was to "hurt" and deride Muslims. It is this particular preunderstanding that shaped their response to the arrival and reception of the novel.

FROM IMPERIAL TO DEMOCRATIC READING

My project here is not only to challenge Western modes of reading and representing Islam but also to promote a sort of training that enables students and scholars to read texts about Islam with an eye toward the preferences, prejudices, and anxieties of a Muslim reader—in other words, to understand why works like *The Satanic Verses* and others cause such deep anguish and anger among Muslim readers. Dismissing the grievances of general Muslim readers constitutes an imperial act of reading, an act that presupposes that Western modes of reading are the standard, that Muslims will understand the texts "better" if they could read them like their "enlightened" Western counterparts. In fact, Rushdie himself engages in this "training" of the reader in one of his own essays that I discuss at length in chapter 6.

Here I am highlighting, albeit briefly, a strategy to transform ourselves from imperial readers into democratic readers. And in order to accomplish this transformation, we will have to train ourselves, when it comes to texts about Islam, to read in an empathetic mode, to put ourselves in the metaphorical shoes of the Other, and then read the text from the socially constructed expectations of an average Muslim reader. Only such a practice would enable us to become the kind of democratic reader that I am attempting to theorize and promote in this book.

Rabinowitz, in further elaborating the practice of authorial reading, also dwells on the prejudices and preferences of authorial audiences. He states, for example:

> But these authorial audiences, whatever their distance from actual readers, certainly have their own engagements and prejudices. To join the authorial audience, then, you should not ask what a *pure* reading of a given text would be. Rather, you need to ask what sort of *corrupted* reader this particular author wrote for: what were the reader's beliefs, engagements, commitments, prejudices and stampedings of pity and terror! (26)

It is evident that even when we attempt to read a work or a text as an authorial audience, the audience addressed by the author, our own preferences and prejudices play a vital role in the act of reading and in the process of meaning-making. It is crucial to bear these insights in mind in the process of articulating the kind of democratic reader necessary to read texts about Islam and Muslims sympathetically, for a reading oblivious to its own prejudices will only concretize the socially produced and politically promoted motivations of the author as well as the reader. There is no room in this immanent reading—the reading in which the author and readers share their unacknowledged prejudices—to actually perform a sympathetic reading, a reading that while acknowledging the metropolitan reader's right to read in their own way also accounts for the anguish and pain that the same texts might cause to the Muslim reader. For a reading to be truly humanistic and democratic, an accounting of what such an act of reading does to the Muslim reader's realm of consciousness and feelings is absolutely significant, and it is only through this accounting and acknowledgment that an act of reading can be transformed from an imperial act to a democratic act.

I have briefly touched upon Fish's explanation of interpretive communities in the introduction, and the kind of reader that I am proposing in this chapter will also emerge only after the logic of the interpretive community is enhanced to include, within the community's general repertoire, some functional knowledge of the meaning-making processes within Muslim societies. I assert this because, if one looks at what I have discussed above carefully, the deeper structures and ideologies within which we exist as readers have the power to determine, and at times overdetermine, our reading practices. So, any change in how the poetics of incitement is received will have to be structural and would require English departments to include at least a basic knowledge about Muslim reading practices as part of the intellectual training of graduate and undergraduate students.

I can trace my own development as a reader and consumer of texts clearly to its formative roots in my own education. Before I came to the United States and went through formal training in reading and an informal immersion in American culture, I approached Western literary texts with the repertoire of reading strategies that had been developed within the formative environment of my own primary culture. For example, even though I had read the collected works of Mark Twain while deployed in the mountains of Pakistan, my grasp of Twain lacked a deep historical and cultural understanding, and I was in a way "reducing the texts" according to the preferences and prejudices of my own culture. But after living in the US South and after obtaining ten years of formal education in US universities, my understanding of these same texts became more sophisticated and nuanced. This change did not happen on the level of language, for I already had a highly developed fluency in English, but simply because formal education, reading, and immersion in southern culture enabled me to read the texts with more nuanced intellectual tools. Furthermore, I was also able to read the problematics of these texts within the logic of the history of American racism and its history of slavery. For me to truly understand Twain, I not only needed advanced English-language skills but also a deep and sophisticated knowledge of American history and slavery and a clear understanding of the racism of Twain's time and the state of contemporary racism in the South. Imagine a student like me only writing about these texts from the cultural matrix of my own primary culture. Any professor of American studies would have encouraged or *required* me to learn more about American history to understand Twain on a more sophisticated level. We expect this of our students all the time. Thus, when it comes to literatures that rely on Muslim history and culture, a similar degree of understanding of Islamic history, philosophy, and specific cultural setting should be absolutely necessary. This would apply to simple readings of the texts but also to more sophisticated scholarly work and higher-level pedagogy related to such texts as well.

Simply stated, a scholar trained in democratic criticism should be able to read Rushdie's *The Satanic Verses* not only as the author's intended Western audience but also as the Muslim reader whose cultural raw materials created the conditions necessary for the creation of the novel. Therefore, a simple question to ask ourselves is this: Will our graduate students, currently being trained as critics, read the novel and understand why certain parts of it might be troubling or painful for Muslim readers? If the answer is a resounding "yes," then there is no need for this book. But if the answer is not so clear, then there is need for more thought, reflection, and writing on this subject. In that sense, this book is simply a humble attempt by someone with an understanding of both Western critical traditions and the meaning-making processes of a generalized Islamic world.

Another important aspect concerning reading practices is the ability to empathize with others or, in other words, to see the text and the world that it creates from the point of view of others. Walter Slatoff considers this a significant aspect of readerly practices. He writes,

> If the only way we can deeply comprehend or feel the experience of another is through identification, our range of response is limited by our ability to empathize; if we can feel for and with merely by understanding another's predicament and point of view we can probably have a wider range of experience. (52)

Slatoff goes on to suggest that empathy based only in identification with the subject matter is problematic because it requires the reader, while reading about another, to "put himself in his shoes" (52). In my understanding, true empathy can only be developed under such a scenario if we can become the Other. However, Slatoff, suggests that "true connection and love can only occur when the otherness of the object is fully recognized and accepted" (52). A democratic reader, therefore, would not only rely on a degree of sameness or a common core of preunderstandings to empathize with those reading the same text differently but would attempt to hold the impossible position of approaching a text with their own preunderstanding but then expand their repertoire to understand why others are reading and responding to the same text differently. A democratic reader, thus, will not only read texts according to their assumptions but will also be able to understand, and maybe empathize with, readings performed by others that may not match their own engagement with the text.

Most importantly, a democratic reader will have at least a cursory understanding of the sociality of personal and collective responses to representations of Islam originating in the West. So, if a novel or other text causes an uproar, public protests, and, in some cases, actual violence, the important aspect of a cross-cultural reading of the response would be to first understand why such a response occurred to in the first place. Dismissing such reactions as atavistic or simply politically motivated is, in my opinion, a misleading way of reducing the Other through one's own meaning-making processes.

READING AND DISCIPLINARY TRAINING

This brings me to the question of disciplinary training, especially in Western English departments. Those of us who work and teach at metropolitan universities have already done the work essential to teaching humanities in such institutions: no matter where we are from, as diasporic postcolonialists, we teach our subject matter with a clear and deeper understanding of the meaning-making processes of our host countries. In fact, one could say that without this deeper knowledge of the culture and history of our host countries, none of us would be considered worthy of employment. Furthermore, unlike our metropolitan colleagues who have no reason to show any particular expertise in other areas of the world, we cannot afford to simply rely on the cultural and aesthetic assumptions and preferences of our own primary cultures. Ngugi wa Thiong'o touched upon this lopsidedness of metropolitan institutions years ago. Let me reiterate one of his major observations about the structural inequalities between the literatures of the metropolitan West and those of the rest of the world, in his case African literatures:

> Currently no [Western] expert on the so-called "African Literature" need ever show even the slightest acquaintance with any African language. Can you imagine a professor of French literature and culture who does not know a single word of French? (156)

I suggest that a similar situation exists when it comes to knowledge and understanding of Islam and Islamic cultures, especially when texts about Islam are taught in most English departments. While I provide a detailed discussion of what, in my view, constitutes the

Muslim scared in the next chapter, I will try here to share my own experiences of teaching *The Satanic Verses* at the undergraduate level at my current institution.

At my institution, we offer a course titled Banned Books, which usually deals with issues related to books banned for various reasons within the US school system. A few years ago, I developed a proposal for this course, but instead of using the usual US-based texts, I decided to teach a course centered around the novel and attendant circumstances related to *The Satanic Verses*. While designing the course, I had some of the following important factors in mind: (1) I wanted to teach the text with all its intricacies and substance. (2) I wanted students to learn about basic aspects of Muslim cultures, especially the general approach to permissible norms. (3) I also wanted students to learn about Indian and Pakistani culture and about the history of early Islam. And (4) I wanted students to learn about the Rushdie Affair and read it as an event with some knowledge of the Muslim response.

Keeping the above goals in mind, the course had to have a component on historical knowledge about the setting as well as about Islamic history, Islamic jurisprudence, and a historical and cultural understanding of the Muslim response. The aim, however, was not to convince students to forgive the acts of aggression against Rushdie and his affiliates by Muslim hardliners but to understand the nature of anguish felt by everyday Muslims. I believe this latter aspect was important for my students to learn to understand and care for the Other without effacing their global differences. I, therefore, encouraged students to research different areas: Muslim history, basic tenets of Islam, the history of the Rushdie Affair itself, and so on.

As a result of all this careful planning and in-class exchanges, my students came out of the course not only having read a wonderful novel but also understanding and maybe empathizing with the feelings of everyday Muslims whose anguish and pain they could now, at least partially, comprehend.

Now let me point out what it took for me to teach the novel. I had to be aware of both the Western tradition of freedom of expression—not that that is not part of the symbolic historiography of Islam, for to speak against tyranny *is* considered a pious act in all sects of Islam—as well as the meaning-making processes of everyday Muslims. I also had the capacity to read the text from the place of a Muslim subject and feel the pain and anguish at the depictions of the Prophet, his wives, and his companions. I read the novel with my secular training but also from the point of view and preunderstandings of an everyday Muslim. I could inhabit this ambivalent space because I was privy to the meaning-making process of both cultures. I am not suggesting that all students in the United States should be able to perform this identity, but that for anyone to write seriously about such texts or teach them, they will have to develop a repertoire like this or else they will teach such texts only to accentuate and reinforce a global hierarchy of knowledge for themselves and their students.

Note that, according to Paulo Freire, such courses and instruction must not come across as the "banking concept of education" (72), which, for Freire, is a model of pedagogy that suffers from "narration sickness" (71). In this method of teaching, according to Freire,

> The teacher talks about reality as if it were motionless, static, compartmentalized, and predictable. Or else he expounds on a topic completely alien to existential experience of the students. His task is to "fill" the students with the contents of his narration. (71)

Now, in teaching texts about the Islamic world, a reality mostly "detached" from metropolitan students, in my experience, the best method is fostering an atmosphere that turns students into participants. While I shared my knowledge of the subject with students, the students themselves were active participants. For example, one major assignment in the course was a group presentation. The students chose their topics from a range of possibilities related to the course and then conducted active research as a group before presenting this research to the class. The most significant learning outcome from this experience was that each group of students, through their research, became an "expert" cluster in the class, and this enabled me to engage the class in student-centered, in-class discussions. I found the class exciting, and the main reason for this was that not only did students participate in their learning they also related the experience of their reading and research to the realities of their daily lives, especially with issues related to racism and the rights of minorities and other marginalized constituencies.

So, it goes without saying that the construction of the democratic reader, within the confines of a classroom, will certainly require an informed pedagogy; if instructors rely only on the primary texts, then they will, perhaps inadvertently, end up solidifying preexisting misconceptions or prejudicial views.

So, the democratic reader, as I am imagining it, would emerge only through the kind of pedagogy that encourages a certain degree of empathy for one's local and global Others. In that sense, then, critical and informed pedagogy plays an essential role. Any literary education that relies only on a Eurocentric, formalistic model would only result in concretizing the insipient prejudices and preferences of students and scholars in training. Next, I would like to discuss, albeit briefly, Mark Bracher's work on issues of pedagogy and the significance of informed pedagogy in enabling students and readers with the capacity to empathize with their global and local Others.

LITERATURE AND THE CARE OF OTHERS

In one of his essays, while challenging normalized assumptions about the transformative power of humanistic and literary studies, Bracher attempts to answer the question about literature's capacity to create compassion for others. He offers his views on this possibility in literary studies by way of a response to Martha Nussbaum and certain claims that she makes in two of her major works. The reason I am delving into this is because the creation of the democratic reader that I am attempting to theorize within the context of my project, the creation of a compassionate self in our students and scholars, is an absolutely significant precondition.

Bracher highlights three kinds of judgment on the part of a reader of literature, that, according to Nussbaum, are "necessary and sufficient to produce compassion" ("Educating" 30): "That another person has a serious need or is experiencing significant suffering . . . That the other is not responsible for this suffering or need . . . and that the other's well-being overlaps significantly with one's own" (30). These are the three judgments that, according to Bracher, enable Nussbaum to suggest that "when people make these three judgments (explicitly or implicitly) they feel compassion, and when one or more of these judgments is absent, the compassion is either vitiated or absent entirely" (30).

For Bracher, however, while these three judgments might play a role in shaping a reader's feelings toward their global Others, he also suggests that "there is no clear evidence that empathy for characters [in a book] leads to greater empathy for real people" (31). This conclusion about Nussbaum's claims and three compassion-producing judgments leads Bracher to pose the following questions, questions also relevant to my attempt at theorizing a democratic reader of texts about Islam. Bracher ponders "[h]ow the study of literature might promote the capacity and tendency to make the three compassion-producing judgements when they are warranted by facts" (32). In other words, does literature produce these compassion-forming habits and practices simply by accident, or do we need specific training or education to make them possible. Bracher offers the following as a viable mode of addressing the problem of prejudice:

> Research in social cognition . . . indicates that certain faulty cognitive structures that control social information processing are

largely responsible for the three incorrect compassion-inhibiting judgments about others. Studies also demonstrate that when these faulty structures are replaced by more adequate ones that produce more accurate and comprehensive perceptions and judgments of others, the result is greater compassion and assistance for others. (32)

This assertion by Bracher is in line with other works such as, but not limited to, that of David Miall who has also attempted to theorize empirical reading practices that at least attempt to trace "what occurs during literary reading" (25). Bracher, however, offers an even more convincing and comprehensive body of work that aims at transforming our habits of receiving texts, focusing on ways to teach literature in a way that makes it "actually" transformative. Of course, I am employing Bracher's work here because it enables me to articulate how the strategies he theorizes in terms of a broader spectrum of readers apply specifically to the acts of reading texts about Islam, a practice I have termed democratic reading and democratic criticism.

Returning to Bracher, I think the main crux of his argument within the logic of the text that I am invoking here is the basic assumption that literature can be and must be mobilized to create and encourage compassionate and empathetic subjectivities. Of course, if one disagrees with this mode of literature pedagogy, then this argument is of no value. But for those who are invested in the ameliorative function of literary studies, Bracher's insights could be extremely useful. While discussing the nature of individual prejudices, Bracher points to certain identity-building schemas, according to research in the study of cognition, that predecide (much like the preunderstandings discussed in the beginning part of this chapter) our responses to our local and global peers. According to Bracher and the research that he cites, "the cognitive schemas are general knowledge structures that comprise multiple types and forms of knowledge concerning a particular category"

(32). Bracher designates four kinds of operative knowledge that inform our perception of others:

> The basic types of knowledge include propositional knowledge (based in semantic memory), knowledge of particular instances and events (based in episodic memory), prototypes (generalizations or averages of these particular instances and events), and information-processing scripts (based in procedural memory). (32)

Out of all four kinds of knowledge discussed by Bracher that inform the schemas upon which our edifice of self and perception of others are built, prototypes play a major role in assigning value to outside groups. I will, therefore, discuss only this aspect of Bracher's theorization here, as this particular mode of perception is most intensively operative in the reception of Muslim- or Islam-based texts. For his explanation, Bracher uses the example of perceiving Africa and Africans. He starts his argument as follows:

> When it comes to perceiving and judging Others . . . the type of knowledge that often plays the main role in guiding our assessment of them is the stereotype, which is a prototype that is automatically (and usually unconsciously) activated whenever we process information about a particular category of person. (33)

The prototype is activated, of course, because it forms part of the cognitive schema that already shape our perception, but it also then forces us to see the world through that preestablished schema. Using the African stereotype as an example, Bracher argues that because of this operative stereotype, "even today when many Westerners think Africans, their perception, judgment, emotions, and actions are governed by their prototype (stereotype of Africans)" (33). Now, with a few modifications, we can apply the same perceptive principles to the reception of African Americans within the United States and, in the case of my inquiry, perception of

Muslims, Islam, and all things Muslim-related. Now, of course this prototype and this mode of perception must originate somewhere, at least that was my thought when I first encountered Bracher's text. Bracher argues that the creation of such prototypes, and their attendant generalization, depends upon the "contrast between one's prototype of the Other and one's prototype of the Human", and that the latter almost always signifies "the prototype of one's own group" (33). In other words, for a typical Western reader within the context of my study, almost all encounters with Islam-inflected texts would already predispose them to read about the Muslim world or Muslim characters—historical or fictional—from this dichotomous prototypical view of the human (they themselves) and the dehumanized Other (the Muslim). Now, this operative system of identity is so deeply embedded in our consciousness that mere information will not inspire the Western reader to interpret the text differently. More facts, in this case, are not likely to render the Muslim subject more human; in fact, if we follow Bracher's earlier work on identity, forcing such knowledge upon students would actually make them more defensive, and often belligerent, about their views and stances.[1]

This conception of the Other as less human relative to one's in-group is also layered and complex. According to Bracher, there are "two basic forms in which out-groups are perceived to deviate from the category of Human" (35), and these two kinds of "dehumanization" can be understood as follows:

> The most common form involves denying that the Other possesses uniquely human (UH) qualities that distinguish humans from other animals such as "cognitive sophistication, culture, refinement, socialization . . . and self-control. The other form of dehumanization denies that the Other possesses certain qualities that are central to human nature (HN), such as interpersonal warmth, drive, and vivacity.[2] (35)

Let us just pause here and ponder the metropolitan responses to the Rushdie Affair. It is obvious that the deriding of the protests and the "pedagogical pronouncements" proffered to Muslim readers fall into these two categories: the masses were either irrational, thus not fully human, or not sophisticated enough to read the text as their Euro-American counterparts could.[3] The Muslim stereotype, especially that of the Muslim reader, can easily be plotted along these two categories of dehumanization. The question, then, is simply this: How must we untrain our thought processes and perform the kind of readings that do not fall prey to these schematic and preinscribed prejudices? This is where Bracher's work becomes absolutely crucial to my project and to the larger project of pedagogy related to the Muslim sacred and works produced using Muslim raw materials.

So, if we already understand that reading can enable us to generate certain compassion-raising practices, and that in order for an act of reading to be transformative one must first free oneself from compassion-inhibiting schemes, then the next phase, of course, is to learn to change our modes of perception. This change, however, cannot be accomplished at the surface alone, for actual change requires a shifting of preestablished schemas. Bracher provides an account of this "liberating" process. In his words, "the key to increasing the defining element of cosmopolitanism—helping different others who are in need—is thus to increase people's recognition of their sameness and overlap with Others" (36). This might seem like an easy project, and perhaps well within the normative claims of literary studies, but there are, as Bracher points out, certain complicated steps involved in transforming our reception of texts about others to more understanding and empathetic modes of reading; they cannot just be accomplished simply by offering "more evidence and logical argument" (37). Here is how Bracher articulates the process that would enable our students to see their global Others as equals and as equally human:

It requires replacing not just faulty propositional beliefs about Others but also multiple nonpropositional forms of knowledge. These nonpropositional forms of knowledge include, prototypes, exemplars, and information processing routines. Prototypes, the most familiar form of which is the stereotype, are models incorporating what are taken to be the most typical features of members of a given category. . . . Exemplars are individual instances of a particular category, and they occur in the same multiple forms as prototypes, which in fact are formed out of exemplars when similar exemplars reach a critical mass.[4] (37)

Now, what Bracher is offering us here is a sort of cognitive mapping of the process of reception and perception of others. If our understanding of others is filtered through internalized prototypes and exemplars, and if that information is filtered through preestablished meaning-making processes (information-processing routines), then no amount of superficial, factual information—propositional knowledge—will impact the understanding of the reading subject, as the nonpropositional deep structures will already decide the meaning of the sign for them. In other words, if a reader already enters a text about Islam with preestablished stereotypes of Muslims, even if they feel sympathy for a Muslim character in the novel, that will not lead to a real sympathetic view of Muslims because the scripts that make the world of Islam intelligible to them have not been altered. The key to reaching a better understanding and in creating an empathetic reader—what I have called *democratic readers*—is to work toward altering and reshaping preestablished schemas. In Bracher's words, "preventing the dehumanizing and overlap-obscuring cognition of the Other, then, requires more than just getting people to subscribe to correct propositional knowledge concerning the full humanity of the Other" (40).[5] Now, literature, can be a great tool in accomplishing this deep "cleansing" of one's schemas of distrust of the other, but only if literature is taught carefully and with a purpose. Here, of course, the same general rules discussed by Bracher would apply to metropolitan readings of Muslim texts.

For Bracher, literature, if carefully taught, can play a huge role in transforming our view of the other. Toward the end of his chapter he offers a few methods of employing some techniques to unleash the transformative potential of literature and the humanities. Bracher suggests:

> One of the most basic and most important things teachers can do to promote these corrective processes is to select texts that provide multiple corrective exemplars for each of the prototype categories. . . . Simply having students read such texts, however, will not usually be sufficient to alter their faulty prototypes of the Other. (41)

So, concerning the reception of Muslims and Islam, the first step must be to use texts about Islam that offer some form of commonality and offer characters with whom readers can find something in common. Otherwise, the text, even if it relies on Islamic history, will end up only solidifying the preestablished prototype of Muslims. But, as Bracher suggests, that alone would not be sufficient. For a real change in perception and reception to occur, after encountering "the corrective exemplars" students must "*also recognize these textual elements as corrective exemplars and encode them as such in their memories*" (41; emphasis in original). This can be accomplished in many ways, but a few examples would be assigning extra readings or making assignments that encourage looking at the comparative representations of characters and their real-life exemplars. Either way, the process of reading would involve not just encountering the text but also creating a sort of catalogue of one's encounter with the text and an exploration of one's views of the Other followed by an exploration of the nature of those views. So, the literature about the Other, in this sense, always involves not only mastering the content but also reflecting on one's own meaning-making processes. The key to all this, according to Bracher, "is to look for self-other overlap, similarities" (43).

So, to sum up Bracher's argument, our deep understanding of the Other can only be made palpable if we are trained to read the Other from the point of view of looking at commonalities, and after this first step, acts of reading—and teaching—should involve exploring and altering one's own biases, even before the act of reading. In order to really transform our reading habits about Islam and to make the process of reading, teaching, and writing about texts about Islam different, we will thus have to not only transform our reading practices and learn more about Islamic history and meaning-making processes but also question our own assumptions and preunderstandings when it comes to our engagement with Muslim cultures and texts. Furthermore, this "training" would involve first exposing ourselves to texts that provide and reinforce positive exemplars and then, after having modified our schemas, move on to more complicated texts that offer more complex and negative representations of our global Others. In other words, *The Satanic Verses* should probably not be the first text one teaches about Islamic history or culture, for it would probably reinforce prejudicial views of Islam. That is why, when I teach the book, I first build up students' repertoire of propositional knowledge and request they ask themselves these two important questions:

Why do I think the way I do?
Why do I feel the way I do?

Bracher, besides offering other strategies, also suggests that developing students' "metacognition" can be enhanced by encouraging "students to keep a diary recording their cognitive encounters (in memory, in imagination, or in actuality, as well as in reading) with the other" (42), which eventually will help them in "identifying how the various information-processing acts they engage in work either to obscure or to apprehend the Other's humanity and sameness with themselves" (42).

I believe, when it comes to the poetics of incitement, this strategy of reading along with a catalogue of one's own reception of the texts would be crucial in developing a repertoire of reading practices that enables metropolitan students and scholars to read Muslim works more compassionately and carefully. Thus, overall, what I have encouraged in this chapter is a mode of training our students that emphasizes that engagement with texts is never really unmotivated, and that in order to really understand Muslim texts more comprehensively and more compassionately we do not only need factual (propositional) knowledge, but that we also need to discover the very deep schemas and preunderstandings that predispose us to read and teach texts about Islam in certain ways. Only after this thorough training and care will we be able to teach Islam, Muslim cultures, and the lives of Muslims in the real world with a certain degree of care, understanding, and compassion. And when we can do that, when we can approach Muslim texts with such propositional and nonpropositional sophistication. Then, and only then, will we become democratic readers.

CHAPTER 2

A GENEALOGY OF THE MUSLIM SACRED

In all cultures, the prevalent norm always mediates the degree of permissibility and prohibition of one's actions. In this sense, the sacrosanct is the very limit of permissibility, just a shade away from what is forbidden or labeled blasphemous. As such, Islamic cultures have their own logic of permissibility. But before I attempt to explore this realm of permissibility and prohibition, I must first define my terms. When I invoke Islamic cultures, I am, of course, performing a grand act of abstraction. The scope of this work does not allow me to deal with all Islamic cultures in their geographical and temporal specificity. For all practical purposes, my generalized use of "Islamic cultures" basically suggests all cultures that foreground Islam as a mode of understanding the world and to understand the degree of permissibility of one's actions within it are Islamic. When I mobilize the term *Islamic*, this precisely is the abstraction at play. When I feel a need to offer concrete examples, I will certainly inform the reader that I am moving into a specific and concrete explanation from my hiding place in the abstract.

But let us consider, on the highest level of abstraction, what constitutes the basic tenets of the Muslim sacred. But before doing that, let us first attempt to grapple with the term *sacred* itself. Just like most other concepts in this work, my grasp of the word will also be flawed, fluid, and often contradictory, for the sign, as we know it, never arrives at the end of meaning: the most we can achieve, if we are lucky and attentive, is a fleeting charge of moving along, over, above, and outside a long, endless chain of significations. My views of the sacred are caught in yet another web of discursivity and thus require a slight detour into the explanation of the terms listed in the title of this chapter, "A Genealogy of the Muslim Sacred."

WHAT IS GENEALOGY?

A few words about the term *genealogy* and my reasons for using it. Those who have read Michel Foucault already know that the term originates in his work, inspired by the work of Nietzsche. 1 am using it with some modifications. Foucault defines his genealogical method at various places, so one can pick and choose. 1 have decided to rely on the following discussion of the method by Foucault: "Well, 1 think it is the coupling together of the bruised scholarly knowledge and knowledges that were disqualified by the hierarchy of erudition and sciences that gave discursive critique . . . its essential strength" (*Society* 8). One could then argue that genealogy, for Foucault, is a sort of mixed retrieval or a multipronged offensive: always launched against the edifice of normalized, powerful discourses but with the weapons provided by the discourses that had been silenced in the totalizing realm of dominant discourses. Thus, a genealogical approach is a foregrounding of "subjugated knowledges" (8) in order to render the dominant discourse unstable or moot, if that is possible. In other words, Foucault further explains, "[W]e can give the name 'genealogy' to this coupling together of scholarly erudition and local memories, which allows us to constitute a historical knowledge of struggles" (8). A genealogy, therefore, must tell the untold story, must retrieve silenced knowledge, but must do so in the face of the dominant discourses and not as a voice in the jungle where no one is able to hear its ramblings. A genealogy therefore must retrieve buried knowledge and then take into account how this buried weapon bruises the very body of normalized power and structures.

So, when I attempt to retrieve a genealogy of the Muslim sacred, I must do that on both these accounts. I must provide a brief review of how this sacred is constituted at the higher level of abstraction by Muslim religious scholars, by governments, and by institutions; but also, to complicate the picture, I must also provide, at least on the abstract level, an accounting of how the people, wherever they may be, experience and account for the Muslim sacred. How the people respond to the poetics of incitement is shaped and structured by this strange mixture of high and low, sacred and mundane. On a higher level, my attempt is also a challenge to the normalized hierarchy of literary studies itself, which has mostly viewed all things religious or spiritual in the realm of literary interpretation as suspect.

THE SACRED

To define the sacred, I rely on a much more conventional source. The following definition of "sacred" from the OED seems most apt for my purpose:

> Of things, places, of persons and their offices, etc.: Set apart for or dedicated to some religious purpose, and hence entitled to veneration or religious respect; made holy by association with a god or other object of worship; consecrated, hallowed.

The Islamic sacred, both in erudite scholarship and in its popular versions, relies heavily on these connotations of the meaning of the sacred. In the ensuing pages, I attempt to discuss the modes of defining and normalizing the sacred and then come back to my main point about importance of this "buried knowledge" against the backdrop of the normalized knowledge of literary theory discourse.

What is sacred in Islam and why? What defines the sacred? What sources are used to differentiate the sacred from the mundane? These are some of the questions that need to be answered first. To answer these questions, we will take a long detour into the history of Islamic philosophy and jurisprudence.

Just as the Western canon of literary criticism draws heavily upon its classical philosophical sources, Islamic practices of interpretation are deeply affected by the history of Islamic thought, early Islamic sources, and current interpretations of the sacred as informed by classical sources. According to Seyyed Hossein Nasr, "The Islamic philosophers meditated upon" the definitions of philosophy, "which they inherited from ancient sources and which they identified with the Qur'ānic term *hikmah* believing the origin of *hikmah* to be divine" ("Meaning" 22). Roughly translated from classical Arabic, *hikmah* can mean "[w]isdom, sagacity, philosophy, rationale, underlying reason" (Cowan 196). The term *philosophy*, used interchangeably with hikmah, was adopted into Arabic as *falsafah*. In fact, Nasr also asserts that despite the later changes in the philosophical vocabulary of the Islamic world, "*hikmah* and *falsafah* continued to be used" ("Meaning" 21) even during the later and widened phases of Islamic philosophy.

Despite the Greco-Roman influences on Islamic philosophy, Nasr suggests that Islamic philosophy, in all its stages, does also stay purely Islamic at least in its conception of itself and in terms of its functionality within Islamic life. Nasr broaches this subject as follows:

> The very reality of the Qur'ān and the revelation which made it accessible to a human community had to be central to the concerns of anyone who sought to philosophize in the Islamic world and led to a source of knowledge not only of religious law but of the very nature of prophetic consciousness which is the recipient

of revelation (*al-wahy*) had to remain of the utmost significance for those who sought to know the nature of things. How were the ordinary human means of knowing related to such an extraordinary manner of knowing? How was human reason related to that intellect which is illuminated by the light of revelation? . . . Such questions as the hermeneutics of the sacred text and theories of the intellect which usually include the reality of prophetic consciousness remain, therefore, central to over a millennium of Islamic philosophical thought. ("Inspiration" 28)

Despite its insistence upon a fixed core to Islamic philosophy, an assertion that I do not wholly agree with, the above passage does highlight two central issues of Islamic philosophy: (1) the human capacity to access truth through reason alone and (2) the importance of the hermeneutics of the Sacred Text. Only God, according to this approach, can reveal the truth through direct revelation. The process by which this is accomplished is called *al-wahy*. In its classic and current definition, *wahy* means the "inspiration, revelation" (Cowan 1057). This revelation, however, in terms of the prophetic tradition, does not involve an active rational seeking on the part of the recipient; it is rather more of a one-way flow of knowledge from the divine to its chosen vessel. In this process, the figure of the Prophet is just a conduit to relay God's word to His chosen people. But what redeems this passive state of reception of the sacred in the state of "prophetic consciousness" is "the type of manhood that he [the Prophet] has created, and the cultural world that has sprung out of the spirit of his message" (Iqbal, *Reconstruction* 112).

The hermeneutics of the Sacred Text is the second most important aspect of Nasr's explanation of the role of Islamic philosophy. Since the figure of the Prophet receives divine wisdom—hikmah—through a revelation of the truth by the divine, the Qur'ān, then, as a record of those revelations, becomes the path toward understanding the mind of God. Islamic philosophy, therefore, is geared toward a detailed hermeneutics of the Sacred Text in which the status of the Qur'ān as a revealed text is taken as axiomatic, but the question of interpretation is kept open, as interpretation is the only mode of reaching and understanding the mind of the Absolute. Thus, while the content of the Qur'ān is fixed and recorded, its interpretation and meaning cannot be fixed—all innovation in Muslim thought takes place through the act of interpretation. It is this emphasis on the nature of the Qur'ān as the physical manifestation of God's will or as a sacred code upon which most of the energies of Islamic philosophy are spent. This is one reason the Qur'ān as a sacred text has never been dislodged from the apex of Islamic philosophy. Over the centuries, then, Muslim philosophers and theologians have focused on articulating a correct or more nuanced science of interpretation.

SOURCES OF ISLAMIC INTERPRETATION

There are basically four main sources of Islamic interpretation: the Qur'ān, the Hadīth, *Ijmā*, and *Qiyās* (Farrah 185–88). In degree of importance, the Qur'ān holds primacy. Thus, when a scholar needs to interpret a question of Muslim daily life or a particular legal issue, the first place to look for a law or an injunction is the Qur'ān. The Hadīth are the recorded sayings of the Prophet and are the second most important source for such knowledge. If nothing can be found in the first two sources, then scholars rely on the use of *Ijmā*:

> In its true sense *Ijmā* involved the practice of seeking the consensus of the community on any issue of ritual or other religious practice or observance. *Qiyās* or "analogical deduction" is the way belief or practice gains official credence and support on the grounds that it is similar to a practice or belief clearly embodied in the Qur'ān, Sunnah, or *Ijmā* (187).

The modes of interpretation also depend heavily on the rules articulated by various interpretive communities or schools of Islamic interpretation. As mentioned earlier, the main aim of Qur'ānic exegesis was to interpret the Qur'ān as a message from God in order to reach the "intended" meaning of the text, hence an act of interpretation aimed at understanding God's intentions. The various schools of interpretation—*madhāhib*—became significant "sometime in the course of the third Muslim century" (189). Based on the teaching of four major juridical scholars, these madhāhib differed on questions of interpretation but had no major differences insofar as core Islamic concepts were concerned. The four major early Sunni madhāhib include *Hanafite*, *Mālikite*, *Shāfi'ite*, and *Hanbalite*. Out of these, the Hanafite was the earliest school of interpretation founded by Imam Abu-Hanīfah (d. 767) and "reflects the views of the jurists of Iraq . . . manifesting considerable toleration in the use of *ra'y* (private opinion of the jurist)" (190). Mālikite, the next school, was founded by Imam Mālik Ibn-Anas (d. 795) and depended "more on the traditions associated with the Companions of Muhammad than with the Prophet himself. When it came to conflicting traditions, Mālik and his followers after him simply made an arbitrary choice" (190). The Shāfi'ite school, founded by Imam al-Shāfi'i (d. 820), relied heavily on the Hadīth to reach juridical opinions. In fact, it was al-Shāfi'i "who elevated the authority of the Hadīth to its position of pre-eminence" (191–92). Hanbalite, the fourth and by far the most conservative school, was founded by Imam Ahmad ibn-Hanbal (d. 855). This is the school of interpretation that underwrites the Wahabi doctrine designated as an official interpretation by the Kingdom of Saudi Arabia. Besides these four major schools of interpretation, there is also the tradition of Imam Ja'far Sādiq, whose teachings guide the various sects of Shi'a Islam.

These four Sunni schools of interpretation play an important historical role in the development of the Islamic science of jurisprudence.[1] Important to note in the explanation of the four madhāhib is that their differences arise only from the questions of interpretation and the subsequent implementation of the rules thus articulated. They have, however, no differences on the core issues of Islam. Thus, through the commentaries developed and recorded by these scholars, four different modes of Islamic interpretation are concretized and eventually normalized in particular geographic regions of the Islamic world.

In modern Islamic debates, there are now two major schools of interpretation: one group believes that all that needed to be explained has already been explained by the above-mentioned four schools of interpretation. These scholars are known as the *taqlidi* scholars, the ones who follow what has been decided before them. Another larger group of scholars believes that since the Qur'ān is a living text, its interpretation cannot be fixed and must therefore be reinvigorated with the increase of human knowledge and experience. These scholars are called the *tajdīdi* scholars.[2]

The application of the science of reading into daily life is certainly premised on the idea that the Qur'ān-as-living-text was meant to offer humankind the ultimate wisdom of God for them to shape their lives accordingly. The whole purpose of the hermeneutics of the sacred text is to understand God's intentions, and even when no clear answer is provided, the other methods must certainly, at least, attempt at reaching the intentions of the divine. Islamic philosophy thus relies on an acute philological attempt at reading the text as closely as possible.

Critical readers in the Islamic world are not caught in an unchanging and hermetic tradition of reading, but when it comes to reading the appropriations of Muslim raw materials by metropolitan authors, the average Muslim reader should not be expected to completely transcend their cultural rules of inclusion and permissibility. That would be similar to expecting a member of one reading community to read according to the rules of another community. Conversely, for metropolitan critics, reading a text about life in the Islamic world without any knowledge of the meaning-making processes prevalent in a particular part of the Islamic world is like walking blindfolded on the edge of a dangerously twisting precipice. If the role of the humanities is, as Gayatri Spivak suggests, "the empowerment of an informed imagination" (*Other* 2), then as humanists of the twenty-first century, it is our duty to not just inform ourselves of the subtleties of these technical modes of reading but also to incorporate them in our curricula in order to allow our students to become more engaged and intellectually attentive readers of texts. If we fail, the results would be similar to those evidenced in metropolitan readings of Rushdie's *The Satanic Verses*, a text I will discuss in the next chapter.[3]

The entire project of Fiq'a in Islam is to separate the clean from the unclean and to differentiate between the permissible and the impermissible. Fiq'a, therefore, traditionally provides a tripartite model of differentiation: *halal* (permissible), *haram* (forbidden), and *munkir* (something in-between). The entire project of commentary and explication, therefore, is meant to clearly articulate what is permissible, what is forbidden, and what falls in-between. It might sound slightly archaic to discuss this explanation of reality, but to a large extent these issues of permissibility and impermissibility still form an important part of an average practicing Muslim's life. The decisions that are otherwise taken for granted in the Western world are not so transparent and involve a juridical explanation of their permissibility. One could say that the Muslim mode of experiencing modernity is slightly more complex than those of their counterparts living in Western democracies. In the West (and I am aware of this grand generalization of the term "West"), subjectivities are formed and perform in a legal framework: by and large an average subject in the West lives their life aware of legalities and illegalities. There is, of course, some form of moral reasoning involved as well, but what is legal is usually assumed to be morally right.

For a Muslim subject of modernity, the question of legality and morality is a complex one: what is permissible under the law of the land must also be filtered through the litmus test of permissibility in the Sharia. This tension, often present in countries that have developed their legal systems in the tradition of their former colonial masters, bears upon many everyday decisions. It is when modern law somehow develops a clash with the spiritual aspects of a Muslim's life that a Muslim subject seeks scriptural and interpretative guidance. That is why the earliest Islamic websites were the Fiq'a sites, where the readers could post a question of faith or a query about everyday life and seek a scholar's opinion on it. This opinion is called a *fatwa*—a term erroneously translated as "verdict" in the Western press. A fatwa is not necessarily a verdict but a juridical opinion which must be written and proclaimed in accordance with laws of Islamic jurisprudence. While any Muslim scholar can write and issue a fatwa, only the sovereign in an Islamic state has the power to make a fatwa legally binding. But in the postmodern privatization of power, fatwas are now also implemented, sometimes by force, by the sociopolitical groups that fill the legality gap in the absence of clearly established governance by national governments.

When a scholar is asked for an opinion on a religious matter, or if a scholar feels like giving a *suo moto* opinion, the opinion cannot just be a statement. The fatwa, as a genre of writing, must follow certain established norms depending upon the general conventions or rules of jurisprudence specific to a certain school of thought. This, then, makes it imperative for me to touch upon formalistic and interpretive strategies involved in issuing a fatwa.

For a fatwa to be issued, a scholar either must feel a need to give a general opinion in response to some large-scale upheaval or, in another context, write an opinion on a particular issue as requested by a second party. Needless to say, this practice in itself can be abused and has been abused frequently: sometimes scholars take it upon themselves to issue a fatwa and then encourage their followers to implement it (Ayatollah Khomeini's fatwa against Rushdie is one such example); in other cases, the sovereign can use the *ulma* to request the kind of fatwa needed to stabilize the rule and power of the sovereign. So, just like any other juridical opinion, the fatwa and its impact also depends on the immediate context and the political state of the *enunciating subject*. So, what I am attempting to discuss is the idealized state of issuing a fatwa, which is not necessarily always the norm.

Let us look at one of the most significant fatwas issued in 1803 in India by Shaikhul-hind Shah Abdul Aziz Dehlavi:

> In this city [of Delhi] the *Imām al-Muslimīn* wields no authority, while the decrees of the Christian leaders are obeyed without fear [of the consequences]. Promulgation of the command of *kufr* means that in the matter of administration and the control of the people, in the levy of land-tax, tribute, tolls and customs, in the punishment of thieves and robbers, in the settlement of disputes, in the punishment of offenses, the *kāfirs* act according to their discretion.... There are, indeed, certain Islamic rituals ... with which they do not interfere. But that is of no account. The basic principle of these rituals are of no value to them, for they demolish mosques without the least hesitation and no Muslim or *Dhimmī* can enter the city or its suburbs except with their permission.... From here to Calcutta the Christians are in complete control. (Metcalf 46)

There are two important aspects of this particular fatwa, both crucial to my inquiry: (1) the purpose of the fatwa itself and (2) the context of its proclamation by the leading religious scholar of the time. Barbara Metcalf explains both these aspects of the fatwa quite brilliantly in her work. But first, it is important to understand that Shah Abdul Aziz Dehlavi was not just a voice in the jungle; he can issue this fatwa because he has the institutional prestige (as the leading scholar of his time in India) and the symbolic power (accrued by being the leading scholar) to pronounce or to act as an enunciating subject. Furthermore, since he has countless followers and students in India, it is obvious that his followers and students will pay attention to his verdict and then, in the absence of a Muslim government, conduct their lives under British rule according to the explanation of the transformed public sphere offered by the scholar.

The context is extremely important. Political and administrative control of most of India had passed on to British hands, and within this context, Shah Abdul Aziz Debhlavi, according to Metcalf, wanted the Muslims of India "to recognize that the organization of the state was no longer in Muslim hands" (51). Furthermore, the fatwa is also a living example of the role of *ulama* in an India no longer under Muslim rule and thus, Metcalf suggests, the fatwa also declares implicitly that "if the state no longer provided a hierarchy of courts and personnel to administer Muslim law, then only the 'ulama could fill what was evidently a troublesome legal void" (51). This is a brief example of the appropriation of the public sphere by private citizens and ulama when the political order fails in Muslim lands or when Muslim rulers are supplanted by European colonizers. It is this tradition of keeping the practices and spirit of the faith alive, despite the altered political circumstances, that shapes the current developments of parallel religious spheres of power within the Muslim world.

Furthermore, a fatwa is not just an arbitrary declaration by a cleric; it is rather a well-argued legal document, of which the cited language of the fatwa above is a great example. Generally, when a question is posed to a scholar, the scholar must first look for an answer in the most authentic sources of jurisprudence. The two most important sources of the sacred in Islam are the Qur'ān and the hadīth. The Qur'ān, as is obvious, is the Muslim sacred text, and the hadīth are the authentic collections of the recorded sayings of the Prophet Muhammad.

My explanation of Islamic jurisprudence, a sort of contrived and failed one, proves, to some extent, that there are no easy stages to colonial encounter, that time does not travel on its inexorable journey to a Eurocentric present. Just after the king in Delhi is sacked and exiled by the British, the symbolics of a Muslim life alter in India. These symbolics are crucial for understanding the Muslim response to the rise of the British Empire. The sacking of the king is not only a political upheaval; it is also a spiritual and juridical crisis. Technically, when there was a Muslim king, no matter how ineffectual, the symbolics of a Muslim life could be maintained under a fiction of Muslim sovereignty.

There are two ways in which the king's sovereign power is expressed within this time and space: economic and spiritual. The king is king because the coin is struck in his name. This is crucial given that the Mughals were extremely jealous of coinage production, and punishments for illegally striking coin under their jurisdiction were extremely harsh, for the circulation of coin needed to be the monopoly of the sovereign, and it also expressed the political and economic reach of the sovereign. The spiritual aspects of the sovereign's reach were expressed in the weekly Friday *Khutba* (sermon). There are two parts to the Khutba: the first is formulaic and represents an idealized incantation about the Prophet, the early caliphs and Muslim tradition. But traditionally, the second Khutba was always said in the name of the ruling caliph or king. Thus, when Mughal coinage is replaced by that issued by the East India Company, and when there is no king in whose name the Khutba could be issued, the dynamics of the realm shifts and there is a need to rearticulate Muslim life under these circumstances. The most important question, then, is whether or not India is still Darul-Islam, the abode of peace, or has it, by ceasing to be a Muslim-ruled entity, become Darul-Harb, the place of war? Much is at stake in this rearticulation, for if India has become Darul-Harb, then exception must become the norm because the land has entered a state of exception.

The fatwa by Shah Abdul Aziz Dehlavi is probably the most crucial document and pronouncement in the early British era, especially since the British were forced to mobilize counter-fatwas and counternarratives in an attempt to render impotent the verdict given in this fatwa. It is, therefore, critical to discuss what discourse enables this fatwa and under what symbolic economy the scholar, Shah Abdul Aziz Dehlavi, can make a pronouncement so profound that it symbolically transforms India from one form of habitus to another.

First, within Indian discourse of Islamic knowledge, Shah Abdul Aziz Dehlavi (1703–1823) holds prestigious status as an *alim* as well as a *sayyid*. Called Shaih-ul hadīth (an appellation applied only to the name of scholars who possess deep knowledge of the hadīth), the scholar has the institutional prestige and the knowledge to become what Foucault terms an "enunciating subject." And while he no longer has the political power behind his knowledge, the symbolic power of his stature as a scholar enables him to issue this politically powerful opinion even after the demise of Muslim power in Delhi. This power to pronounce judgment—a judgment that transforms public perception of a whole way of life—can only be understood if one has some insight into the discursive framework of the symbolics of this enunciation. We must, therefore, dismount our powerful, lofty, Eurocentric steeds and dredge through the meaning-making processes particular to this one pronouncement in order to really do this inquiry justice. In other words, we must play a little with the signifier but remain within the rules of the game as articulated by the system within which the enunciation was made. Our reading must be temporally and spatially immanent and must not rely on a lazy transcendent model that reduces all acts of speech to metropolitan speech.

This state of exception, I strongly believe, has always existed within the Islamic political system. The sovereign does ascribe to themself the rights to a safe and protected life, and even a cursory overview of Islamic history is enough to suggest that Muslim biopolitics emerges immediately after the establishment of the first Muslim state and precedes the rise of biopolitics in Europe by centuries. But there is also a permanent tension in the normalization of sovereign power within Islamic political systems. While the caliphs, sultans, and kings rule with absolute power, their power is always subject to public scrutiny from religious scholars. And despite the sometimes-violent attempts to silence this dissent, the ulama have traditionally taken the responsibility to keep the sovereign "honest" in most, if not all, Muslim political systems.

When the political system collapses in India, the parallel parapolitical system with its own hierarchies and symbolics of power becomes even more highly developed and powerful. That is why many historians read the fall of Muslim political power as the beginning of the rise of a more resilient and powerful public discourse of Islam and definition of Muslim life. Shah Abdul Aziz Dehlavi is thus not a mullah on the fringes of a Muslim-governed India but rather, due to the lack created by the political ouster of the Muslim king, the central figure in defining the Muslim way of life. The power to pronounce Muslimhood and to shape perceptions of the British-imposed system becomes privatized and resides in the mosque and the madrassa rather than the political court of any king. Because of this, the current state of ulama and their willing warriors and enforcers is nothing new and falls within a valorized tradition of dissent against oppressive governments. Thus a fatwa can be a legal verdict but also an incitement to action if offered in a space and time when there is no Muslim political power in existence to mediate, implement, or reject them.

The question of power and the role of the sovereign must also be settled here. In most Islamic cultures, the sovereign never really incorporates the entire body politic within the boundaries of sovereign law. In fact, there always remains an ideological (and sometimes geographical) frontier beyond the grasp and influence of sovereign power. The ulama and religious leaders use this space, this fold in the fabric of power, to create and articulate a discourse that automatically functions in response to and sometimes as a monitoring force over the laws of the sovereign. When proclaimed in this space and from this enunciating position, a fatwa becomes a verdict and does not just function as one of several juridical opinions.

Sometimes history is inescapable. This split between the power of the sovereign and the enunciative power of the ulama appears immediately after the first four caliphs of Islam. The reason the first four caliphs are called the Rashideen is primarily because, in the eyes of Muslim historians, since they were immediate companions of the Prophet, their rule was a pure expression of God's will and the Prophet's teachings. This belief also is historically constructed and normalized. Even during the times of the four pious caliphs, political differences were present and often led to deadly confrontations. But by and large, Muslim historians and theologians have either smoothed these historical wrinkles or glossed them over to create a picture of pure, uncomplicated, virtuous, and ideal rule. Thus, the split between the power of the sovereign and the word of scholars is always traced beyond the first four caliphs and becomes a supplementary historical trace in Muslim historiography. While most accounts of Islamic history are dynastic and explain the world through the policies and power of a particular caliph, king, or sultan, the narratives of resistance are always offered through the actions of ulama who historically challenged the practices of the sovereign during different stages of history. This parallel flow of two competing powers that sometimes comes together is also important to retrieve and discuss when dealing with Muslim historiography and the construction of the Muslim sacred.

Another important aspect of sacred and sacral systems relates to the kind of emotional and social structures that depend on them. In the end, the basic tenets of faith or belief provide the very scaffolding upon which is structured the entire edifice of a culture and civilization. That is why defenders of such systems respond so vehemently to all acts of symbolic and material aggression, for if the scaffolding is proven to be faulty or weak, the entire edifice becomes unsustainable. Furthermore, all normative systems, at some point or another, make critiques of the norm a sinful or an undesirable act. Thus, in religious practices there is always a natural tendency from precariously reasoned beliefs to dogmatic and often irrational beliefs in the sacred. Ibn Khaldun argues that when the entire edifice of a system is built as such, then "the arguments for the articles of faith hold the same position as the articles of faith themselves and that an attack against them is an attack on the articles of faith, because they rest on those (arguments)" (145).

The Muslim sacred, therefore, contains a kernel of "revealed" truth that is further augmented by the theological exegesis and acts of interpretation offered by different theologians as well as past and contemporary scholars. Even in its most bizarre articulations, the question of the Muslim sacred is never resolved through arbitrary opinion: the opinion is always propped up by the institutional prestige and the enunciating acts of the appropriate enunciating subjects. In short, the Muslim sacred is highly discursive, but the discourse has a tendency to offer itself, within the logic of certain schools of Muslim theology, as literal truth. Yes, I know I am now entering very murky territory, and I must explain my method.

Simply stated, I am trying to explain the articulation of the Muslim sacred not from the place of political or sovereign power (even though they play a vital role in it too) but rather from the periphery. The postcolonial Muslim sacred, I argue (beyond a few cases like Saudi Arabia), is often defined in opposition to state policy and is offered and enforced by private enunciating subjects and their followers. The Muslim sacred of today is no longer the sole domain of the state but rather has been posited in the tradition of those who are remembered as the ones who had defied the power of caliphs and sultans. This is the space that the ulama and their powerful foot soldiers assign themselves. To sufficiently understand this, we need to seek a historical understanding of the buried knowledge or the popular tradition of valorizing resistance to the dictates of the kings and sultans.

There are two larger historical currents about most Islamic societies: (1) the official dynastic histories of the caliphs, kings, and sultans, and (2) the popularized stories of righteous imams and scholars who defied the sultans and caliphs in order to "save"

Islam from contaminating influences. It is this set of buried narratives that provides the self-serving historical narratives for the construction of radical Islamist identities. Along with their constitutive functions relative to Muslim identities, these narratives also provide a historical genealogy of the tradition of resistance against the corrupt or corrupting influences of the power of the sovereign.

There are quite a few stories that are repeatedly told as exemplary instances of resistance by righteous scholars against the so-called un-Islamic dictates of the sovereign. The oft-repeated story of Imam Ahmad bin Hanbal is one such story in the Middle Eastern context; the narrative of the life of Mujaddad Alif Sani of Sirhind is one pertinent to India. I find it apt to delve a little deeper into these narratives to retrieve the buried knowledge about the popular construction of the Muslim sacred.

Against the backdrop of official historiographies often either commissioned by the kings and caliphs or written by their court historians, there is a stream of historical mythologies, texts, and tales that offer a sort of buried treasure of resistance from various historical figures, from the saints to the scholars. It is similar to the *Book of Martyrs* or tales of saints in the Christian tradition. There is a certain logic to these texts and stories. Often, it seems, at moments when faith is in decline and the political system is at its weakest and most unguided, someone emerges to restore the faith. Thus, when Muslim political systems collapse and are replaced by those of the colonizers, these buried texts and forgotten scholars and leaders are retrieved and become an unofficial corpus for the restoration and reformation of Muslim communities. In the ensuing pages, I will discuss some of these historical figures and the importance of their retrieval and mobilization for the restructuring of Muslim societies.

First, I would also like to point out that fatwas by scholars play an important role in the hegemonic project of the Empire. In fact, since the British Empire relied on counter-fatwas in favor of the Empire, Muslim historians developed two distinct terms to separate the real scholars from those who had become foundational scholars. Scholars deemed true to the cause of Islam were called *Ulma-e-Haq* (the scholars of truth) while those supporting the colonizers were termed *Ulma-e-Su* (the scholars of untruth). This distinction between the two kinds of scholars is still invoked by many popular political and scholarly figures in the Islamic world today.

Going back to British attempts to normalize their hegemony in India, the British also sought scholarly opinions about the legality of their rule over Muslims in India. W. W. Hunter cites a sample of these fatwas in his book about Indian Muslims. Provided in two appendices to his book, the fatwas declare, contra Shah Abdul Aziz Dehlavi, that India had not lapsed into Darul-Harb after the fall of the Muslim political order. I provide one of these fatwas as an example below:

The Questions posed to the Ulma:

> What is your Decision, O men of learning and expounders of the law of Islam, in the following: Whether a Jihad is lawful in India, a country formerly held by a Muslim ruler, and now held under the sway of a Christian government, where the said Christian Ruler does in no way interfere with his Muslim subjects in the Rites prescribed by their Religion, such as Praying, Fasting, Pilgrimage, Zakat, Friday Prayer, and Jama'at, and gives them fullest protection and liberty in the above respects in the same way as a Muslim Ruler would do, and where the Muslim subjects have no strength and means to fight with their rulers; on the contrary, there is every chance of the war, if waged, ending with a defeat, and thereby causing an indignity to Islam. (218)

The fatwa:

> The Musalmans here are protected by Christians, and there is no
> Jihad in a country where protection is afforded, as the absence of
> protection and liberty between Musalmans and Infidels is essential
> in a religious war, and that condition does not exist here. Besides,
> it is necessary that there should be a probability of victory to
> Musalmans and glory to the Indians. If there be no such probabil-
> ity, the Jihad is unlawful.

By Maulavi Ali Muhammad, Maulavi Abdul Hai, Maulavi
Fazlullah, Muhammad Naim, and Maulavi Rahmatullah, all of
Lucknow, Maulavi Qutb-ud-Din of Delhi, Maulavi Lutfullah
of Rampur. (218–19)

This strategy to seek counter-fatwas, or juridical opinions, at least
in India, was also used by other religions. For example, in the case
of Hindus, British officials approached the Hindu clergy to seek
their opinion in favor of an imperial law or policy. Incorporating
the opinions of native scholars, or Ulma, was crucial to the hegemonic project of the Empire. In almost all cases in which Muslim
scholars "served" the interests of the empire, they were termed
Ulma-e-Su by their opponents and by the public. In other words,
as the Muslim political order collapsed, the Muslim public sphere
became even more open to and welcoming of the opinions of Ulma
and scholars. And this influence of the scholars, I have suggested,
has its own history and genealogy within the discursive history of
Islam.

There are two such public Ulma whose opinions and writings
were offered and popularized in opposition to their Muslim rulers
and whose followers still wield immense power in their respective
communities of the Islamic world today: Imam Ahmad bin Hanbal
and Mujaddad Alif Sani of Sirhind.

Imam Ahmad bin Hanbal's teachings now form the core of Sharia law in Saudi Arabia. Founder of the Hanbaliya school of inter-

pretation (the last of the major schools), bin Hanbal was born in "164 AH [780 CE] in Baghdad" and, because his father died young, "was raised as an orphan" (Al-Khattab xvi). It is important to note that bin Hanbal was the last of the great jurists, and when he entered the arena of jurisprudence, his stance needed to be much different from that of the established school. While he had a large number of ardent followers, he gained his symbolic power not only through his work on the hadīth and Sunnah but also because of his opposition to Al-Mamun, the Abbasid caliph, and his successors. It is this resistance to the imperatives of the sovereign that garners him his space within the Muslim symbolic universe and ultimately launches his career as the last of the great imams, great enough to be the founder of Hanbal madhab, the one that happens to be the official doctrine of Saudi Arabia.

There are four major schools of jurisprudence and Islamic inter-pretation: Hanafi, Sha'fai, Maliki, and Hanbali. Out of these, the Hanbali madhab, established after the death of bin Hanbal, tends to be the most conservative and literalist in its approach to ques-tions of religious interpretation. According to most scholars, "the Hanbalis adhere almost to the literal injunctions of the Qur'an and Hadith" (Farah 194). My point here is not to explain the Hanbali madhab but to trace the rise of its founder within the mythology of scholarly resistance to political imperatives. The greatest historical narrative of legitimacy associated with bin Hanbal is his opposition to the caliph Al-Mamun. The *mihnah*, or questioning, was initiated by the caliph after he, on the advice of *mutzillah* scholars, had made the "createdness of the Qur'an"[4] the official doctrine of the Abbasid Empire. After doing so, the caliph also instituted a mihnah under which all religious scholars were questioned to prove their stance on the issue of the "createdness of the Qur'an." It was bin Hanbal's confrontation with the caliph and his functionaries that becomes, due to his refusal to accept official doctrine, the ultimate legitimiz-ing grounds for bin Hanbal's rise to prominence as a true imam. It is, therefore, his steadfastness under the mihnah that is the kind of historical retrieval against the grain of official histories that is mobilized to create role models for future extragovernmental conduct of Muslim scholars and their followers.

Saudi scholars (all Hanbalites) explain the performance of their imam under the mihnah as follows:

> Imam Ahamad continued to narrate *hadeeth* and issue *fatwas* until 218 AH, when the caliph al-Ma'moon declared his views that the Qur'an was created and issued orders that the scholars be tested concerning their opinions on this issue. But Imam Ahmad remained steadfast in his view that the Qur'an is the word of Allah and not created. He was taken to al-Ma'moon in chains, but when he reached as-Raqqah, news came of the death of al-Ma'moon . . .
>
> Among the things he said when he was being tested during the *mihnah* was: "If the scholars remain silent on the grounds of dissimulation (*taqiyyah*), and the ignorant do not know, when will the truth be manifested?" (Al-Khattab xvii–xviii)

The ultimate narrative of resistance involves an injunction, trial, or torture by a powerful political figure and its defiance by a righteous scholar or imam. It is this narrative of resistance that becomes one of the main mobilizing myths in all forms of radical resistance in the Islamic world both during colonial rule and in the postcolonies. In the case of bin Hanbal and his madhab, things become even more complex after his doctrine is officially adopted in the Kingdom of Saudi Arabia. But my point here is not to delve into a discussion of the Saudi system and the impact of Abdul-Wahab[5] in the adoption of Hanbalite jurisprudence, but rather to retrieve a genealogy of the creation of resistance myths within popular Islamic tradition.

The second figure in Islamic history is Mujaddad Alif Sani of Sirhind. In India the popular narrative of Sani is yet another example of a narrative that works under the same symbolic construct: a king (Jalauddin Muhammad Akbar) has declared a certain kind of religion to be the official religion of India, and a religious scholar emerges to contest this declaration in the popular domain and is considered the "savior" of Islam in India. The only difference between this narrative and the one about bin Hanbal is that while bin Hanbal belonged to the strictest and most literalist school of Islam, the Mujaddad belongs, loosely, to the Sufi and mystical tradition of Islam. While discussing the importance of Sani for the survival of Islam in India, his biographer, Muhamad Masood Ahmad, quotes the opinion of Shah Walliullah about the Mujaddad as follows:[6]

> It is all because of Hazrat Mujaddad's efforts during the times of Akbar that we still hear the sound of the azan from our mosques and wiriness Muslims praise the God and his Prophet in mosques and at shrines. Had the Mujaddad not challenged Akbar and initiated the renaissance of faith there would have been neither the sound of the azan nor any religious education in the madrassas. (40)

Note that there is no scholarly consensus on the Mujaddad's role in singlehandedly defeating Akbar's Deen-e-Illahi. In fact, according to Sheikh Muhammad Akram, even before the Mujaddad wrote his famous letters about the king, "The apostasy of Akbar had already been defeated" (quoted by Masood Ahmad, 281). However, it is undeniable that Mujaddad's mythical role in preventing the fall of Islam during the times of Akbar and his son Jahangir has become a part of popular lore and, scholarly disputations notwithstanding, he is seen as the historical figure who challenged Akbar's Deen-e-Illahi. It is this popular belief in the role of a Sufi scholar that endures and creates precedence to follow that is crucial to understanding the constant rise of such human subjects within the Muslim tradition of reform and challenge to political systems.

Even Muhammad Iqbal, the most influential poet-philosopher of India, writes about the Mujaddad and offers him as an example to the often-corrupt peers and Sayeds of Punjab:[7]

I visited the grave of Shaikh Mujaddad
That dust patch filled with light under the skies
That dust that shines brighter than the stars
That dust that hides that man of secrets
The one who did not bow his head to Jehangir
And whose presence warms the hearts of the faithful
The savior of wealth of the millat in India
The one whom God gave timely warning! (*Baal-e-Jibreel* 158–59)

Note that I have already pointed out that the Mujaddad's place as the ultimate "savior" of Islam is already historically contested, but facts lose their ground when the logic of historical mythmaking takes over. In Iqbal's poem, the poet not only acknowledges that the sheikh had saved Islam in India but he also compares him to other sheikhs of his time who do not measure up to expectations. Not only is a historical figure mythologized, he also becomes a standard against which the conduct of all others is measured. In the end, such historical appropriations create an aura of expectation for scholars and make semiotic and material resistance against oppressive, non-Islamic government actions worthy of emulation and repetition. It is within this mythologization of the heroes of Islam that the divide between the established political order and the resisting figure of the religious leader is crystallized and offered up for use by future generations.

Of course, this at first may seem irrelevant to my project. What is the significance of knowing that there is a parallel and unofficial tradition of mythologizing and narrativizing Muslim history? Since my intention in this chapter is to highlight how the popular Muslim senses of the sacred are constructed, I rely on some examples of unofficial historical retrievals and the effects of their mobilization. Within these narratives, a sense of popular justice and popular norms emerges that is not dependent upon official doctrine and often, in fact, works in opposition to official political doctrine. Thus, on the whole, even if Muslim governments might agree about a certain imperative, there are always currents within Muslim societies that have their own alternative norm, and sometimes this norm becomes the national or the political norm, as has happened in Iran and Saudi Arabia. Knowing that this kind of divide exists in Muslim societies is crucial when attempting to gain a clear understanding of Muslim reactions to the West in general and the poetics of incitement in particular.

It is crucial for metropolitan readers and critics to understand the aspects of the Muslim sacred that are mobilized against the poetics of incitement, for without knowing what causes the material-semiotic responses to the poetics of incitement, only an uninformed, incomplete Eurocentric perspective of such phenomena informs metropolitan readers. This Eurocentric perspective oversimplifies the complexity of Muslim responses, reducing all reading practices to a Western, universalist mode. There are some essentials for a clear understanding of the Muslim reception of texts that constitute a poetics of incitement—that is, texts that satirize, parody, and mock God, the Qur'ān, or the Prophet and his immediate companions; texts that sexualize the lives of the wives of the Prophet or the companions of the Prophet; works that trivialize persons—historical or contemporary—who are considered friends of God and who are prominent religious scholars; and texts that satirize or trivialize established religious practices or places.

I am not suggesting that metropolitan readers should hold the same view as their Muslim counterparts; that would be asking them to do the same as they ask of Muslim readers. I am suggesting, instead, that metropolitan engagements with Muslim responses to transgressive texts should not simply rely on Western senses of the sacred or an overreliance on the mythologies of freedom of expression. They should, rather, have nuanced opinions regarding the reception of these texts with an understanding of what mobilizes general Muslim responses to the poetics of incitement. Beyond these sacrosanct subjects, the official as well as popular Muslim histories are filled with instances and examples—some discussed above—in which prominent and everyday Muslims have risen against the dictates of a government or rulers, and such acts are valorized and mythologized even in contemporary poetry and fictions produced in the Muslim world.

So, in order to fully understand what these transgressive texts do, how they are received, and why one must have some basic awareness of the official Muslim sacred as well as its popular forms, a simplistic understanding of Islamic history will certainly not suffice. A genealogical understanding of Islamic history—an understanding that combines official and buried knowledges—is absolutely necessary to understand Muslim responses.

Some may suggest that this means every reader of texts about Islam must become a scholar of Islam as well. My answer, of course, is that this is not necessary. I do not expect scholars in the West to become professional scholars of Islam. Instead, what I do expect is for them to have the same kind of deep cultural knowledge about Islam to perform the kind of reading of which they are expected to get through the great works of Western literature. Especially for literary critics, media pundits, and teachers of literature, a deep understanding of the Muslim sacred is absolutely necessary, for only then can they teach, consume, and talk about the poetics of incitement with a meaningful degree of cultural complexity. The absence of such knowledge would only force them to reduce all such texts according to their own preestablished modes of meaning-making, which would not enable them to fully under-stand the complex nature of Muslim responses to the books, car-toons, and movies that increasingly make Islam a primary topic through appropriation.

What I propose is what Jonathan Culler calls a "semiotic of reading," albeit a slightly different and non-Eurocentric semiotic of reading. For Culler, interpretation should not only be about judg-ing correct readings but also about acknowledging that "various readings are the product of interpretive conventions that can be described" (67) and that "this project [of describing various interpretive conventions] is disrupted whenever one slips back into the position of judge" (67). And if we claim to be "judges" of texts about Islam, then we must, at least, know the very logic of the sacred within Islam, with all its historical and geographical permutations.

CHAPTER 3

INCITEMENTS

Salman Rushdie and the Quixotics of Reforming Islam

> *The attempt at reclamation goes even further than this. . . . The very title, The Satanic Verses, is an aspect of this attempt at reclamation. You call us devils? It seems to ask. Very well, then, here is the devil's version of the world, of 'your' world, the version written from the experience of those who have been demonized by virtue of their otherness. Just as the Asian kids in the novel wear toy devil-horns proudly, as an assertion of pride in identity, so the novel proudly wears its demonic title.*
>
> —Salman Rushdie, "In Good Faith"

When *The Satanic Verses* (1988) was published and became controversial, Salman Rushdie offered a series of explanations about writing and publishing his novel. For lack of a better term, I use the term *quixotics* to capture the absurd nature of Rushdie's claims about the novel. Simply explained, the term, for me, refers to the kinds of after-the-fact claims that one offers to justify and rationalize an act.

Before I begin my discussion of Rushdie's argument about the novel, it seems appropriate to provide a sampling of passages and sections that were either deemed objectionable or blasphemous by Muslim readers and critics.

About the Prophet:

His name: a dream-name, changed by the vision. Pronounced correctly, it means he-for-whom-thanks-should-be-given, but he won't answer to that here; nor, though he's well aware of what they call him, to his nickname in Jahilia down below—*he-who-goes-up-and-down-old-Coney.* Here he is neither Mahomet nor MoeHammered; he has adopted, instead, demon-tag the farangis hung around his neck. To turn insults into strengths, Whigs, Tories, Blacks all chose to wear with pride the names they were given in scorn; likewise, our mountain-climbing, prophet-motivated solitary is to be the medieval baby-frightener, the Devil's synonym: Mahound.

That's him. Mahound the businessman, climbing his hot mountain in the Hijaz. The mirage of a city shines below him in the sun. (*Satanic* 93)

About the Prophet's Companions and the Qur'ān:

In the grip of a self-destructive unhappiness the three disciples had started drinking, and owing to their unfamiliarity with alcohol they were soon not just intoxicated but stupid-drunk. . . .

Salman the Persian got to wondering what manner of God this was that sounded so much like a businessman. This was when he had the idea that destroyed his faith, because he recalled that of course Mahound himself had been a businessman, and a damned successful one at that, a person to whom organization and rules came naturally, so how excessively convenient it was that he should have come up with such a very businesslike archangel, who handed down the management decisions of this highly corporate, if non-corporeal, God. . . .

What finally finished Salman with Mahound: the question of the women; and of the Satanic Verses. Listen, I'm no gossip, Salman drunkenly confided, but after his wife's death Mahound was no angel, you understand my meaning. . . . The point about our Prophet, my dear Baal, is that he didn't like his women to answer back, he went for mothers and daughters, think of his first wife and then Ayesha: too old and too young, his two loves. . . .

[Salman] Here's the point: Mahound did not notice the alterations [to the Qur'an]. So there I was, actually writing the Book, or rewriting, anyway, polluting the word of God with my own profane language. But, good heavens, if my poor words could not be distinguished from the revelation by God's own Messenger, then what did that mean? What did that say about the quality of the divine poetry? (*Satanic* 117, 364–67)

About the Prophet's wives, the account includes, in the dream sequence still, poet Baal's sojourn in the brothel called the Hijab, his naming of his consorts after the names of the poet's wives, and a parody of the defamation incident against Ayesha, the Prophet's wife.[1]

These are some of the passages and references that most Muslims—fundamentalists and progressives alike—found to be offensive and hurtful. There is an entire catalogue of Muslim responses to these passages. Contrarily, there are long-winded defenses of these passages and Rushdie's right to publish them by Rushdie's apologists and other metropolitan defenders of free speech. My point here is not to contest these appropriations and discussions of the passages[2] but instead dwell a bit on Rushdie's own defense and explanation and then provide my own views on the subject.

RUSHDIE'S ARGUMENT

In a wonderfully crafted and eloquently argued essay about Muslim responses to the "offensive" nature of his book, Rushdie argues for the inoffensiveness of his "offensive" novel under several rhetorical registers.[3] In his essay, Rushdie invokes, in sequential manner, the list of objections raised regarding the novel from unnamed, generic Muslim sources and then offers his own refutation of those claims.

Of course, the first question that comes to mind is: How does writing an essay in English serve the purpose of refuting these objections, given that most of the Muslim public that Rushdie hopes to address does not read in English and are not professional literary critics? The essay is an explicatory note as well as a patronizing didactic argument for the potential Muslim reader of English. In a way, the essay's imagined reader is already a Muslim who would at least read the novel and do so with the tools of Western literary criticism, for any other mode of reading, it seems, would not render the authorial intentions of the author correctly. Furthermore, the only "true" interpretation of the text is supposed to be what Rushdie himself offers and, therefore, all contrary readings are either ill-informed or inadequate. Rushdie's self-defense, therefore, depends upon an extreme and immutable form of legitimacy of authorial intention, an intention mobilized and normalized at the cost of the reader's right to read and interpret according to their own modes of reading and meaning-making. In other words, to really "get" what the novel intends, according to Rushdie, the Muslim reader must become an informed critical reader with a Western mode of reading as their *primary* and *only* reference.

In this didactic piece, Rushdie starts with a discussion of the novel as a genre. In other words, he wants his (English-reading Muslim) readers to understand that *The Satanic Verses* is neither a "work of bad history" ("In Good Faith" 393) nor an outcome of an "international capitalist-Jewish conspiracy" (393) but rather a work of fiction. In other words, unless the naïve Muslim reader can differentiate between fact and fiction and unless they understand the generic subtleties of the novel, they are, somehow, likely to miss the point. Muslim anger and anguish, therefore, is simply an outcome of a gross misreading that is further aggravated by the propaganda of religious pamphleteers. The purpose of Rushdie's essay, then, is to offer an explanation to Muslims by way of a pedantic lecture about fiction and about the novel as a generic form.

While Rushdie asserts that he is "not trying to say that *The*

Satanic Verses is 'only a novel' and thus need not be taken seriously"
(393), he also expects his readers to know the very generic specificity of the novel in order to truly understand what he intends in
terms of meaning. Note that his emphasis still is on explaining and
establishing authorial intent as absolute. In Rushdie's words, the
novel can be described as follows:

> If *The Satanic Verses* is anything, it is a migrant's-eye view of the
> world. It is written from the very experience of uprooting. Dis-
> juncture, and metamorphosis (slow or rapid, painful or pleasur-
> able) that is the migrant condition, and from which, I believe, can
> be derived a metaphor for all humanity. ("In Good Faith" 394)

It becomes obvious that the novel belongs to a specific genre of
postmodern fiction, and in order to comprehend it, Rushdie suggests, we must first be privy to its specific point of view (POV): that
of a migrant. In other words, anyone who does not read the novel
through this lens—a lens now provided by the author himself—
would miss the point and misconstrue its meanings. Note that
this extreme privileging of authorial intention completely forces
the reader to read the novel as the author wishes it to be read.
If one were to suggest this to a metropolitan reading audience,
most critics would not accept it, as a complete concession to the
author's own version of the text would essentially render literary
studies meaningless; the study of literature would be reduced to
interviewing authors in order to reveal "true meaning."

Next, Rushdie goes on to explain another aspect of his novel:
the characters. Like the POV, readers are expected to read the characters a certain way in order to understand the novel. By now one
is expected to follow the directions based on the generic specificity
of the novel in conjunction with author-provided character analysis. Note that such constricting suggestions will never really be
welcomed by metropolitan readers and critics:

Standing at the centre of the novel is a group of characters most of whom are British Muslims, or not particularly religious persons of Muslim background, struggling with just the sort of great problems that have arisen to surround the book, problems of hybridization and ghettoization, of reconciling the old and the new. (394)

So, after educating the reader about the generic specificity of the novel itself and the authorial POV that drives the narrative, readers are now supposed to read the characters a certain way or else, it is implied, the true meaning of the novel is lost, especially on those who oppose the "intermingling with a different culture" (394) that novels purport to promote. Thus, unless readers read the novel in sympathy with authorial intent and the kind of politics of identity that the author and his characters privilege, the reading would somehow not and could not be valid. This imperial imperative to assert only a certain kind of reading as valid would also be dismissed by metropolitan critics.

Having laid down the basics of how to correctly read his novel, Rushdie goes on to express what kind of book the novel has been declared to be by critical Muslim readers: one "containing nothing but filth and insults and abuse" (395). Rushdie now argues that the book is not what Muslim readers think it is. In other words, it may have insults and abuse in it, but that is not what the book is truly about. The book is, in Rushdie's words, "a work of radical dissent and questioning and reimagining" (395). But, somehow, even though it is a reimagining by the author, it must also be read, despite the so-called insults, as a work of cultural reimagining by the readers. For Rushdie, if Muslims could somehow forget about the abuses and insults contained in the book, then a more fruitful reading can be performed. Rushdie implores:

You see, it's my opinion that if we could only dispose of the 'insults and abuse' accusation . . . then we might be able, at the very least, to agree to differ about the book's real themes, about the relative value of sacred and profane, about the merits of purity and those of hotch-potch, and about how human beings really become whole: through the love of God or the love of their fellow men and women.

And to dispose of the argument, we must return for a moment to the actually existing book, not the book described in the various pamphlets that have been circulated to the faithful, not the 'unreadable' text of legend, not two chapters dragged out of the whole; not a piece of blubber, but the whole wretched whale. (395–96)

It is obvious that for Rushdie and his opponents to have a rational conversation, a certain compromise must be reached. Sadly, this compromise requires the "offended" party to forget the offense in order to acknowledge the author's defense, thus rendering the social dimension of the novel meaningless, as the author himself attains the status of grand interpreter. What the author desires is that the work should be read as a whole, and only then should a value be assigned to its content or the intention of the author. This suggests that ultimately, even for Rushdie, the work is an organic whole, and in order to opine about it, one must evaluate the whole and not just select portions. If Muslim readers put aside their readerly prejudices and all responses exterior to the text, then they could, somehow, understand the noble intent of the author. Note that this reading technique is also external to the text itself as the author is attempting to impose a particular mode of reading on his skeptical audience.

Now if we go by the classic definition of the text as a logical whole and remember the pitfalls of the intentional fallacy, we already know that there is no need on the part of the reader to seek authorial explanation beyond the text, as the text itself contains what the author intended. Thus, by this logic, even if Muslim readers were only focused on the text itself, the text would still be offensive and it could then be construed to be the very intention of the author, because the text, in such a phenomenological approach to reading, is the ultimate intention of the author printed on a page. Authorly advice notwithstanding, the text could only be rendered inert or inoffensive if readers were to understand it exactly as directed by the author: an act akin to following the directions on a medicine bottle. But reading does not work this way and never has. A reader can only read the text informed by cultural norms, readerly assumptions, and prejudices that constitute their own reading practices. To insist on a different kind of reading—the kind of reading that the author desires—is an imperial act that would never be accepted within the norms of metropolitan reading practices.

What would Rushdie accomplish if readers were to pause and give the text a chance? Such a reading would need a clear understanding of the novel as a genre as well as guidance from the author himself. We have Rushdie's own words on this kind of reading:

> *The Satanic Verses* is the story of two painfully divided selves. In case of one, Saladin Chamcha, the division is secular and societal: he is torn, to put it plainly, between Bombay and London, between East and West. For the other, Gibreel Farishta, the division is spiritual, a rift in the soul. He has lost his faith and is strung out between his immense need to believe and his new inability to do so. The novel is 'about' their quest for wholeness. ("In Good Faith" 397)

It is fairly clear that the only way to understand the novel and reach the author's intent is to clearly understand what the novel is about: the struggles of its two main characters. Of course, for Rushdie, this understanding is crucial, for only if one were to read the novel as a whole with this knowledge of its main characters can one read beyond the insults and abuses, for then the insults and abuses could be placed on the characters and not the creator of the text.

It is obvious that the Jahiliyya chapters are mostly enacted through Gibreel Farishta's dreams, and in order to truly understand what they mean, one ought to be educated in reading this character more acutely. And as Rushdie suggests, "Gibreel's most painful dreams, the ones at the center of the controversy, depict the birth and growth of a religion something like Islam" (398) and, in Rushdie's words, the "purpose of these sequences is not to vilify or 'disprove' Islam, but to portray a soul in crisis" (399). Of course, this makes sense. How else could Rushdie portray a character who is going through an extreme crisis of faith? But then there is the question of language that Farishta uses in his dreams, the language in which the dreams unfold to him. Rushdie's answer to this is to offer a narrative of stylistic consistency; in other words, the dreams are offered in such coarse and insulting language because "the waking Gibreel is a coarse-mouthed fellow" (399) and, it seems, his dreams had to have some kind of lexical correspondence with his waking self.

But this is sadly ironic: for if one were to see all the abuses and curses only from the eyes of the characters, then inserting authorial intent in the act of interpretation is the last thing one would want to do. Of course, this leads one to ask another concomitant question: Why such an insistence on authorial intent? Considering the charges leveled against Rushdie by some of the Muslim clergy, the only defense could be to prove beyond a doubt that Rushdie had no intention of insulting the Prophet or the Prophet's wives and hallowed companions. This essay and many other interviews with Rushdie are not only explanations and explications of the novel but also a form of legal defense. While I would otherwise be skeptical of inserting authorial intention in the act of interpretation, here Rushdie's insistence on explaining his intentions and "training" the readers about how to read his novel are fully understandable.

Having explained where the novel is set and how to read the actions and thoughts of his characters, especially Farishta's dreams, Rushdie then proceeds to explain how it would help dispel the concerns of his Muslim readers and help them see clearly that the chapters are not actually offensive but rather consistent with the dreams of a deranged and tortured character. After this general explanation of the characters, the tone, and the setting, Rushdie attempts to rescue certain specific aspects of his representation of Islam. He goes on to explain the references in the novel to the companions of the Prophet and the dream sequence about the brothel (which, in my view, was the most disturbing scene to most Muslims) by addressing the question of the sacred and the profane and by explaining that all these events—the Jahiliyya chapter—happen as part of dream sequences of a very disturbed character.

Furthermore, Rushdie asserts, "the scene in which the Prophet's companions are called 'scum' and 'bums' is a depiction of the early persecution of the believers, and the insults quoted are clearly not mine but those hurled at the faithful by the ungodly" (401). Similarly, concerning the most disturbing representation of the brothel, Rushdie suggests, "what happens in Gibreel's dreams is that the whores of a brothel take the names of the wives of the Prophet Mahound in order to arouse their customers" (401). Rushdie answers the question asked by so many Muslims about why such a description of the brothel is necessary by stating that

> [t]hroughout the novel, I sought images that crystallized the opposition between the sacred and the profane worlds. The harem and the brothel provide such an opposition. Both are places where women are sequestered, in the harem to keep them from all men except their husband and close family members, in the brothel for the sue of strange males. . . .
>
> The two struggling worlds, pure and impure, chaste and coarse, are juxtaposed by making them echoes of one another; and, finally, the pure eradicates the impure. (401)

This explanation makes perfect sense to anyone attuned to modernist and postmodernist modes of writing. But this explanation, other than privileging a Eurocentric mode of representation, does not explain anything to Muslim readers in accordance with their meaning-making practices. What Rushdie finds apt and so crucial to his attempt at combining the profane and the sacred is simply not done by most Muslim writers. Needless to say, even though there are thousands of challenges to the assumptions about women's roles in the Islamic Sharia, all of those arguments are made from within and without any attempts at parody, irony, or any other artistic artifice. Rushdie's explanation is rather an assertion that his mode of tackling the issue—with a predominantly Western artistic device—should be accepted as the norm by Muslim readers. If they fail to understand the text as such, they are simply bigoted and illiterate.

Furthermore, within this essay, Rushdie invokes the all-important question concerning the right to criticize the norm and the religious dogma by way of suggesting that what he is doing is part of (or ought to be) a critical tradition in Islam. While developing this argument, Rushdie also provides the all-instructive reason for assigning the designation "Mahound" to the Prophet, by suggesting that it is akin to owning the insults of others as our own and making them a part of the accepted lexicon of a particular society or social group. But for such insults to become acceptable, a larger consensus within the community is needed, and that acceptance must come from within the community. A normalization of insults cannot be enacted by the work of an elite author using postmodern parody to write about the most sacred aspects of a religion that he, self-declaredly, has abandoned. Thus, one cannot read the transformation of Muhammad into Mahound as internal to the logic of the larger Islamic community, for no such adoption of the insulting term as a valorized one exists in Islamic history and letters. Rushdie absolutely lacks the cultural caché to render the term acceptable, for he is, after all, writing from outside of the Islamic community due to his non-Muslim status, even though he was born in a Muslim family.

Rushdie's stance about the nature and importance of his work becomes even more quixotic when he makes the most complex issues of Islamic jurisprudence a part of his polemic. He asserts:

> To those participants in the controversy who have felt able to justify the most extreme Muslim threats towards me and others by saying that I have broken an Islamic rule, I would ask the following question: are all the rules laid down at a religion's origin immutable forever? How about penalties for prostitution (stoning to death) or thieving (mutilation)? How about the prohibition of homosexuality? How about the Islamic law of inheritance, which allows a widow to inherit only one eighth share, and which gives to sons twice as much as it does to daughters? ("In Good Faith" 400)

Naturally, Rushdie is not the first one to ask these questions; there are other more scholarly engagements with these questions, and these rules are perpetually under different kinds of challenge and stipulation in Muslim societies already. Muslim theological tradition also provides hundreds of years of history of dissent and commentary on these issues. The difference, however, is that these critiques come from within and use the vocabularies of dissent but with due deference to the sanctity of the expected historical, symbolic, and sacred roles of various individuals within Islamic history. Thus, the practice of criticism and revision within the Islamic tradition has its own logic and norms of respect and permissibility, and if one defies this logic, positive reform remains impossible. Instead, conflict becomes the end result. For any critique to be effective, it must come from within the norms of Muslim discourse and cannot be affected through a work that already undermines its own logic and its own seriousness through a parodic "historiographic metafiction."

One could say that the reception of *The Satanic Verses* cannot just be reduced to a question of intolerance but should also be connected to the question of form and genre. That brings us to the extremely imperial nature of Rushdie's project: a British-based author writes a book touching upon the most sacred concepts in Islam and then hopes to be heard dispassionately in Muslim nations simply because the place in which he writes happens to be tolerant of such writing. This is just another way of saying that the only "true" present is the "universal" present of the metropolitan West, and the only civilized part of the world happens to be where enunciations such as Rushdie's are accepted without reservations. In other words, Rushdie implies, if you have a problem with his way of seeing it, you are somehow not advanced enough as individuals and as a society.

THE REFORM TRADITION IN ISLAM

Keeping in view what I argued and explained in the last chapter, one must approach the question of permissibility and sanction with a clear understanding of the Muslim sacred and the rules of permissibility within it. Also, one must rethink the attempt to reform and represent and keep in mind the rich tradition of reform already ongoing within Muslim societies.

I will discuss here, albeit briefly, two texts that have successfully challenged the most contentious issues within the Islamic sacred and have not only created a meaningful space within Islamic discourse but have done so without any sanction and without any threats of apostasy or murder: *Haqooq-e-Niswan* (Rights of women) by Maulaman Mumtaz Ali in 1898 and *Woman and Islam* by Fatima Mernissi in 1987. Both these texts, one by a male Muslim scholar from India and the other by a female Muslim scholar from Morocco, focus on the issues related to the rights of women in Islam. Both succeed in their radical attempts, because they argue their points from within the Islamic tradition and tackle the issues in a language that does not rely on any cosmetic rhetorical flourishes and engage with the subject using the kind of seriousness and respect that is the norm in Islamic theological writing. In other words, these authors can broach and discuss serious issues because they do so within the logic of Islamic religious discourse. As such, their radical thought might be challenged but it cannot be regarded as contentious until read.

I discuss these two authors and their works, briefly, to highlight the importance of writing from within the scholarly and cultural tradition of a field that is always in the process of being challenged. This demonstrates why these two authors are acceptable even though their challenge to Muslim orthodoxy, in terms of substance, is more radical than Rushdie's. I know at this point, I need not offer this comparison, but it would serve my readers well if they could see the difference in comparison.

Both these authors embark on their scholarly journeys to refute the traditional interpretations of the Qur'ān and the hadīth, mobilized by conservative scholars to justify the secondary role assigned to Muslim women. Ali provides an explanation and then an extended discussion of the misreading of a particular passage from the Qur'ān while Mernissi provides the archaeological details of a few hadīth that are often mobilized to keep women out of the political public sphere.

Mernissi begins her inquiry with an anecdote, where in response to a question about women's roles as leaders, she is silenced through the invocation of a single hadīth: "Those who entrust their affairs to a woman will never know prosperity!" (1). This encounter, in which a sacred text silences her even before she has uttered her question, sets her on a quest to inform herself "of this Hadith and to search out the texts where it is mentioned, to understand better its extraordinary power over the ordinary citizens of a modern state" (2). Note that Mernissi's quest is somewhat similar to that of Rushdie, for the latter is also trying to write about the place of women in Muslim society, which he goes on to seek and then extrapolate from another set of Qur'ānic verses in his novel. The difference, however, relates to form: while Mernissi takes it upon herself to seek the answer through her diligent and patient research within the field of Islamic exegesis, Rushdie resorts to a flashy, self-reflexive, and playful novelistic narrative. The difference, therefore, is not the content (for Mernissi's content is more radical, arguing against a normalized worldview about women in her culture)—the difference is the tone.

Mernissi broaches a radical question from within the logic of Islamic theology and then goes on a quest to challenge the very pronouncement that fixes women's roles. Her work is effective because she challenges Islamic theology from within a preexisting tradition of exegesis. She does not want the peripheral aspects of her challenge to undermine her argument. Rushdie, on the other hand, is not concerned with writing within the established exegetical tradition. His tone and style exceed the normalized discourse, thus making his work inherently transgressive. While there is a lot of thunder in his novel, it fails to become a catalyst for positive change within Islamic cultures because of this very transgressiveness and its place outside of normalized Muslim discourse. Now, I am not suggesting that Rushdie is trying to reform Islam, but he is offering a criticism of it, and my point is that such criticisms work only if they follow the norms within the logic of permissibility in Islam. In fact, it further pushes quite a few Islamic nations to more extreme positions. I am not suggesting that Rushdie's novel was meant to reform Islam, but that kind of claim is implicit in a work that attempts to rewrite the very basic assumptions about one of the world's three major monotheistic religions.

So, how does Mernissi argue her point? Having encountered public misogyny and being forced to accept it through the invocation of a hadīth, Mernissi shares her plan of action as follows:

> My misadventure in a neighborhood grocery store had more than symbolic importance for me. Revealing the misogynistic attitude of my neighbors, it indicated to me the path I should take to better understand it—a study of the religious texts that everybody knows

but no one really probes, with the exception of the authorities on the subject: the mullahs and imams. (2)

In Mernissi's estimation, no playful representations of the sacred and the taboo would create solace for her and other women in the public sphere of a democratic Muslim state; this space must be opened by a thorough understanding of the methods of exegesis followed by a deeper reading of the sacred itself from within the culture where it is invoked. Writing from a place outside the discourse of the Muslim sacred would be necessarily futile and lack the discursive capital to affect positive reform.

I am not suggesting that this should have been Rushdie's approach. What I am suggesting is that, stylistically speaking, no matter how sympathetic Rushdie might have been to Islam, by mocking and satirizing sacred aspects of Islam, his work becomes a kind of cautionary tale and serves to enhance the very gendered hierarchies that the novel challenges. On the other hand, Mernissi's work, because of the respect accorded to questions of faith, creates a discursive space within the preestablished discourse of the Islamic sacred to create a place for Muslim women within the public sphere.

The case, either way, must be proven from within the tradition itself, for anything asserted from outside is necessarily invalid within the internal logic of Islam. Mernissi's quest is to see if the hadīth in question (that those who entrust their affairs to a woman will know prosperity) is authentic. It is crucial to answer this question, for finding the veracity of the hadīth is crucial to changing and validating the scholarly consensus on the rights of women in Islam as well as to advocating and abrogating public roles for women. Similarly, the author must also follow the normalized method of research and exegesis, for she does not want her argument to be weakened by a lack of knowledge and adherence to the method itself. In other words, if she does not inhabit the persona of a religious scholar, then her argument will be received as invalid due to its nonscholarly and amateurish nature.

What I am trying to assert here is that there are more cogent and eloquent challenges to the patriarchal appropriations of Islam, and that some of these challenges *actually changed* material conditions and politics within the Islamic world. The two texts that I have chosen clearly affect sociopolitical change. Toward the end of her book, having followed the trace of meaning through a mountain of Islamic political scholarship, Mernissi finally gives us her views about the normalization of *hijab* and the silencing of women as active agents in Islamic society by retrieving the silenced history that underwrote hijab during the times of the Prophet. Both Mernissi and Rushdie reiterate one particular event in their works: the incident regarding Aisha,[4] the Prophet's wife, called "al-ifk" (the lie) by Muslim scholars and called "the affair of the necklace" by Orientalist scholars (Mernissi 177).

Rushdie, in a characteristically postmodernist fashion, invokes the incident through the voice of Salman, an unreliable character within an already unreliable dream sequence by Gibreel Farishta, who is going mad. The scene is staged as a drunken conversation between Salman and Baal, the god of fertility and weather. I provide both representations here to highlight the importance of tone as a rhetorical strategy. In Rushdie's account:

> Ayesha and the Prophet had gone on an expedition to a far-flung village, and on the way back to Yathrib their party had camped in the dunes for the night. Camp was struck in the dark before the dawn. At the last moment Ayesha was obliged by a call of nature to rush out of sight into a hollow. While she was away her litter-bearers picked up her palanquin and marched off. She was a light woman, and, failing to notice much difference in the weight of that heavy palanquin, they assumed she was inside. Ayesha returned after relieving herself to find herself alone, and who knows what might have befallen her if a young man, a certain Safwan, had not chanced to pass by on his camel. . . . Safwan brought Ayesha back to Yathrib safe and sound; at which point tongues began to wag, not

least in the harem, where opportunities to weaken Ayesha's power were eagerly seized by her opponents. The two young people had been alone in the desert for many hours, and it was hinted, more and more loudly, that Safwan was a dashingly handsome fellow, and the Prophet was much older than the young woman, after all, and might she not therefore have been attracted to someone closer to her own age? "Quite a scandal," Salman commented, happily.

"What will Mahound do?" Baal wanted to know.

"O, he's done it," Salman replied. "Same as ever. He saw his pet, the archangel, and then informed one and all that Gibreel had exonerated Ayesha."

Salman spread his arms in worldly resignation. "And this time, mister, the lady didn't complain about the convenience of the verses." (*Satanic* 387)

This is, of course, an interesting postmodern rendering of a recorded historical event in the style that Linda Hutcheon terms "historiographic metafiction" (5–6). Of course, being a postmodern rendering of history, there is a certain degree of playfulness in its tone. But there are also certain strategic imaginative alterations that render the entire incident out of context for Muslims as well as for Western readers, even though it works fine within the logical drive of Salman's obsession with Mahound and all things related to Mahound. Also, important to note here is that for Salman, it is Mahound who is bent upon reassigning the public role of women within the culture of his new religion, for the Prophet, we are told by Salman, "didn't like his women to answer back" (*Satanic* 366) and thus the strict rules about hijab, in this interpretation, is a result of the Prophet's latent misogyny.

Note that, stylistically, Rushdie not only transforms the incident into the Prophet's supposed misogyny, but he also assigns the narration of the event to a nonreliable character. In the recorded incident, at least in all major accounts of it within Islamic tradition, Aisha speaks for herself and tells her own story.[5] How substituting

Aisha's own historical voice with that of an unreliable character helps the cause of Muslim women in any pragmatic sense, which the novel implicitly argues, is anyone's guess.

For Mernissi, this incident is a pivotal point in Islamic history and she narrates and discusses it with the seriousness and care deemed absolutely necessary, and she also places the incident within the political context of its time and traces its implications for the future of Muslim female subjects. Mernissi retrieves the historical account of Aisha's late return, accompanied by "Safwan ibn al-Mu'attal, a young Companion who, having found her *en route*, escorted her" (177), to the Muslim camp. This incident was "enough to unleash a veritable campaign of defamation against Aisha, orchestrated by the leader of the Hypocrites."[6] "Abdallah Ibn Ubayy" is supposed to have started his whispering campaign against Aisha (and thus indirectly against the Prophet) by exclaiming upon Aisha's arrival: "A'isha can be excused for what she just did; Safwan is handsomer and younger than Muhammad" (178).

Now, Aisha's own account in the history I cited above is longer, and there is a long period of doubt and separation between her and her husband. Eventually, however, the Prophet takes a public stance on the issue. Mernissi renders this public defense of Aisha in the following words:

> The matter took on such importance that the leader of the young Muslim state decided to broach the subject publicly. He mounted the *minbar* and spoke thus to the assembled believers in the mosque: "How does somebody dare to throw suspicion on the house of the Prophet of God? It was one of the rare occasions in our Muslim history on which a political man came to the defense of his wife instead of taking sides with her accusers. (178)

The figure of the Prophet, in the actual historical account retrieved by Mernissi, performs his actions within a tumultuous political situation in Medina, and the incident gains extreme importance because in the process, the Prophet must resort to tribal customs to respond to Aisha's accusers. And thus, "with his action in the mosque [in defending Aisha] he transformed a simple rumor into a matter of tribal responsibility: the tribe to which the defamer belonged had to take charge of punishing him" (Mernissi 178). It is crucial to understand that this public intervention by the Prophet, further augmented by seventeen Qur'ānic verses revealed in support of Aisha, ultimately decided the public life of women in Islam. Until then, according to Mernissi, the Prophet had worked toward a "private life mingled with public life" (178) in which women would have had a natural public role. But after the incident and the rumors, the Prophet's "entourage presented a slaveholding solution to him: protect women—free women only—by veiling them. The slaves remained unveiled" (178). And "in a city on the brink of civil war . . . the anti-slaveholding policy that Islam sought to promote was officially abandoned—at least as far as women were concerned" (179). Since not everyone could be protected from public harm, "protection would be limited to those who were free" (179) and therefore hijab are introduced to separate free women from slave women. This is how "*hijab* incarnates, expresses, and symbolizes this official retreat from the principle of equality" (179) that until then had been the main project of early Islam.

The incident of Aisha is not only a peripheral event that can be valorized or parodied without import: it is the turning point in the egalitarian message of Islam, and to understand it with that kind of deeper cultural and historical knowledge is important not only for metropolitan readers but also for those in the Islamic world who are continuously fighting for the rights of women. One needs, in other words, more than just an artistic rendering of the event, a rendering that serves no purpose other than to lend the author some critical acclaim.

Like Mernissi, who reads an important hadīth critically, Maulana Mumtaz Ali, in his 1898 work *Haqooq-e-Niswan*[7] [Rights of women], published over a century before Rushdie's novel, challenges and refutes all rational and theological arguments against the so-called inferiority of women. His work not only challenges patriarchy but also literally opens the Indian public sphere for women's education and their involvement in the public domain. From the very outset, Ali is aware that he is broaching a controversial subject, and he also mentions the perilous nature of his work in the preface. He knows that "these ideas would be considered a mimicry of the British and a hundred pens would come together to oppose me" (2). But he finds expressing these ideas is important because "expressing these thoughts and acting upon them would work to improve our cultural condition and that is why I am daring to publish these words" (2). In Ali's view, "even if the rights of one single old woman are protected by my writing, then I would have earned my reward" (3).

He begins his argument by highlighting the most entrenched patriarchal prejudices about the rights of women in Islamic society:

> Most of the customs and beliefs of our society are based in the false idea that men are rulers over women. Since women are created to provide comfort to men, the men, therefore, have the same rights over them as they do over other property. Or that Women's rights cannot be equal to men.
>
> Now if men only believed this because of their own personal prejudices without offering any logical support for this claim, then I would have not cared much about it. But the problem is that men consider this false claim to be divinely inspired and logically proven. Therefore, the purpose of this work is to refute these baseless claims about inferiority of women. (4)

This is a declaration of extreme import. Ali challenges the very basis of gender division in Islamic theology and proposes to challenge both the so-called logical as well as theological arguments used to claim male superiority over women. His purpose, as will become clear in his later discussion, is to argue from within the

Islamic tradition with the purpose of opening the public sphere to Indian Muslim women. He then provides a list of all the arguments made to support claims of male superiority over women:

1. Men have relatively more physical prowess than women, which gives men an edge in all things that require physical strength. Since governance requires such physical strength, it therefore belongs to men.

2. Just as men are stronger in physical strength, so are they in mental strength. This is why women in all historical cultures have been considered mentally inferior. This is evident from women's proclivity to superstition, their lack of foresight, and their tendency to be disloyal in their relationships.

3. Just as governance is the most superior of all the worldly things, the Prophethood is the most superior blessing in the realm of the spiritual, and God has always bestowed this blessing on men alone. No woman has been sent as the messenger of God.

4. In religious terms, the Qur'ānic verse "Arrijal o qawwa-moona alannisa" (Al-Qur'an 4:34) is quoted and is trans-lated as "Men are the rulers of women."

5. Another false assertion often made is that God created Adam first and then created woman for his comfort. Therefore, women, having been created to comfort men, must act and live subservient to men.

6. Also used, to bolster the claims of male superiority, are the Qur'ānic verses that declare two female witnesses equal to one male witness, and similarly the verses about the rights of inheritance, women inheriting half of what men inherit, are also used to prove men's superiority.

7. The right of a man to marry four women simultaneously is also offered as proof to suggest that God has granted *more comfort* to men, thus proving them superior to women.

8. Similarly, in heaven men have been promised *hoors* (beautiful women) while no such promise has been made to women.

Note that this list is not just derived from official theological sources. This is also consistent with the laundry list offered by pretty much all men who want to assert male superiority over women. Thus, not only is Mumtaz Ali aware of the general attitude of men toward women during his lifetime but also offers a distilled list of male privilege and prejudice against women. He then goes on to refute all these claims.

I will not repeat his entire argument here, but it is important to discuss at least one part of his challenge to faulty readings of the oft-cited Qur'ānic verse: "Arrijal o qawwamoona alannisa." Usually translated as "Men are rulers over women," this verse has the same legislative power as the hadīth cited to Mernissi by her male neighbors. I personally experienced the hostility of the followers of a great Pakistani scholar when I pointed out that the main noun in the verse—*qawwam*—has never been used to mean *Hakoomah* or *Malukiyya*, the two terms often used in the Qur'ān to refer to political power. Had I read Ali then, my response to those scholars would have been much more effective. The Arabic text of the whole verse is often cited to bolster claims of male superiority: "Arrijal o qawwamoona alannisa bima Fadl Allah b'aduhum ala ba'd wa bima anfiqoo be amwalhum." Traditionally, this verse translated into Urdu and Persian says: "Men are rulers over women, for God has given *some* 'superiority' over *some* as support them with their means" (emphasis added). Ali challenges the traditional translations and commentaries of the verse in question as follows:

The scholars suggest, while explaining this verse, that men are superior in two ways: One, because they are (essentially) mentally and physically stronger than women and second because they provide for women. But I do not agree with this explanation. . . .

First, to translate *Qawwam* as "Rulers" is incorrect and other than Maulana Shah Abdul Qaqdir, no one else has used this particular translation. Secondly this translation does not clarify as to who is the *some* (*Ba'd*) in the first instance and who in the second. If men are meant at the first instance and women at the second, then all men having privilege over all women cannot be supported. If it is meant to be men at both instances then one cannot really prove that some men have privilege over other men and even if it could be proved then how does this prove that men also have privilege over women. (15–16; emphasis mine)

Ali's challenge to the translation occurs on two levels: (1) simple translation and (2) in-depth explanation of the pronouns *B'ad* used in the verse. He first provides a genealogy and etymology of the word *Qawwam* (translated as "ruler") and proves beyond a doubt that lexically, as well as in reference to other usages within the Qur'ān itself, the term *Qawwam* is never used as a cognate for *hakoomat* and thus cannot be translated as hakoomat/rulership in this particular instance. In other words, this translation happens only when men read this verse with their own preexisting gender biases. Ultimately the first clause of the verse "Arrijal o qawwamoona alannisa" cannot really be translated as "Men are rulers over women" but should instead be translated and understood as "Men are protectors/supporters/sustainers of women." Note that even though this is still a form of benevolent sexism and fairly patriarchal, this simple translation transforms gender relations from one defined by power to one defined by love, for if men are protectors/supporters/sustainers of women, then the nature of this relationship is based not in power but in their love, responsibility, and obligation to women. And, legally speaking, if one has obligations to another, then the matter is not necessarily about superiority of one over another but rather about one's rights to the support and love of another. One could also conclude from this that the verse obliges men to play their supporting roles toward women, which, incidentally, would assign them to the very secondary role that women have been traditionally assigned in Muslim societies.

Arriving as the last part of the verse, where those who provide for others are mentioned, Ali again refutes traditional claims about male superiority over women. Having established that the pronoun *B'ad* could refer to men or women, he then goes on to ask a set of questions:

> Imagine, the father provides for his sons and a master provides for his servant. Does this mean that the master has privilege over the servant? What if the case was reversed and the servant became the master? Would he then become inherently more privileged? Similarly, if all men are superior to women [The word used is *Alrijal* and not *Al-Muslimoon*] then does it imply that Abu Jh'el [one of the chief opponents of the Prophet] would have privilege over Hazrat Khadeeja [the first and the most revered wife of the Prophet]? (17)

In the end, one by one, Ali challenges and refutes all statements about the superiority of men through a judicious reading of sacred Islamic texts. This again clarifies that in order to bring about any lasting change in Islamic tradition and its popular manifestations, a certain process or method must be followed. Just as Mernissi takes up the persona of a Mujtahid, a scholar, and argues her point from within the tradition using the vocabularies of the tradition and the rules of exegesis approved and prevalent within that tradition, Ali also forwards the cause of women's rights by using the same strategies. In fact, Ali was trained as a religious scholar and "was closely associated with the founders of Deoband School and the intellectual legacy of Shah Waliullah" (Minault 148). His solutions, therefore, originate from within the tradition of Islamic jurisprudence.

There are material consequences for such diligent works of exegesis. Such works create a space within the corpus of Islamic explication and commentary for others to draw upon. Just as conservative scholars rely on more traditional explanations of the sacred and rules of conduct, progressive scholars use such works as their sources and points of reference to open a space within Muslim discourse to mobilize their own liberal and liberating enunciated speech acts. Thus, as Muslim theology and jurisprudence works through legal and theological precedence, the works of people like Ali and Mernissi, then, become prominent references in the fight against patriarchy.

Within the context of colonial India, Ali's work is crucial because it creates an argument for women's education through his book as well as through his magazine, *Ta'leem-e-Niswan*. Thanks to this, the first generation of female public figures and female Muslim leaders were produced within the discursive space made possible by the work and activism of Ali and other such scholars. As I have discussed elsewhere,[8] this trend toward female education and its importance for the Muslim culture of India was an important trope in the reformative work of other scholars and writers. In fact, the first and one of the most popular Urdu novels of its time, *Mirat-ul-Uroos*, published in 1869, also made a case for female education. The only difference between the novel and early attempts at women's liberation is that Ali argues from his position as a religious scholar and refutes the theological and logical claims offered in support of male superiority. While the novel does so from an outsider's perspective, it is this discourse from within that lends Ali's work added weight and depth.

There is a need for such works that respond and challenge the established hierarchies from within the religious debates surrounding Islam. Such works, beyond effecting immediate change, provide legal precedence for future fights about equality and women's rights. There was and is something unique about Islamic cultures and their colonization: all conquered or colonized Islamic societies were societies with living, written records of their own histories, a vast corpus of juridical and legal commentaries, and a strong belief in the immutability of their sacred texts. The colonial experience always placed Western power in stark relief with Muslims' own history and meaning-making processes. In most cases, then, anticolonial struggles rely on a sort of return to religious tradition to posit a political identity in opposition to the hegemonic and dominant project of the West. It is in this movement that conservatives in anticolonial movements attempt to evict the liberating and contaminating influences of the West to forge a "purely" Islamic identity.

As a result of this purist retrieval, postcolonial national identities in most Muslim postcolonial states transition through various stages of development or devolution: the nationalist movement usually is headed by a more cosmopolitan or Westernized elite who, sometimes in opposition to the Islamist elite, lead the way; but eventually, Islamist factions take over the national narrative to rewrite it in a way they deem appropriate for a Muslim state. One can discern these tendencies in places as far apart as Algeria and Pakistan.

Within this discursive space, advancing a mode of argument for women's rights using largely Western strategies tends to be ineffective. Within the logic of a historical retrieval of an unsullied precolonial past, Western-defined women's rights become the ultimate point of contest, the ultimate place of sanction by the patriarchy. The only way to make room for equal rights for women is to create that space from within Islamic history and theology itself. That is why the works of Mernissi and Ali are crucial and significant. These texts provide a reference from within Islamic tradition to bolster claims for women's equality. Thus, in colonized cultures that possessed written records of their precolonial heritage and, in the case of Islam, which contained a long history of theological-political debate, the colonial encounter unleashes an arduous return to the precolonial systems of thought and meaning-making. In other words, colonial encounter inhibits the natural flow of local time into the future and tethers possible future imaginings to a precolonial past. This is not an automatic, reactionary response to colonial imperatives but is instead a result of those with enunciative power within the colonized culture to use their prestige to recuperate, articulate, and perpetuate the return to a purist past contra colonial imperatives.

Consequently, Islamic cultures place an increasing emphasis on articulating a less Western identity in favor of a heightened Islamic identity, both on an individual and a social level. Most Muslim scholars understand the hegemonic project of the colonizers and, in turn, mobilize a response to it. Abul A'ala Mawdudi, for example, explains the specific conditions of colonial encounter as follows:

> The nature of the clash between Islamic civilization and the Western civilization is quite different: Certainly, the Western civilization is in no way better than the Islamic civilization. In a clash with Islam, no power in the world can succeed. But where is Islam? The Muslims possess neither the Islamic way of life, nor the Islamic conduct, nor Islamic thought. The real Islam exists neither in the mosques nor in the shrines of the saints. The Muslims neither follow true Islam in their personal lives nor in their collective social lives. Thus this conflict is not between Islam and the West but rather between the ossified and static Islamic civilization and a strident, energetic, and fluid civilization, a civilization that has the light of knowledge and fire of action. And that is why Muslims are constantly in a state of retreat. (*Tanqihat* 26)

It is with these thoughts in mind that Mawdudi exhorts Muslim scholars for a renewal of Islam and makes it his own mission to do so. His simple solution to combat the decay of Islamic civilization and its retreat from the West is to encourage all Muslims, through his work, "to seek the true source of Islamic education and to go back to the pure sources of Islamic civilization" (29). The solution, it seems, manifests as a journey back in time to make the present referential to the past. Furthermore, a future that emphasizes the past is articulated due to the present's contamination by the overpowering presence of Western civilization. Thus, over a lifetime of work, Mawdudi not only rethinks modern Islam but also provides a whole body of work that creates a way forward for political and social Islam in the twentieth century. His legacy still lives on as a guiding force for the most organized Islamist political party in Pakistan, the Jamaat-e-Islami. In order to provide a complete way forward and to fully articulate his position, Mawdudi also writes a whole book on the concept of "state" in Islam. Entitled *Islami Riasat*, the book explains, within the light of Islamic principles as well as acceptable norms of modernity, the path toward a workable and modern Muslim state, of which, it seems, Pakistan becomes an example and a working experiment. Even before he had finished writing his book on the Islamic state, Mawdudi was already offering his solutions to the problems of Islam and Western modernity in his occasional journalistic pieces. In one such instance, he provides a detailed account of his argument in favor of a Muslim state. In 1944, a Hindu reader of Mawdudi's public writings asked the following questions:[9] What would be the status of Hindus within the Islamic state (*Islami* 545)? What is the difference between the rights of *Ahl-e-Kitab* (people of the book) and the *Dhimmis* (546)? Will the Qur'ānic rules apply both to Muslims and Hindus (546)? The answers that Mawdudi provides to these questions, though very well argued from an Islamist theological perspective, provide an opportunity to glean the limitations and possibilities of a modern Islamic state.

In his answers, Mawdudi distinguishes between the material functioning of the government (and within that the needless hierarchies of class and religion) and the ideological basis of a future Muslim state. In his view, "since the future Muslim state is based in certain valid principles, then all who agree to those principles would be equal citizens" (547), and those who do not believe in the same foundational principles would thus "naturally become Dhimmis" whose protection would be "the responsibility of the those who govern" (547). While answering the second question,

Mawdudi asserts that the only difference between the Dhimmis who are Ahl-e-Kitab and those who are not is that the "Muslims cannot marry any women from the latter group; other than this their rights as dhimmis are equal" (547).

In answer to the third question, Mawdudi describes two kinds of Dhimmis: "Those who have entered the nation through a treaty and those who become part of it through default" (547). In the case of the former, the rules of the negotiated treaty will decide their place in society. In the case of the latter group, their "legal rights will be the same as those of Muslims" (547). Similarly, for as long as their personal laws do not directly confront the laws of the nation, "their personal law shall be given preference" (547).

What is crucial to understand here is not whether there ought to be such a qualitative division within the Islamic countries (in fact I am opposed to any such divisions), but that at a certain point in Islamic encounter with the West, all questions about the future of a Muslim political system become inherently connected to a valorized and imitable past. A nuanced understanding of modern Islam, therefore, must be understood if we are going to attempt a reading of texts about Islam and the Islamic world as responsible scholars.

There is no dearth of writers and scholars in the Islamic world who, in one way or another, respond to the imperatives of Western colonialism and modernity by seeking guidance and comfort in an idealized past. My point is that any attempt at challenging or rearticulating the Muslim sacred, Muslim history, or Muslim grand narratives from a purely postmodern and Western perspective does not occur in a vacuum. Such works are received by and reacted to within an already existing discourse of Western epistemic violence and the native Muslim response. Thus, even before these words and works are consumed, understood, and discussed, they fall within a preexisting intellectual, social, and political milieu. Hence the response to Rushdie and his novel. This also implies that, just as the works by Mernissi and Ali produce certain enabling conditions for modernity in Islam, Western works critical of Islam unleash their own peculiar set of consequences, especially since they also fall within the predesignated space of a Western history of intellectual intrusion into the Islamic world and outside of traditional Muslim exegetical discourse itself.

There is yet another area of contention related to the publication and readerly consumption of *The Satanic Verses*: the novel as a genre and the mobilization of a specific part of Muslim history as part of the two historical chapters in the novel. What we are told repeatedly, by Rushdie and his defenders, is that Muslims are not reading the novel correctly. This, of course, implies that if Muslim readers could read the novel with certain specific assumptions, and in the light of guidelines provided by Rushdie himself, they would not feel so outraged. This suggests that Muslim outrage about the novel and its content is somehow attributable to Muslims' lack of civilized reading skills. In other words, Muslims are deemed intolerant because they fail to read and respond to the novel the same way that their "enlightened" Western counterparts do in accordance with their own preunderstandings. But these assertions defy the very internal logic of the generic imperatives of the novel, particularly the historical novel. It is, therefore, also appropriate to discuss, albeit briefly, certain aspects of the novel in general and the historical novel in particular.

THE NOVELISTIC FORM

For Mikhail Bakhtin,[10] the novel as a genre is as "yet uncompleted" and "continues to develop" (3) which is why it is difficult to clearly explain its generic characteristics. Bakhtin provides a description of the novel by comparing it to the "completed" genre of the epic.

While discussing the complexities of a theory of the novel, Bakhtin also makes the following, slightly dated, claim:

Of all the major genres only the novel is younger than writing and the book: it alone is organically receptive to new forms of mute perception, that is, to reading. But of critical importance here is the fact that the novel has no canon of its own . . . only individual examples of the novel are historically active, not a generic canon as such. (3)

At this point, the novel does have a certain canon, but it still is the only genre that continues to develop and is consumed primarily through the act of silent reading. Despite its late arrival and provisional generic status, Bakhtin asserts the novel also affects and causes a novelization of other genres. In a way, then, "parodic stylizations of canonical genres and styles occupy an essential place in the novel" (6).

Since the novel itself is in touch with the contemporary and fluid, it forces other genres to become open to change. The novel is not only a "novel" genre in itself, but it also causes innovation and change in other older and "completed" genres. This happens partly because the novel is grounded in contemporary reality. Being an open and developing genre, "it reflects more deeply, more essentially, more sensitively and rapidly, the reality itself in the process of its unfolding" (7). Being a genre of the new and changing world, the novel, for Bakhtin, affects other genres, and by anticipating its own development and the "development of literature as a whole" (7), it makes itself the most important genre "as an object of study for the theory as well as the history of literature" (7).

Of "particular interest," Bakhtin suggests, "are those eras when the novel becomes the dominant genre, for all literature is then caught up in the process of 'becoming,' and in a special kind of 'generic criticism'" (5). These eras include the Hellenic period, the late Middle Ages, and the Renaissance (5), but the most important era is the beginning of the "second half of the eighteenth century" (5). During this time, according to Bakhtin, the novel "reigns supreme" and all other genres are, in one way or the other, "novelized" (5).

Bakhtin explains his main project—articulating a viable theory of the novel—as follows:

> I will attempt below to approach the novel precisely as a genre-in-the-making, one in the vanguard of all modern literary development. I am not constructing here a functional definition of the novelistic canon. . . . I am [rather] trying to grope my way toward the basic structural characteristics . . . that might determine the direction of its peculiar capacity for change and of its influence and effect on the rest of the literature. (11)

Bakhtin is not relying on earlier theoretical definitions of the novel, the normative and generic, but rather is attempting to provide a mode of defining that takes into account two important aspects of the novel: (1) the novel as a genre in the making and (2) the novel's immediate relationship with contemporary reality as it unfolds. With these factors in mind, Bakhtin provides us with three basic characteristics of the novel: (1) its stylistic three-dimensionality, (2) the radical change it effects in the temporal coordinates of the literary image, and (3) the new zone opened by the novel for structuring literary images—namely, the zone of maximal contact with the present (contemporary reality) in all its open-endedness (11).

The first characteristic is explained through its connection with the "multi-languaged consciousness realized in the novel" (11). The three characteristics are interrelated "organically" and historically situated and, as Bakhtin points out, "powerfully affected by a very specific rupture in the history of European civilization: Its emergence from a socially isolated and culturally deaf semi-patriarchal society, and its entrance into international and interlingual contacts and relationships" (11). The rise of the novel is inherently catalyzed by a widening of the linguistic repertoire and by Europe's contact with and awareness of other cultures, even those outside Europe. The novel, being a genre of the contemporary and the present, is deeply affected by these changes. This is what Bakhtin calls the "active polyglossia" (12) of the world of novelistic representation.

Bakhtin does not offer *polyglossia* as something completely new. In fact, he suggests that polyglossia "had always existed" (12) but it "had not been a factor in literary creation" (11). In his view, even though classical Greeks "had a feeling both for 'languages' and for the epochs of language, for the various Greek literary dialects . . . but creative consciousness was realized in closed, pure languages" (12). This could be very easily compared to high Arabic literature: even though Arabic has several regional and class-based dialects, most traditional Arabic language is still written using classical Arabic, as it is considered the only suitable language for what is considered "high literature."

The rise of polyglossia is linked directly to the rise of a polyglot world—the material conditions of contemporary time that, as we have already learned, inform the novelistic mode of writing. This suggests "the new cultural and creative consciousness lives in an actively polyglot world" (12) and, as languages compete with each other, the "period of national languages, coexisting but closed and deaf to each other, comes to an end" (12). All this, according to Bakhtin, sets "into motion a process of active, mutual cause-and-effect and *interillumination*" (12). Thus, in this polyglot world, new "relationships are established between language and its object (that is, the real world) . . . [which] has serious consequences for already established and completed genres as they were formed during the eras of closed and deaf monoglossia" (12). This changed condition is, in effect, the ideal precondition for the rise of the novel: "the novel emerged and matured precisely when intense activization of external and internal *polyglossia* was at the peak of its activity; this is its native element" (12). Since the novel emerges in the world of polyglossia, the novel has the capacity of "developing and renewing literature and in its linguistic and stylistic dimensions" (12). This concludes Bakhtin's discussion of the first of three basic characteristics of the novel: "Its stylistic three-dimensionality" (11).

Bakhtin then moves on to discuss, in comparison with the epic, the other two distinguishing characteristics of the novel: (1) "The radical change it effects in the temporal coordinates of the literary image" and (2) "[t]he new zone opened by the novel for structuring literary images, namely, the zone of maximal contact with the present (with contemporary reality) in all its open-endedness" (11). To make this comparison more fruitful, Bakhtin first describes the basic characteristics of the epic: a national epic past (absolute past) serves as the subject for the epic. A national tradition (not personal experience) serves as the source for the epic. And an absolute epic-distance separates the epic world from contemporary reality—that is, from the time in which the singer (the author and his audience) lives (13).

These three constitutive features serve as a comparative grid upon which Bakhtin plots the rise and description of the novel in comparison with the epic. It is important to first understand his discussion of these characteristics, as our understanding of his theory of the novel depends on it. The main features of the epic, according the Bakhtin, are as follows: (1) the epic concerns itself with a national heroic past, a world of "beginnings" and "peak times" in national history. (2) The epic is always a poem about the past, never the present. (3) The epic has an "authorial position" that is "of a man speaking about a past that is to him inaccessible, the reverent point of view of a descendant" (3). (4) The epic includes a singer and listener situated in the present, but "the represented world of the heroes stands on an utterly different and inaccessible time-and-value plane, separated by epic distance" (14). And (5) the epic concerns itself with national tradition, as the space between the singer-listener of the present and the heroes of the represented epic past is "filled with national tradition" (14). Thus, as we understand it, the narrative content of the epic is always from an absolute past, underwritten by a shared national tradition. While the singer-listener inhabits their contemporary time, the story itself is located in the past and is always about a past. To render the past contemporary, by eliminating epic distance, would mean "to undertake a radical revolution, and to step out of the world of epic into the world of novel" (14). The epic is a "completed" and "finished" genre, in which "the memory, and not knowledge . . . serves as the source and power for the creative impulse" (15). The novel, in comparison, "is determined by experience, knowledge and practice" and is related to the present and looks toward a future (15). Bakhtin also suggests that the reason the epic is a closed genre is because the past it contains is "monochronic and valorized" (17). For this reason, one cannot destroy this boundary between the absolute past and the contemporary without destroying the epic as a form.

Since the epic past is closed off from any other influences, it is preserved "in the form of a national tradition" (16). Now, the important thing is not the factual truth of this tradition but rather its representation as "sacred and sacrosanct," demanding from all "a pious attitude toward itself" (16). This valorization of tradition, in a way, predefines the respect accorded to the epic and the language used to narrate it. This is the third main characteristic of epic that Bakhtin discusses. In his view, "the epic world is an utterly finished thing, not only as an authentic event of the distant past but also on its own terms and by its own standards; it is impossible to change, re-think, or re-evaluate anything in it" (17). It is this immutability that defines the epic's absolute epic distance. Bakhtin further asserts: "This distance exists not only in the epic material . . . but also in the point of view and evaluation one assumes toward them; point of view and evaluation are fused with the subject into one inseparable whole" (17). Therefore, the epic world is constructed "in the zone of an absolute distant image, beyond the sphere of possible contact with the developing, incomplete and . . . rethinking and reevaluating present" (17). This epic distance is challenged only with arrival "on the scene of an active polyglossia and an interillumination of languages" (17). As explained above, the time of the epic is sacred and "high" compared to the narrative time of the novel, which is of a "lower order in comparison with the epic" (19). The contemporary and the low, Bakhtin suggests, was "subject of representation only in low genres" (20). The authentic "folkloric roots of the novel are to be sought" (21) in laughter. It is in parody and laughter that the high world of gods and legends is "contemporized" and "brought low" (21). Thus, for Bakhtin, the novel, as opposed to the closed and high form of the epic and a genre in constant flux, is informed by its precursors and opens the narrative form to further change and experimentation.

With this brief detour and the understanding of the novel as a genre that it provides us, we can now return and take another reinformed look at Rushdie's highly allegorical novel.

THE SATANIC VERSES AND GENERIC CONVENTION

When Rushdie introduces Muslim historical characters within the fictionalized world of his novel, he crosses the boundary from the "epic mode" to the novelistic narrative. His use of history is also guided by a large degree of play and parody. Play and parody are deeply present in novelistic representations in Rushdie's book. For his Muslim readers, this practice clashes with the very idea of the Muslim sacred. One cannot force Muslim readers to relinquish their respect for established and normalized histories and the place of certain personages in those histories simply because the novel has reached a different stage of development in the West. This cannot be explained away to an audience that is currently in the process of retrieving a useable sacred past against what they view as an all-encompassing, imperial Western discourse. One could argue, therefore, that the Rushdie Affair is also based in different understandings of history and modes of representation.

What further complicates the matter is the fact that *The Satanic Verses* is not a realistic novel but a quintessentially postmodern one. I rely here, by way of explanation, on Hutcheon's work on postmodern poetics. We know, through a cursory generic understanding of the novel as genre, that *The Satanic Verses* is neither a realistic novel nor a historical novel. It is, in fact, a postmodern novel and, therefore, must be read with a certain understanding of commonplace postmodern tropes and devices. Reading it as realistic fiction would be a categorical mistake, leading readers to meanings unintended by the author. But even this statement, along with Rushdie's own explanation of the novel, yet again tethers the reader to a particular mode of reading. In other words, the only way a reader can adequately understand the novel is if he or she follows the instructions provided by the author in conjunction with a deep knowledge of what constitutes postmodern fiction. Such stipulations are *not* similarly imposed upon the metropolitan reader if they are asked to read a novel from or about Islam. So while metropolitan readers can read novels about Islam with their own set of readerly tools, Muslim readers are expected to transcend their own modes of reading and meaning-making and are then expected to read works such as *The Satanic Verses* as if they are "universal" Western readers and Western texts are themselves "universal" texts.

It is a fact, at least for those trained in critical readings in metropolitan universities, that our interpretations of novels also depend upon the periodization of novelistic narratives. To read a realistic novel as a modern novel or to read a postmodern novel as a realistic or modern novel would be a mistake because the reading would involve faulty assumptions. An understanding of the stylistics, aesthetics, and poetics particular to certain historical periods is essential to comprehending and interpreting specific novelistic subgenres. Understanding *The Satanic Verses* as a postmodern novel is crucial for arriving at a meaningful interpretation. It is, therefore, important to at least point out some basic attributes of postmodern fiction. My purpose here is to point out that reading and receiving postmodern fiction is an acquired skill and while we may deride those in the Western academy for reading texts without a knowledge of the techniques involved, expecting average Muslim readers to know and master these skills is a bit too far-fetched. Furthermore, it is important to understand that what Rushdie does in this postmodern text is something that may be normal within metropolitan literary circles but may be subject to extreme censorship and sanction within the Muslim sacred. Just because the West has reached a certain point in its aesthetic development in which such subjects are permissible does not mean that it is the universal norm, nor should it imply that the entire world has informally entered the postmodern epoch.

In her highly regarded book, Hutcheon begins her discussion of postmodernism by asserting that it "is a contradictory phenomenon, one that uses and abuses, installs and then subverts, the very concepts it challenges" (3). In other words, postmodernism does not claim to have a stable episteme but rather plays with, parodies, and satirizes established modernist storytelling techniques. For Hutcheon, postmodernism is "fundamentally contradictory, resolutely historical, and inescapably political" (4). But the return to history or historical narratives in postmodernism is "not a nostalgic return; it is a critical revisiting, an ironic dialogue with the past of both art and society" (4). The most crucial term relative to her book's argument is "historiographic metafiction." She defines the term as follows:

> By this [historiographic metafiction] I mean those well-known and popular novels which are both intensely self-reflexive and yet paradoxically also lay claim to historical events and personages. In most of the critical work on postmodernism, it is narrative—be it in literature, history, or theory—that has usually been the major focus of attention. Historiographic metafiction incorporates all three of these human constructs (*historiographic metafiction*) is made the grounds for its rethinking and reworking of the forms and contents of the past. (5)

It can then be construed that in postmodern historiographic metafiction, the works not only play with form but also with established historical narratives and attempt to re-present them with a sort of nonnostalgic, parodic, and playful attitude. Furthermore, Hutcheon also points out that this kind of representation can often "reduce epic tragedy to the bathos of the mechanical and debased" (5). Thus, when Rushdie explains his technique and intent, he is aware of the techniques that underwrite his narrative and, within the context of Western postmodernism, his explanation makes perfect sense. The problem occurs when he and his apologists expect the same degree of understanding from average Muslim readers. This expectation is blatantly imperialistic. It announces to potential Muslim readers, in several ways, that the novel as a genre has reached a different level, and this level, this mode of representation, is *universal*. Muslims should either accept it or teach themselves how to read the novel as intended by Western readers and authors. But has Western postmodernism really become the universal norm? Have all grand narratives vanished and been replaced by the petite narratives that Lyotard discusses?

Even metropolitan critics disagree on the meaning(s) of postmodernism within the academy. And while for many philosophers and critics most literary novels tend to fall within the postmodern paradigm in one way or the other, we are still in modernity, and modernity, to borrow Habermas's phrase, is still an "incomplete project."

But my point here is not to discuss or resolve the modernism/postmodernism debate. Instead, I am suggesting that the above-mentioned attributes of the postmodern are not universal and hence not necessarily universally accepted as truth by Muslim readers.

I have already explained in the previous chapter a brief genealogy of the Muslim sacred. Works like *The Satanic Verses* do not arrive in a vacuum: they are received as texts read through the meaning-making processes of various Muslim cultures. These cultures, as I have also discussed, are mostly postcolonial and rely on cultural and political narratives that were developed in response to colonial imperatives. Most of the people from these cultures can therefore not read the novel from culturally transcendent or neutral places. The works are always judged against the sociocultural matrix within which they are offered. And within that matrix, there is no room for bathos, no room for parodying sacred historical personages, no matter how craftily they are represented. And while the sacred and the profane do exist within Islamic literary production, the sacred is not to be conflated with the profane. Figures like the Prophet, his wives, or his early companions cannot so easily be transformed into real-life, fictional characters with their insecurities, sexualities, or transgressions. The absence of such literary licenses in fictional works from the Islamic world does not imply that Muslim cultures are less advanced. Rather, it means that the experience and representation of the sacred is different and that there are limits to what one can and cannot mobilize as raw materials for the purpose of literature and art in Muslim societies.

While I am generalizing here, even within the Muslim sacred there are major differences over questions of interpretation involving the sacred text. I have provided two such examples of the differences above. Ironically, works like *The Satanic Verses* tend to give more voice and power to the very forces in the Islamic world that the West yearns to vanquish or at least manage while weakening those who may not be totally hostile to certain positive aspects of Western modernity. In the end, *The Satanic Verses* ends up strengthening the more intolerant within Muslim societies, often resulting in the enactment of harsher laws.

THE MATERIAL CONSEQUENCES OF
THE SATANIC VERSES

This brings me to the next phase of my discussion: the material consequences of Rushdie's use of Muslim raw materials for a postmodern novel. While its publication became highly controversial within metropolitan culture and created its own "culture war"—which was further compounded by the Ayatollah Khomeini's fatwa against Rushdie—the publication of the novel had drastic consequences within the Islamic world, especially in Pakistan where it served to bolster arguments for stricter blasphemy laws.

Much has been argued concerning Pakistan's infamous blasphemy laws, but one crucial aspect is rarely highlighted—the context within which an additional provision was added:

> Section 295C (1986), which carries the death penalty or a life sentence for those who, "*by words, either spoken or written, or by visible representation, or by any imputation, innuendo, or insinuation, directly or indirectly, defiles the sacred name of the Holy Prophet Muhammad.*"

Note that capital punishment for insulting the Prophet neither exists in the Qur'ān nor was it a part of the Pakistan Penal Code (PPC). It was added to the PPC not as part of the Islamization project of then Pakistani dictator General Zia-ul-Haq, as is often believed, but rather through successful litigation by a private citizen, Ismail Qureshi, as the PPC "did not have any specific provision for blasphemy against the Holy Prophet (PBUH), advocate Ismail Qureshi moved the Federal Sharia Court (FSC) in 1984 to prescribe the death penalty for blasphemy" (Rehman 2). In this temporal trajectory, the effort to make blasphemy against the Prophet punishable by a capital sentence was already on its way and preceded the publication of the novel. But further strengthening of this law and its passage by the National Assembly and the eventual removal of a "life sentence as an alternative" happened in a post–Rushdie Affair world. In fact, Qureshi spends quite a lot of time in his sadly triumphal book about the Rushdie Affair and the need for more stringent laws.[11]

It was only after the publication of *The Satanic Verses* that the existence of Section 295 (C) in Pakistan could be totally justified—not just as a caution but also as a preemptive tool for all those who might consider "defiling" the Prophet. The fact that there was no legal recourse against Rushdie prompted the accentuation of pre-existing but rarely implemented blasphemy laws. Thus, Rushdie's incitation, in one way, moved Muslim societies to legislate speech, and it precipitated a chain reaction of sociopolitical events that still manifest, often violently, in Pakistani society.

CHAPTER 4

OTHER INCITEMENTS

Islam and the Metropolitan Opportunists

> *The idea of representation is a theatrical one: the Orient is the stage on which the whole East is confined. On this stage will appear the figures whose role it is to represent the larger whole from which they emanate. The Orient then seems to be, not an unlimited extension beyond the familiar European world, but rather a closed field, a theatrical stage affixed to Europe. An Orientalist is but the particular specialist in knowledge for which Europe at large is responsible, in the way that an audience is historically and culturally responsible for (and responsive to) dramas technically put together by the dramatist.*
>
> —Edward Said, *Orientalism*

In one of her most celebrated and contested essays, "Can the Subaltern Speak?," Gayatri Spivak points out the most troubling aspect of the metropolitan impulse to save the *sati* women from their so-called brown oppressors. According to Spivak, even when these women enter the colonial records through the benevolent intervention of their British saviors, they do not really speak for themselves, and their narratives are subjected to a strange epistemic violence. This same principle applies to Western attempts at fictionalizing historical Muslim women. For example, Aisha happens to be the subject of artistic rendering both in Salman Rushdie's *The Satanic Verses* and Sherry Jones's novel *The Jewel of Medina*. Building on my argument in the previous chapters, here I will discuss the nature of the metropolitan poetics of incitement as a trend in the visual and textual arts and its impact on the reciprocal perceptions between Islam and the West. I understand that I am using, as I have admitted earlier, the terms *Islam* and *the West* as two generalized concepts and would therefore like to highlight again that despite such usages, I am aware of and sensitive to the particularities on both sides.

As I discussed in the previous chapter, when Western scholars and artists use Islamic raw materials for their artistic pursuits, their appropriation unleashes the potential for a multitude of critical and public responses, largely dependent on the receiving audience. I would like to argue here that the success of *The Satanic Verses* and the attention that it gained within the Western academy as well as in the media and public sphere has now elevated the "poetics of incitement" into a specific genre: authors, artists, publishers, and other cultural producers now use such inflammatory poetics not only to serve the arts but to also enhance their visibility and economic viability. In short, controversy sells. Use on television, for example, results in increased viewership. This has become exceedingly profitable in the United States after the 9/11 attacks, the Iraq War, and the rise of ISIL/ISIS.

Usually, these works choose a few aspects of Islamic history and mobilize them, under a generalized artistic license, to offer a "fresh" look at Islam and Islamic history. But since in most of these cases only Western aesthetics and politics are at play, the *horizonal difference* between metropolitan audiences and Muslim audiences is completely effaced. Muslim responses to such works, often reactionary, occur in that in-between horizonal gap that is either inadvertently effaced or purposely mobilized to achieve the desired effects.

When referring to horizonal difference, I am relying on Hans

Robert Jauss's theorization of a "horizon of expectations" and its impact on the reception of literary texts. Jauss introduces the important role of the horizon of expectations as follows: "The coherence of literature as an event is primarily mediated in the horizon of expectations of the literary experience of contemporary and later readers, critics, and authors" (22). Note that, for Jauss, a literary work is not "an object that stands by itself" (21) and, similarly, "the historical context in which a literary work appears is not a factical, independent series of events that exists apart from an observer" (21). Thus, a literary text "becomes a literary event only for its reader who reads this last work" of an author with a "memory of his earlier works and who recognizes its individuality in comparison with these and other works that he already knows" (21). The literary text as an event presupposes this dialogic dance between the reader, the text, and the specific and general contextuality and contingency of itself. A horizon of expectation is, therefore, dependent upon this dialogic engagement with the literary text. But sometimes a gap exists between the aesthetic value of a literary text and the horizon of expectation. Jauss calls this "horizonal change" (25). This change occurs when a literary text exceeds the expected horizon of expectations. It is at this time that the act of interpretation and understanding must account for the horizonal change, and the "difference between the familiarity of previous aesthetic experience and the 'horizonal change' demanded by the new reception of the new work, determines the artistic character of a literary work" (25).[1] This difference, I suggest, also provides varied responses from different audiences, and these responses cannot be clearly understood without accounting for the horizonal difference. Metropolitan authors mobilizing Muslim raw materials for their own artistic purposes either knowingly play with this gap—to create controversy—or assume that the entire world exists on the same horizonal plane.

Furthermore, in truly Orientalist fashion, these artists take it upon themselves to speak for historical Muslim subjects. When they do so, they make certain implicit assumptions, the most prominent of which is that the subjects so imaginatively rendered have been historically silenced. Aisha is one such example—both Rushdie and Jones write about Aisha as if she had been an utterly silenced historical subject waiting to be rescued by them after centuries of neglect. With Jones, the case is even worse, for she Orientalizes Aisha for her Western audiences without paying even the slightest attention to the recorded history of Islam in general or of Aisha in particular. This lack of historical awareness can be gleaned from the declared intent of the author in the preface:

> Join me in a journey to another time and place, to a harsh exotic world of saffron and sword fights, of desert nomads living in camel's-hair tents, of cravens laden with Persian carpets and frankincense, of flowing colorful robes and kohl-darkened eyes and perfumed arms filigreed with henna. (vii)

I need not point out that this opening passage is laden with Orientalist tropes that one expects in a traditional Oriental "tale" about Arabia. And even though for Jones's Aisha is a "role model" (ix), this role model, it seems, can only be represented as a character in a profoundly Orientalized tale of mythologized Arabian land and its attendant intrigues. Of course, my opponents might argue: What is wrong with that? Isn't it salutary for an American author to retrieve a heroic female figure from Islamic history and tell her story in imaginative fiction? Would this not introduce Aisha as an early Muslim protofeminist hero to American audiences and dispel some of the popular views regarding gender roles in Islamic societies?

All such arguments, I agree, are valid, but only within the context of metropolitan utility. In the end, if all these attributes were assigned to the text, all they do is prove, yet again, that the metropolitan writer is like a "dramatist" (Said, *Orientalism* 63) staging a historical show for metropolitan audiences, a show in which

Aisha speaks, but only through the language of the dramatist and often at the cost of her own historical speech. Once again, I must return to Fatima Mernissi, who also retrieves another woman from the silenced history of Islam to make a case for broader rights for women in Islam. The difference, however, is that in her case, even though there are objections to her retrieval, such objections are not about the method of representation but rather about the veracity of her claims. Her intervention happens within the logical form of the Islamic tradition of historical exegesis and cannot simply be dismissed for its tone and irreverence to the subject of retrieval. And, in the end, her retrieval serves the most important function: it supports her argument in favor of equal rights for women in Islam instead of offering a sexualized Aisha for consumption by metropolitan audiences. In the conclusion of her book, after having accounted for the curtailment of women's access to the public sphere in Medina, Mernissi takes us to the triumphant phase of Islam and to the fourth day of the Prophet's triumphant return to Makkah, the day the women of Quraish come to take their oath of allegiance with the Prophet:

> The Women, under the leadership of Hind Bint 'Utba . . . refused to swear the oath to 'Umar, as the Prophet had arranged. Hind pushed him aside and approached Muhammad: "It is to you that we want to swear allegiance and it is with you that we want to enter into agreement." (190)

Mernissi considers this a moment worthy of recovery, for it teaches us that the women of Quraish "were not going to accept the new religion without knowing exactly how it would improve their situation" (191). And, Mernissi argues, this "critical spirit" remained a part of the early caliphate and vanished only during the rule of "Mu'awiya and turning of Islam into a dynastic system" (191). There is something crucial in such retrievals: they provide an alternative cultural memory in opposition to established, normative, patriarchal histories. The important element to note here is that these instances already exist in the recorded history of Islam and need not be invented. Even in her creative rendition of these instances of female agency, Mernissi does not rely on purely fictive or imaginative rendering; she instead retrieves her narrative through the most respected and valorized historical sources.

Retrieving such silenced narratives is crucial to changing our attitudes, for the most potent register in identity formation is the "linguistic register." We cobble our individual and collective selves together through various forms of collective and self-serving narratives. If self-serving narratives can be complicated and expanded, chances are they would have a larger impact on a culture. But if the narratives are being mobilized in a highly contested discursive domain, then their provenance and their history must be impeccable. Thus, when Mernissi is attacked while recounting the story of the Prophet's great-granddaughter Sukayana, who was "celebrated for her beauty, for what the Arabs call beauty—an explosive mixture of physical attractiveness, critical intelligence, and caustic wit" (192), and who "ended up marrying five, some say six, husbands" (192), Mernissi can offer the most authentic sources from within Islamic history and tradition as her references. This does not make her intervention legitimate in the eyes of the orthodoxy, but it does make it more forceful, for she asserts the rights of women with due diligence and with a deep scholarly attention to the details of Islamic historiography.

Compared to such scholarly, theological work, *The Jewel of Medina* is a metropolitan work that relies only on the imaginative rights of an author who disregards history, reception, and horizonal expectations of Muslim readers. *The New York Times* review declared:

> An inexperienced, untalented author has naïvely stepped into an intense and deeply sensitive intellectual argument. She has conducted enough research to reimagine the accepted versions

of Muhammad's marriage to A'isha, thus offending the religious audience, but not nearly enough to enlighten the ordinary Western reader. (Adams 1)

In fact, I would suggest that while the novel has a designated place within the metropolitan publishing scene as a romanticized version of a feminist story and is written in the same vein as other romantic accounts of women from European history, the novel has no meaningful place in the collective imagination of average Muslims. Its lack of place is not due to a lack of Muslim interest in the story of Aisha but rather because this is not an adequate genre to tell such a story in Muslim cultures. No amount of insistence in the West on free expression can change the fact that Muslim readers have the right to expect certain respectful representations of their own "sacred" historical subjects. Muslim readers should not be expected to respond positively to or gain meaning from the kind of experimental writing that Western authors take for granted. The purpose here is not to unpack the intention of the author but to focus on "what the text does, rather than what the text is meant to mean" (Iser 6). In the process, I will trace the author's intention, but this intentionality can best be sought "in manifestations of intentionality expressed in the fictional text itself through its selection of and from extratextual systems" (6). Considering the role of selection as a key to understanding what a text does, Iser explains the process of fictionalization as follows:

> Every literary text inevitably contains a selection from a variety of social, historical, cultural, and literary systems that exist as referential fields outside the text. This selection is in itself a stepping beyond boundaries, in that the elements selected are lifted out of the systems in which they fulfill their specific functions. This applies both to cultural norms and to literary allusions, which are incorporated into every new literary text in such a way that the structure and semantics of the system concerned are decomposed. (4–5)

Thus, a literary text becomes what it is through a process of selection and it is this selection and arrangement of various "elements that are now incorporated in the text are not in themselves fictive, but their selection is an act of fictionalizing" and "the author's choice . . . can be described only in terms of the selections made" (5). But even what the author chooses to "fictionalize" cannot simply be attributed to the author, and we do not need to retrieve the intention of the author to know a work, for "if an act of selection were governed by a set of rules given prior to the act, then the act itself would not transgress existing boundaries but would simply be one form of actualizing a possibility within the framework of prevailing convention" (5). The framework that Jones's novel is working with is the romantic tale of historical retrieval, which allows an author to choose a female historical figure and lend her substance through an act of imagination and the poetics of incitement. Here the poetics of incitement enable the author to apply the elements of a metropolitan romantic novel to the historical figure of Aisha and thus create a layered text, a text that retrieves a female historical figure to foreground her in a mostly male narrative and, at the same time, to touch upon the usual tropes that make the work controversial to an audience that might not be privy to such generic conventions. The text purposefully highlights its own horizonal difference to its Muslim readers. Therefore, while the text falls into an expected horizon of expectations within metropolitan cultures—the romantic tale with exotic and sexualized undertones—it completely violates the expectations of Muslim audiences. I must add that it is this acknowledged horizonal difference that becomes the ultimate space for metropolitan authors who want the work to be more than what it is through its power to enter a controversial domain.

Some passages in the novel point out this horizonal difference and its attendant ramifications. In her rendition of the "incident of the necklace" and the Qur'ānic injunction about seclusion of women, which Mernissi discusses with full historical clarity,

Jones offers the story as a romanticized account of Aisha's desire for Safwan. This is common practice for a metropolitan author, especially when writing historical fiction: historical characters are foregrounded, and the reader is given a glimpse into their imagined thoughts and feelings—creative inventions not available to readers of actual historical sources. The author has the right to do so within the logic of metropolitan literary production, but the author and publisher cannot expect Muslim readers to interpret such representations with the same receptive repertoire as their metropolitan counterparts. What results is that a common creative technique for metropolitan audiences is the ultimate contested area for Muslim readers, and no appeal to the authorial right to represent can change this outcome.

As I discussed in the previous chapter on Rushdie, there is no need to create an imaginative authorial voice for Aisha in this particular instance, unless the purpose is to sexualize her as a character. After all, in every major account of the incident of the necklace, or the "Account of the Lie," she speaks for herself. In Al-Tabari's account of the incident, for example, Aisha recounts her story as follows:

> When the people had mounted, I went out to attend to a need of mine. On my neck was a necklace of mine with onyx beads from Zafar. When I finished, it came undone from my neck without me noticing it. . . . I retraced my steps to the place to which I had gone and looked for the necklace until I found it. . . .
>
> When I came back to the camp, not a soul was there—the people had departed. (59)

Thus, as she covered herself and lay down to wait for someone from the caravan to notice her absence in the litter, she was discovered by Safwan bin Al-Mu'attal al-Sulami, who then safely brought her back to the caravan (59). It was after this incident that the Munfiqun (the Hypocrites) led by Abdullah bin Ubay started circulating the rumor of her romance with Safwan.

Now, for Muslim readers of history, Aisha's account is authentic because it is reported by all major recorders of Islamic history and because she is ultimately vindicated by divine revelation, part of which I discussed in the previous chapter. But in its techniques as historiographic metafiction, Jones fictionalizes this incident. As is common in such fictional reimaginings, elements of history become detached from their historical reference (Aisha's own recorded account) and from the Muslim approach to such subjects: an extreme form of respect accorded to the wives of the Prophet, who are called Ummahat-ul-Muslim, the mothers of Muslims.

Thus, while it makes sense to offer Aisha's interactions with Safwan using the language of desire and to fictionalize for metropolitan audiences who receive the work within a prepared ground of expectation, it is not fair to expect the same kind of reception from Muslim readers. For example, the following is a passage that would be considered harmless in accordance with the norms and expectations of metropolitan readers:

> Safwan's body pressed against mine. I struggled, but he pulled me closer as if we were tied in a knot. "Do you ever quit?" I said, but my words were lost in the wind. He touched his lips to my ear. His warm breath made me shiver. "Never," he said. (Jones 155)

But the same passage fails on two accounts in terms of its reception by Muslim readers: on account of its *faulty historiography* and on account of its *(mis)representation of Aisha*, the very Aisha who speaks with her own voice in the pages of recorded history, defending her honor against the rumors of the Hypocrites. In other words, then, the very rumors that the historical Aisha fought against and spoke against are the ones privileged by Jones to create a fictionalized account of Aisha. For the Western reader, then, a speculative rumor regarding Aisha is concretized by an act of fictionalization; the historical Aisha is replaced by a fictional Aisha, an overtly sexualized version. A Muslim reader would respond to this text quite differently from that of their metropolitan counterparts.

First, in terms of history, we know from Al-Tabari and other historians that the rumor of the affair was started by the Hypocrites, and it took all the Prophet's symbolic power to curb the rumors and to apportion blame to the individuals who had started and perpetuated the rumor. Furthermore, it was within this context that the Qur'ānic verses were revealed to exonerate Aisha of any blame. So, for Muslim readers, even speculating on the subject is sacrosanct as it privileges what has been historically and traditionally considered impermissible within the realm of fictionalization. In fact, the actual account has more aesthetic beauty than Jones's fictionalized account:

> By God, before the messenger of God left the place where he was sitting, there came over him from God what used to come over him. . . . As for me, when I saw that happen, by God I did not become very frightened or troubled, for I knew that I was innocent and that God would not wrong me. As for my parents . . . as soon as the messenger of God came to, I thought their souls would depart for fear that confirmation of what people had said would come from God.
>
> The messenger of God came to and sat up. . . . He began wiping the perspiration from his brow and said" "Rejoice, 'A'isha! God has revealed your innocence." (Al-Tabari 63)

The historical Aisha not only struggled to fight against the rumor but was also ultimately exonerated by the word of God. And, according to Islamic sources, including the source cited above, verses 11 through 20 of the twenty-fourth Surah of the Qur'ān were revealed to stop the rumors and to clear Aisha's name. I am not suggesting that this is a necessarily authentic history against which all other histories of Aisha should be measured. In the end, all histories are recorded and involve acts of human retrieval, bias, and agency. But my point is that in all accounts of the incident, Aisha speaks for herself and is exonerated by the divine word. This is the valorized and official account of Aisha and the scandal. To insist that the rumors were the truth and then allow Jones's fictional Aisha to sanctify them in the shape of an affair or her desire for Safwan does not only erase Aisha's own historical voice but also impacts other aspects of Muslim regard for Aisha. She is, after all, one of the most revered women in Islam. Therefore, when she is represented as an amorous young woman at the mercy of the sexual attraction of one named Safwan, the representation becomes more than just offensive—it becomes an open defilement of the figure of Aisha, which was no small matter in her own lifetime, as is evident from the historical records, and is certainly no small matter for Muslims today. Thus, some deep thinking is needed on the part of metropolitan writers: just because the world has become "global" does not mean that a universal and globalized horizon of expectation exists. Furthermore, while it might be acceptable to use Islamic raw materials for metropolitan works, it does not necessarily mean that such appropriations can necessarily be safely covered under the general rubric of freedom of expression. Just as writers have the right to appropriate and represent these raw materials in fictional forms, readers also have the right to read according to their own meaning-making processes. To insist on only one mode of reading and to reduce every other mode of reading as intolerant or uninformed is itself another form of intolerance: perhaps a more pernicious form too.

On the other hand, in the Muslim world, there needs to be no violent responses to the texts of poetic incitement. Such offenses should never be punishable by death, and extrajudicial threats of physical violence to the lives of "offenders" should not become the norm. Muslims should also understand that representations of Islam originating from certain Western writers must be read, as difficult as the task might be, from the place of the Other. Such habits are necessary in order to live and thrive in today's complex world. I say this after acknowledging that the poetics of incitement exist and continue to thrive in metropolitan culture. The best response from the Muslim world is to avoid reinforcing xenophobic claims already made about Islam and its intolerance of free speech. Furthermore, the rhetorical impulse of Islamic work needs a new form of Kalam, a kind of Kalam that can offer a Muslim perspective without apology—forcefully and without being goaded into the kind of violent response that is incited and hoped for by the publishers and writers of works such as *The Jewel of Medina.*

In fact, one major reason *The Jewel of Medina* did not garnish its expected international uproar was because of the early intervention of those who understood Islamic history and recognized the intent of the novel, as evidenced within its pages. (Authorial intent, in this case, remains secondary.) These learned responses came early: not from the Muslim world but rather from the American academy. If Muslims want to have any impact on metropolitan representations of themselves, they must respond semiotically to acts of semiotic aggression. Material responses, even when peaceful, are often futile in a culture war defined by signs, symbols, words, and meanings.

Even early interventions by American academics became a point of contention. The first review of the novel was by Denise Spellberg, who was later blamed for "killing" the novel and for her alleged encouragement of censorship. In response to this accusation, Spellberg sent a response to *The Wall Street Journal* in which she clarified her position:

> As a historian invited to "comment" on the book by its Random House editor at the author's express request, I objected strenuously to the claim that "The Jewel of Medina" was "extensively researched," as stated on the book jacket. As an expert on Aisha's life, I felt it was my professional responsibility to counter this novel's fallacious representation of a very real woman's life. The

author and the press brought me into a process, and I used my scholarly expertise to assess the novel. It was in that same profes- sional capacity that I felt it my duty to warn the press of the novel's potential to provoke anger among some Muslims.

Spellberg's objections to the novel were on two grounds: (1) its claims to historical accuracy and (2) the possibilities of its hazard- ous reception by Muslim audiences. In a way, then, she was in the ideal position to assign value to the novel: she had the expertise to understand that thin research was being touted as deep research while also being aware of why the novel would be offensive to Mus- lim readers. As critics of Islamic works or works about Islam, we must have at least a basic idea about these issues, otherwise we will judge all such works from a so-called universalist place and then feel offended if readers do not read the works the way we expect them to. With *The Jewel of Medina*, an average novel became more than a novel—it became, yet again, the staging ground for a battle between the right to free speech and censorship. Even Rushdie, now a hardened veteran in this battle, offered his opinion: "This is censorship by fear and it sets a very bad precedent indeed" (qtd. in Bone).

Like the metropolitan reader, the Muslim reader can be encour- aged to broaden their receptive repertoire but cannot be expected to read texts about their own culture with the same (in)sensitivities of metropolitan readers. This would be impossible simply because the history of engagement between the West and the Islamic world is mostly antagonistic. And beyond that, a whole corpus of works, of which I have cited some above, already exist to highlight the historical, material, and intellectual causes of the fall of Islam from global prominence. These texts are read within that discursive space, with an eye toward a checkered and violent past as well as a conflicted present.

Other than the novel's historical inaccuracies, it is the sexu- alization of Aisha and the Prophet that by far create the greatest cause for concern. In most Muslim societies, talking or writing about sex is not as readily accepted as it is within metropolitan cultures. Bear in mind that I am only speaking of the apparent acceptance in the media as well as in literature. To be sure, there is no dearth of highly sexualized stories and writings that appear in local and national languages and generally go unnoticed by the larger public or the censors. But by and large, talking or writing about other people's sex lives or introducing highly sexualized men or women into popular stories transgresses the norm. But writing about the Prophet and his wife—even though historically they were sexual beings—is also discouraged. Furthermore, when this stream of consciousness sexualizes a historically valorized figure like that of the Prophet or Aisha, then the reception becomes even more distressing. Most Muslim responses to the novel, as well to similar works, are not necessarily about the historical veracity of the texts but rather about "profane" representations of what is, to some extent, sacred and sacrosanct. Thus, freedom of expression notwithstanding, just as metropolitan authors and artists hold their right to represent as sacrosanct, so do readers in the Muslim world when they assert their right to read and receive texts according to the meaning-making processes pertinent to their own cultural sensitivities.

But, say my opponents, does all this give Muslims the right to kill or hurt all those who are deemed to have insulted Islam, the Prophet, or his wives? Of course my answer is an unequivocal "no." I am not providing apologies for those who take it upon themselves to condemn others to death through decree or who take it upon themselves to harm those who they deem to be in error. I am instead offering a deeper understanding of what contributes to the formation of this kind of rage, the kind of rage that transforms a reader or a viewer of a text into a potential murderer. As I have discussed earlier, all of this can be attributed to the horizonal differences between the writers and their Muslim readers. Within Muslim societies, there is also a huge gradation of various subjectivities, some of which are more literal than others. The consequence of Theo van Gogh's short film *Submission* (2004) is a case in point. The film, after all, is about the mistreatment of women by men in certain Islamic societies. These Islamic societies, of course, are aware of this abuse, and depending on their political systems and their civic structures, these issues are attended to within these societies as well. The main argument offered by van Gogh's detractors was not that he had dared to represent a private Islamic affair visually as a public act of shaming. After all, there is nothing private about instances of domestic violence in Muslim societies. The main objection had to do with one particular "transgressive" act in the film: the digital inscription of Qur'ānic verses on the naked bodies of four female characters in the film. Was it more important to the director to publicize the state of affairs in Moroccan society as a means of creating empathy for the abused? Or was it to make a sensational, provocative artistic statement? If the intent was the latter, then that means that the work was primarily for metropolitan audiences with no regard to the reception by the very people whose sacred text is mobilized to create art. However, its reception cannot be grounded only in metropolitan aesthetics. At the very moment a writer claims an absolute right to freedom of expression, the reader, on the other end of this divide, also has the absolute right to read the text with the values and prejudices of their own reading community. To insist only on the writer's right to represent while ignoring the reader's right to read, feel, and react is a form of hubris that too often goes unquestioned.

Similarly, while *Submission* and *The Jewel of Medina* at least offer themselves as artistic renderings of the Islamic present and past respectively, popular forms of the poetics of incitement are even more provocative. It seems that attacking Islam and Muslims with the most bigoted and bizarre claims has now become a new norm, a genre in its own right. Within the United States, bashing Islam and Muslims can sometimes bolster faltering political and professional careers:

Bill Maher is a great example of a kind of unapologetic Islamophobia that offers itself as informed critique to a general American public. According to Raya Jalabi, in post-9/11 America, Maher has become an advocate for the ever-popular view that while all religions need to be criticized and identified as antagonistic to liberal principles, Islam is a *singular* affront to liberal values, as Muslims are *uniquely* oppressive and extremist and violent.

Note that Maher is not the only one making such generalized claims: he is in fact in the company of neoconservative scholars such as Daniel Pipes, Michael Palmer, and others. The only difference is that American conservative scholars tend to be deeply nationalistic and offer their lopsided and generalized critiques of Islam as they relate to American national security and traditional American values. Maher, on the other hand, without research or academic credentials, is a self-appointed defender of American liberalism and offers his half-baked generalizations to liberal audiences. Furthermore, Maher justifies these opinions because he, as a comedian and satirist, can claim that he is not necessarily singling out Islam, because he is equally as dismissive of other religions. Thus, just like the bigoted and unenlightened mullahs that he criticizes (along with the one billion or so Muslims), Maher relies on bigoted and prejudicial generalizations about the Other.

What is Maher's general purpose in these pronouncements? Certainly this harsh stance on Islam buffers his credentials as a liberal who is not soft on Islam. On the other hand, his discourse does not serve any useful public function. His discourse consists of mere clichés about Islam and its adherents: easy targets for a late-night comedian masquerading as a political commentator.

There is no doubt that, in addition to its violent factions, Islamic cultures tend to hold deeply negative sentiments about the United States and the West. Attributing these factors to an essentialized Islam is also wrong. In most cases, grievances are political and historical and, as I discussed in an earlier chapter, Islam becomes a mobilizing ideology in crystalizing these views. Figures like Maher, then, point to these instances of violence or protest as examples of the atavistic and violent nature of Islam itself, as if Islam were an infectious disease that contaminates human bodies through mere proximity. Maher's public record indicates that he is an unapologetic "rationalist," and that happens to be the reason for his main opposition to all religions. Thus, as a man of reason opposed to all metaphysical explanations of the real, one should not, it is implied, expect any irrational claims from such a person. But according to all possible permutations of reasoned thought, his views on Islam and Muslims are inherently irrational. For my claim about Maher's irrationality about Islam, I am relying upon the most readily and popularly available philosophical explanation of irrationalism. A person may be accused of irrationality if they are prone to making mistakes of a particular kind or indulging in invalid reasoning; but it is only insofar as one maintains some specific doctrine concerning such things as the status and role of reason or the relevance of rational standards within various domains of experience or inquiry that they can be called an irrationalist. In other words, attention is focused not on an unwitting failure to conform to norms of generally recognized validity but on the explicit repudiation, or putting into question, of such norms in the light of certain considerations or in relation to certain contexts ("Irrationalism").

What makes Maher's claims about Islam irrational, and thus opposed to his stance as a rationalist, are the generalizations that he makes—without much empirical evidence—about Islam. Now, there is nothing wrong with such views being espoused by one who does not claim to be a modern prophet of reason. But when someone identifies with the realm of reason but makes unfounded generalizations about a billion people, this is worth pointing out. In other words, the very mullahs that someone such as Maher would consider irrational and bigoted rely on exactly the same kind of vocabularies and generalizations about the West. Thus, in his zeal to condemn all things Islamic, Maher has become the very thing that he claims to challenge through his diatribes against Islam. Maher has become a mullah of secularism, a *secular fundamentalist*.

Through such actions, metropolitan writers, artists, critics, and comedians fulfill the very expectations that the mullahs and their ilk create about the West. In the end, such metropolitan representations result in strengthening the very fundamentalists that they hope to challenge. In my own exchanges and public talks, the most common questions asked by the most moderate, educated Pakistani Muslims concerns the media coverage afforded to such poets of incitement. When I suggest that not every American is bigoted or has derogatory views of Islam, they ask me, ironically, the same question: Where are the people who condemn such views about common Muslims? Increasingly, in the United States, those who attempt to complicate the discussion about Islam are reduced to terrorist sympathizers or viewed as weak and misguided. This trend is not only common on the American Right but is also being advanced on the American Left by the likes of Maher and others. Islamophobic hysteria appears to be the norm on both poles of the political spectrum, as anti-Islamic sentiment takes precedence in mass media.

In most cases of incitement, the reactionary and sometimes violent responses from the Muslim community itself are deployed as proof of the very things that are associated with Islam: negative actions enacted by Muslims become essentialized and over-emphasized in the poetics of incitement. A Muslim act of terror, for instance, ceases being a singular event and comes to signify the very "essence" of Muslimness. Those in the media and academia who choose to take a more nuanced and complex view of such events often provide culturalist or political explanations, thus placing the violence and the protests within the logic and context of a radicalized Muslim community. In the case of Danish cartoons, for example, an article by Pernille Ammitzbøll and Lorenzo Vidino is a case in point. The writers trace the reaction to the publication of cartoons within the logic of the personal and political ambitions of several local imams. The article also suggests that in the fight for the minds of Danish Muslims, the imams with Saudi money tend to have an advantage over those who do not have foreign donors to build their mosques. But in the article's conclusion, the authors deride the Danish government itself for enabling the radical imams within the Danish nation:

> PET's [Politiets Efterretningstjeneste] policy of short-term obsequiousness may have long-term repercussions. Radical imams use the authorities' endorsement to boost their own status within the Muslim community, portraying themselves as the only ones who can represent and defend it. At the same time, the imams manipulate the relationship, becoming necessary mediators in any contact between authorities and the Muslim community. When, for example, in June 2006, a small right-wing group organized a provocative anti-Muslim protest inside Gellerup, the police dispatched insufficient numbers and had to resort to the imams' help to stop the local Muslim youth from attacking the protesters. If keeping order within the Muslim community is subcontracted to the imams, the state relinquishes part of its authority on its own soil to the benefit of megalomaniacal imams disloyal to Denmark and its democracy.

There is no denying the fact that, even in ideal conditions, police and other disciplinary institutions rely on community leaders to maintain peace. Even in the United States, the police at least attempt to have someone on their staff who can learn from minority communities that are heavily policed. So while it does enable and empower a certain segment of the ethnic elite in Denmark, the Danish authorities, the only other alternative would be to sever their connections with the community or to enable different and more progressive leadership to emerge, and that will only happen if those in the Muslim community in Denmark (and Europe as a whole) achieve a similar level of upward mobility as their European counterparts.

But the problem here is not just of radicalized youth and militant imams. The uproar over the Danish cartoons must also be understood on a much deeper level. That it was a planned act of incitement is clear, even from the statement of the newspaper's editors: the cartoons were solicited to prove a point, to challenge self-censorship resulting from fear of violent and radical Muslim responses. Consequently, only the most insulting and the most transgressive cartoons were chosen.

The cartoons, one representing the Prophet with a bomb on his turban, were not only hurtful in terms of Muslim perceptions of the figure of the Prophet but also functioned as a defamatory representation of the Muslim community in general. All such racial and ethnic stereotypes are highly offensive, and if it were any other community, no newspaper worth its name—unless it happened to be an avowedly racist newspaper—would publish any such cartoons, no matter how deeply committed to freedom of expression. In this case, though, the paper may not be racist, but it does overemphasize its freedom of expression to a point that its representative art becomes a sign of racial and religious bigotry.

Further, the cartoons were an affront to most Muslims on a basic level. In most contemporary Muslim societies, representing the Prophet through visual imagery is forbidden. This has not always been so. In certain sects of Islam, up until the last century, images of the Prophet and his companions were often on display. In Iran, for example, one can still buy posters of Caliph Ali and other members of his household. Injunctions against the depiction of the Prophet and his companions receive their ultimate sanction in Wahabi Islam, but by and large most Muslims are averse to artistic representations of the Prophet. Thus, the "offense" was not just about publishing the image of the Prophet as a terrorist but also about publishing an image of the Prophet, regardless of *how* he is depicted. Of course, this image does not appear free of context: it appears within a contested domain of reception, especially after the Rushdie Affair. For a Muslim, the chances of receiving the image as an unmotivated viewer or reader are extremely reduced, and politics, therefore, becomes a part of the reception itself. And since the reception is political or politicized, responses range from the semiotic to the violent. Furthermore, these instances of incitement—or freedom of speech—might be useful or laudatory for metropolitan artists and writers, but they end up enhancing the power of the very radical groups that the authors and artists rely on to receive the expected response. Every time such works are published, radical segments in Muslim society can employ them as evidence of the impossibility of coexistence with the mores of Western modernity. As a result, even moderate Muslims have a difficult time standing up for the ideals of tolerance and cross-cultural understanding. In fact, the only cross-cultural work that moderate Muslims can perform under such contested circumstances is to claim that anti-Muslim sentiments in the West are not universal. But given the level of vitriol and bigotry at both ends of the global divide, the space for such work is, unfortunately, diminishing at a rapid rate.

I understand that this is an inconclusive discussion. I have neither provided a complete catalog of incitements nor any particular remedies for reducing cross-cultural tensions. Part of this is because I am neither in the business of cataloguing nor in the business of recipe production. I am, however, deeply committed to offering my views about how things are and how they became as such. Ultimately, Muslims and their Western counterparts will have to reach a sort of global understanding, a kind of understanding in which both sides at least "know" why and how the other side thinks and acts. It is only through an understanding of the thoughts and feelings of each other that can provide the possibility of a world with less cross-cultural strife. In that light, I will—albeit tentatively—attempt to provide a mode of literary criticism in the next chapter that may benefit metropolitans and Muslims in working toward meaningful cross-cultural dialogue.

CHAPTER 5

TOWARD A COSMOPOLITAN PRACTICE OF READING

In this chapter, I appropriate the term *cosmopolitan* to empha-size the development of a transcendent mode of reading that involves going beyond one's provincial perspective to incorporate the meaning-making processes of one's cultural others. It is a sort of postmodern modus vivendi in which we may not agree on the universality of our sociocultural principles; however, this mode of reading allows us to learn *why* and *how* others read the same texts in varying ways. This cosmopolitics needs to become normalized on both ends of the global divide. Just as cosmopolitanism presup-poses thinking beyond the borders of one's material and ideological nation, a democratic and cosmopolitan criticism should force us to not only read texts with our own culturally constructed values but also to read and experience texts as our global Others would experience them.

There are quite a few major works on cosmopolitanism. The term itself is often offered either as a response to staunch nation-alist tendencies or, at least, as a possible alternative means of belonging in an increasingly interconnected world. In all cases, one important aspect of being cosmopolitan is understanding intracultural differences and learning to live with those differences. In explaining the nature of cosmopolitanism as an existing praxis, Sheldon Pollock suggests that, in a way, "we already are and have always been cosmopolitan, though we may not always have known it," for "cosmopolitan is infinite ways of being" (12). Thus, to be cosmopolitan, one must be open to seeing and experiencing the world not just from a noncultural or statist perspective but also from a varied perspective that allows some space and consideration for different ways of viewing and experiencing the world. For Kwame Anthony Appiah, one aspect of being cosmopolitan is knowing that "people are different . . . and [that] there is much to learn from our differences" (xv). For some scholars of cosmopolitanism, the concept has a deep philosophical lineage and must be mobilized against the pernicious consequences of insular, statist models of politics. In such discussions, cosmopolitanism is often offered as a sort of antidote to the disasters resulting from statist nationalism. For example, Daniele Archibugi offers a model of "cosmopolitical democracy" that can help us define a "cosmopolitical perspective of humanitarian intervention" within the traditional boundaries of states (10–11).

Of course, there is a problem with this theorization because international "interventions" are undertaken mostly by developed nations and, in some cases, international institutions like the United Nations and its security council are used to legitimize these interventions. But despite its Eurocentric outcomes, even Archibugi argues for a model of thinking about the world that is beyond the strict statist model. Thus, no matter how we discuss cosmopolitanism, it always runs across two major problematic scenarios: its Eurocentricity and its challenge to nationalism. In the former case, one is led to believe that the best and most developed present is that of the metropolitan West and that all modes of life not conforming to its values and standards are necessarily in need of sanction or intervention. Similarly, if nation-states must be weakened to accommodate a cosmopolitan politics, then the denizens of the developing world find themselves completely at the mercy of international forces and corporations. Furthermore, in the case of Muslim nations, Pan-Islamist cosmopolitanism is already emerging as the ultimate challenge to all normalizing national narratives, which are essential to developing modern civic nation-states. Because of this, I use the term cosmopolitan advisedly and with a certain specific emphasis on its significance and utility for performing cross-cultural work and especially for training our students as citizens of this complex world.

This leads me to the next important question: How would we go about training ourselves and our students in reading texts about Islam with a certain degree of knowledge of the Muslim world's meaning-making processes? I have already provided a surface knowledge of the Muslim sacred. Of course, the degree of our engagement with the Muslim world defines the level of required expertise. If we are professors teaching texts about the Islamic periphery, then we must know our subject within the context of its own history and the politics of its production, as well as the context of its reception.

In the end, we must move from focusing on *what the text means*, à la Stanley Fish, to *what the text does*. By doing so, we may explore why it is received differently by different audiences. Only then can we assign any critical value to its reception. If *The Satanic Verses* becomes a contested text, our job is not to ignore this contest or to argue that the text is "not so bad" when read "correctly." Our job is rather to trace the reasons for its contested reception in order to go beyond the text and mobilize it for something beyond itself. Our readings, therefore, must be informed by a specific kind of critical cosmopolitanism and a sufficiently understood cosmopolitics.

For the term *cosmopolitics*, I am indebted to Bruce Robbins, who provides the following observations:

Thinking of cosmopolitics not as universal reason in disguise, but as one on a series of scales, as an area both within and beyond the nation (and yet falling short of "humanity") that is inhabited by a variety of cosmopolitanisms, we will perhaps not be tempted to offer the final word on the dilemmas above. But it is something merely to expose them in their full multivoiced complexity, thereby making it clear at least what justice on a global scale would have to resolve. (12)

I am using the term *cosmopolitics* in a slightly modified form, one more pertinent to literary criticism. In my usage, the cosmopolitical or cosmopolitan criticism would acknowledge that there can be various ways of approaching texts. While some universalist attitudes toward interpreting texts might exist, the reader must be cognizant of the context within which specific texts are received. This form of reading needs to happen at both ends of the global divide. We must become different kinds of readers and receivers of literary texts, for one universal mode of reading and textual reception is no longer sustainable or desirable. The Rushdie Affair was a prime example of mutually exclusive modes of reading at both ends of the global divide. While most Muslims saw it as an affront to their cultural sensitivities as well as a challenge to their concepts of the sacred, most metropolitan critics and writers only saw it from an authorial perspective related to the author's right to free expression. In the ensuing conflict, neither side paused to listen to the voice of the other; neither side took time to understand the readerly circumstances that preconditioned the receptive responses of the other. We who teach literature should do better than that or else we will keep deadening and flattening the texts of the Islamic world according to the conventions and modes of understanding of metropolitan cultures.

Of course, I am not the first to broach this subject, nor the first to hazard an opinion on it. I am, rather, a latecomer: I find myself in the company of some giants of literary theory and criticism. My very idea for a better reading focused on the reception of texts is preceded by what Edward Said famously termed acts of "contrapuntal" reading. For Said, contrapuntal reading is a reading with an "awareness both of the metropolitan history that is narrated and of those other histories against which (and together with which) the dominating discourse acts" (*Culture* 51). I, however, hope to go beyond the history and historical context to mobilize this history in order to understand different modes of reception of the text. It is important to focus on reception because a knowledge of the values that shape our reception of texts can lead us to a broader understanding of cultural differences. A complex mode of reading Islamic responses to postmodernist fiction would thus enable us to understand why Muslims object to certain texts and how such anguish can be caused by certain stylistic and literary choices that are taken for granted within metropolitan cultures. We also know that, postlinguistic turn and semiotic criticism, one must avoid reading signs without context, as this is not a valid path toward the interpretation of and construction of meaning. In fact, that simplistic "pursuit of signs" has now been seriously complicated by structuralist theory. In this regard, Jonathan Culler has some important insights to share.

As stated in the introduction, I read *The Satanic Verses* years after its publication when the book was already imbued with the politics and the controversy that surrounded it immediately after its publication. I read it as an infantry officer in the Pakistan Army. I could only receive the text within the immanent domain of my own culture and its attendant reading practices. My troops and I, despite our three separate sects, were of the opinion that a text called *The Satanic Verses* was offensive to us as Muslims.

In hindsight, I can trace the nature of my own response and pose this question: What made something called *The Satanic Verses* offensive to me prior to reading it? Partially, maybe, it was the very name of the text itself that became a challenge to my cultural sensitivities. Informed both by my own lived experience and the current debates in literary theory, this chapter is an attempt at articulating a mode of reading that could have afforded a somewhat nuanced reading and experience of the book event called *The Satanic Verses*. It is my hope that this attempt will initiate a broader discussion of our reading practices concerning such texts. I must point out that my attempt to articulate this nuanced mode of reading and responding to texts about the Islamic world is a preliminary step, and thus this chapter cannot and should not be read as an exhaustive account of a comprehensive and conclusive methodology of reading.

Before I embark on this journey to retrieve the personal in the service of the public and scholarly aspects of my project, some negative work should be done. This chapter posits itself as an intervention within the field of literary theory as taught in the English departments of North American universities. Its specific audience, therefore, are the students and scholars who study and teach theory and literary criticism. While I use *The Satanic Verses* as a problematic text to explain my views, the chapter is not a close reading of the text itself. The text as discussed is instrumental to my larger purpose of encouraging practitioners of literary theory and criticism to acknowledge that their readings and teaching of Islamic texts require an extensive overhaul.

Now, to the question of generalizations. In the previous and ensuing pages, I often invoked and will invoke two slightly essentialized readers: the Western reader and the Muslim reader. I understand at the outset that these are problematic terms. For the purposes of my argument, the Western reader is an academic reader situated as a teacher or student of literature in the North American university. The Muslim reader, on the other hand, is a Muslim aware of the general history of Islam who practices the imperatives of their faith in daily life, and thus entertains a specific idea of the Muslim sacred. Both these readers, however, even after this explanation, cannot really be fixed or specifically defined, and I would request my readers to read my references to them under *sous rature*.[1]

As stated previously, when I invoke the term *poetics of incite-*

ment, I refer to a specific kind of textual production. In general, these texts are centered on certain core concepts of Islam and attempt to rewrite them according to a purely Eurocentric, secular mode of representation. These texts, as discussed in previous chapters, are usually produced either by diasporic postcolonial authors (Rushdie) or Western authors (Jones) to elicit an immediate counter-response from the Islamic world. These texts are produced under the general rubric of authors' rights to an absolute form of free expression. Four major tropes associated with the poetics of incitement can be: (1) the Prophet Muhammad represented as a fallible character in fiction, as exemplified by *The Satanic Verses*; (2) the Qur'ān as a violent and evil text, exemplified by rhetoric often deployed by fundamentalist Christians and the American Right; (3) Aisha as a sexualized being in historical fiction, exemplified by *The Jewel of Medina*; and (4) Muslims represented as untrustworthy or terroristic, exemplified in film, television, and other popular forms.

This brief and inconclusive lists of tropes about Islam and Muslims is, by its very intent, transgressive. They constitute attempts to challenge Muslim history, beliefs, and the very idea of the Muslim sacred. As a result, the (sometimes violent) Muslim responses to such texts, both material and semiotic, become examples of Muslim intolerance. These responses also help reinforce preconceived notions about Muslims for Western audiences.

This attempt at offering a more nuanced mode of reading is thus aimed at forcing the field of literary criticism to acknowledge that our students can only *meaningfully* and *responsibly* read texts about Islam if they have, at the least, a basic understanding of how best to read these texts. Islamic texts—or any text, for that matter—cannot be read without sufficient awareness of their historical, political, and social context. This requires a different kind of critical consciousness as articulated by Said in *The World, the Text, and the Critic*. While elaborating what he means by critical consciousness, Said asserts that the contemporary critical consciousness stands between the temptations represented by two formidable and related powers engaging critical attention. One is the culture to which critics are bound filiatively (by birth, nationality, profession); the other is a method or system acquired affiliatively (by social and political conviction, economic and historical circumstances, voluntary effort and willed deliberation). (25)

The role of one's filiative and affiliative identity is crucial to the kind of critical strategies one finds normative and acceptable. In Said's view, filiation is inherently primordial, while affiliation is generated through learned experience. For literary critics, this could mean associating one's critical practice with a certain school of thought or critical method. Said also asserts in the same work that, at times, the critic is so heavily invested in their affiliative practices that their affiliation becomes a sort of filiation. Secular criticism, for Said, implies an attempt to transcend the limiting structures of a rigid affiliation to a particular method. Thus "the inevitable trajectory of critical consciousness is to arrive at some acute sense of what political, social, and human values are entailed in the reading, production, and transmission of every text" (26). It goes without saying that a critical consciousness unwilling to transcend its own limitations ends up practicing a sort of fundamentalist criticism and is diametrically opposed to Said's idea of secular criticism. Fundamentalist criticism is therefore a complete denial of the recognition of the Other, even when the works being interpreted appropriate raw materials from the culture of the Other. The texts, Said also suggests, "have ways of existing that even in their most rarefied form are always enmeshed in circumstance, time, place, and society—in short, they are in the world, and hence worldly" (35). The privileging of a writer's right to represent over the reader's right to respond according to their own "worldliness" is, therefore, at the least, problematic.

It goes without saying that the material and semiotic responses to the publication of *The Satanic Verses*, both from the Islamic world and from the metropolitan West, form a huge and complex corpus, and quite a few scholars and critics responded to the controversy to highlight the nature and causes of Muslim anguish in response to the novel. Because the material responses—the protests and book burnings in London and elsewhere—were amply covered by the media and need no further explanation at this point, 1 will provide a brief overview of the semiotic responses to the arrival of the text. My discussion of these texts, however, is highly selective and should in no way be considered an exhaustive discussion of the critical responses to the novel.

Immediately after the publication of the book and in the wake of the Rushdie Affair—including the Ayatollah's fatwa against Rushdie—Spivak published an article, which was later published in her book *Outside in the Teaching Machine* (1993).[2] In this essay, Spivak reads the book in a layered manner involving questions of authorial intention, a close reading of the text, and the political ramifications of the text's reception in Iran (but also with a tangential connection to particularities of Indian Islam). Spivak's brilliant analysis is key to understanding the novel and its reception. It is also crucial because it points out the world's emphasis on the figures of Rushdie and the Ayatollah at the cost of neglecting the rights of Muslim subaltern women in India whose rights were curtailed by a selective application of Islamic law. 1 am attempting to go beyond this reading in order to understand, as stated earlier, why the text became so problematic for average practicing Muslims, hence my emphasis on articulating some kind of a method to approaching literary texts about Islam.

In another timely article, Amir Mufti also reads the impact of the text within the context of Islamic politics, according to which the discussion about the novel and its reception "is dominated by the literalist and universalizing discourses of fundamentalism" (107). Mufti also views the novel as an intervention into the politics of the Islamic public sphere and suggests that the novel, by refusing to treat established Islamic norms as axiomatic, "throws into doubt the discursive edifice within which 'Islam' has been produced in recent years" (107). While I find Mufti's discussion of the novel enlightening and enabling, I find it apt to move beyond the political aspects of Islamic fundamentalism and Western secularism (I use both these terms, of course, in a highly generalized sense) to theorize, albeit tentatively, a critical approach that allows the metropolitan reader to understand the nature of the offense caused by the novel and other texts of incitement and to grasp the attendant anxiety and distress that it produced in the lives of average Muslims. In other words, I attempt to theorize a "translation of values" (Mazrui 117) between metropolitan readers and their Muslim counterparts.

Quite a few book-length works were published about the Rushdie Affair. While I cannot possibly account for all such works, I will briefly touch upon some textual responses to the book's publication and the ensuing controversy. In their appraisal of the Rushdie Affair, Ziauddin Sardar and Wyn Davies respond with a particular emphasis on the sensitivities and cultural heritage of the Muslim world. Offering their work as a critique of modernity's (Eurocentric) secularization process, the authors read the imperial imperatives involved in metropolitan responses to Muslim rage and anguish as follows:

> The outraged response to the acts of defiance by a marginalized minority who have no entrée to the levers of power is positive proof that it is through art and the *Book* that the project of modernity has been brought into being, that secularism will brook no interference with its dominance. (11)

Even when scholars respond to the disjuncture between the metropolitan majority and the Muslim minority reception of the book, the burden of proof—proving that it is a marginalized community burning books—still lies with the critic attempting to challenge the absolute reliance on free expression that underwrites a project like

The Satanic Verses. Most critics' energies are spent recuperating and articulating the political and material causes of Muslim rage, and any attempt to inspire metropolitan readers to read the book, or at least experience its arrival, from the place of their Muslim others is completely foreclosed. And even though Sardar and Davies published their response in 1990, the book failed to gain much traction in metropolitan academic circles, partially because the authors themselves were not deeply entrenched within academia. Beyond this lack of academic capital, I believe their book lacked proper recognition because they posed a challenge to the Western poetics of incitement that clashed with metropolitan assumptions. In fact, immediately after the Ayatollah's fatwa against Rushdie, Muslim scholars within the metropolitan world and those sympathetic to Muslim causes were forced to speak on behalf of Rushdie, which was obviously the apt thing to do; nevertheless, it seems all efforts within metropolitan culture were geared toward safeguarding Rushdie's public persona and his right to free speech. *For Rushdie* (1994), a collection of essays by Muslim and Arab scholars in defense of free speech, was an outcome of this sort of cultural pressure. I am not suggesting that these writers offered their support to Rushdie under duress, but that there is no doubt in my mind that part of this was a response to the question, now often invoked concerning the "War on Terror": *Why are Muslim scholars silent against Khomeini's fatwa?* The book's reactionary project is painfully clear from its preface:

> This book aims to break into this whole unhappy state of affairs and give prominence to a school of thought . . . both little known and largely misunderstood in the West. . . . It is at this point that we have now assembled a hundred prominent names from both the Maghreb and the Arab East, as well as from Iran, Turkey, the Sudan, Bangladesh, and the Muslim countries of former Soviet Union; included are writers, thinkers, artists, filmmakers. They are, for the most part, men and women of influence and renown,

and they have all been brought together here to testify in favor of Rushdie. (Abdallah 3)

This book project was thus undertaken in the service of metropolitan anxieties about the silence of Islamic intellectuals regarding the fatwa. The burden of this representation is again on Muslim scholars, for they, while their people are protesting in the streets, must offer a so-called civilized response to the affair. In doing so, they silence the very people and places that gave them the "influence" and "prominence" that the editors so eloquently describe in the passage cited above.

This brief overview of the critical literature produced after the publication of *The Satanic Verses* is in no way exhaustive, but one could glean from this sample a recurrent pattern: the arrival of the text is either read within the political climate of the time, and then the politics are highlighted to rationalize Muslim popular responses to the book or, as in my last example, a sampling of Muslim intellectuals is provided to suggest that not all Muslims are as uncivilized as their brothers and sisters in the street. There is, however, no corresponding effort on the part of metropolitan critics, scholars, or pundits to suggest some deeper understanding of Muslim rage and anguish.

In another interesting article, Feroza Jussawalla suggests that one of the problems with the reception of Rushdie's novel is that it was "working within an Islamic tradition that does not conform to the particular strain practiced by the late Ayatollah Khomeini, his work drew the fatwa from Iran" (53). The problem in such a reading of the arrival of the text is that the so-called "Mughal/Muslim/Indian" (54) Islam that informs Rushdie's narrative techniques has altered and given way to a more fundamentalist strain. Hence, if one could only retrieve and foreground the "Islamic" narrative tradition that Rushdie is relying on, one could, according to Jussawalla, argue that "Rushdie would have not thought of himself as blaspheming but rather would have seen himself as doing the

Muslim community" a favor (57). Though I find Jussawalla's claims about a post-Mughal monolithic Muslim Indian culture problematic, I believe that her attempt to read Rushdie within the controversial space of Rushdie's imagined Islam, the cosmopolitan strain of Indian Islam, and the fundamentalist strain of Islam attributed to his readers is still more nuanced and deserves attention. Readings such as these allow readers to acknowledge the cultural and ideological strains within Islam that prove crucial to performing a more nuanced reading of the text and enhance the level of engagement by metropolitan readers.

This leads me to a brief discussion of the poetics of incitement within the context of the Muslim sacred. Muslim responses to the poetics of incitement are not just about individual readings— rather, they are acts of reading informed by an awareness of the Muslim sacred. Specific Muslim communities form unique interpretive communities not much different from those theorized by Stanley Fish that I discussed in the introduction. Thus the question of Muslim responses to the poetics of incitement is also a question of power: members of secular, metropolitan reading communities expect Muslims somehow to transcend the limitations of their own particular interpretive communities and read the texts of incitement from the point of view of their metropolitan counterparts. This, I must assert, produces a one-way conversation, for metropolitan critics and writers do not feel the same need to transcend their own interpretive communities and read the texts from the point of view of their Muslim audiences. There is then a need to develop a more inclusive and democratic critical consciousness.

In his posthumously published book *Humanism and Democratic Criticism*, Edward Said again insists on a more democratic and inclusive mode of philological criticism. In arguing his point, Said briefly mentions the comparative equivalences of Western humanism and its Judaic and Islamic counterparts. Concerning the importance of the humanistic tradition of reading in Islam, Said suggests:

Suffice it to recall briefly that in Islamic tradition, knowledge is premised upon a philological attention to language beginning with the Koran . . . and continuing through the emergence of scientific grammar in Khalil ibn Ahmad and Sibawayh to the rise of juris-prudence (*fiqh*) and *ijtihad* and *ta'wil*, jurisprudential hermeneutics and interpretation. . . . All these [practices] involve a detailed scientific attention paid to language as bearing within it knowledge of a kind entirely limited to what language does and does not do. There was . . . a consolidation of the interpretive sciences that underlie the system of humanistic education, which was itself established by the twelfth century in the Arab universities of southern Europe and North Africa, well before its counterpart in the Christian West. (58)

The question that arises from this brief reference to the Islamic interpretative tradition is simply this: How many practitioners of literary criticism are aware of this history, and how many of them ever incorporate this knowledge into their critical engagement with literary texts, especially those concerning Islam? Taking Said's brief reference as a point of departure, I suggest that there is a need to incorporate at least a basic knowledge of Islamic reading practices in our critical work while also emphasizing the importance and necessity of this inclusion within the context of the current production and consumption of literary texts. I am in no way implying that "Islamic practices of reading" or "Islamic hermeneutics" exist in a pure form, nor am I suggesting that the practices of reading in the Islamic world are universal or eternal. Nevertheless, there is a historical and philosophical core to particular modes of interpretation that form part of the critical tradition of the Islamic world. Knowing these core ideas is vital for a more democratic and humanistic critical practice in the twenty-first century.

There are two major reasons for insisting on broadening our critical and philosophical repertoire in order to enhance modes of critical reading. First, Islam has now become one of the most intensely studied subjects in the social sciences, and the Western world has never been as connected with the Islamic world as it is now, at least not since the era of pre–World War II high colonialism. Second, several literary works now focus on the Islamic world or are written by diasporic Muslim authors from both metropolitan cultures and the global periphery. It is, therefore, no longer advisable to read these texts using a Eurocentric philosophical mode of critical reading. In the ensuing pages, I will first explore the genealogical core of "Islamic hermeneutics" and then highlight its importance by discussing the metropolitan critical reception of *The Satanic Verses*.

I begin with the title of the book and its translation into three major Islamic languages: in Urdu, *Shaitāni Ayāt*, in Arabic, *Ayāt al-Shaitāniyya*, and in Persian, *Ayāt-e-Shaitāni*. *Ayah* as a descriptive noun is invariably used to designate the individual verses of the Qur'ān. Thus, on the surface, the title conveyed, particularly for my soldiers and myself, a sense that the book's main intent was to label the Qur'ān itself a satanic product. Even without having read the book, its title was laden with a deeply cultural semantic trace, especially when read in translation. The title became a major impediment to an initial engagement with the book's content. In Pakistani newspapers, for example, editors first translated it as *Shaitāni Ayāt*, but later, finding the term deeply troubling and offensive, decided to translate the title as *Shaitāni Manzōmāt*, or the *Satanic Compositions*; however, the newly translated title never caught on.[3]

For me, being a product of a deeply Islamic subculture, an engagement with the content of the book required a relatively heroic undertaking. I had to bracket out the markers of my immediate cultural methods of signification and adopt the reading habits and critical insights of a purely Eurocentric mode of interpretation. It was at the cost of my insular social self and my adoption of a more complex, humanistic, and liberal point of view that I could, at least, dare read the book. Similarly, for a Western reader to find some sympathy for my personal anguish about the offensive nature of the book would require that reader to transcend their own cultural and critical matrix and look at the text from the context of the particulars of my experience and knowledge base. In such a scenario, the only effective and comprehensive reading of the text could be accomplished in what Homi Bhabha, in another context, calls the "third space of enunciation" (37), where the self and the other come together to perform what Said terms the "heroic act of first readings" (67). Any reading that did not include a trace of the other was deeply flawed.

My second reading of the Rushdie text—one informed by my own cultural heritage and the modes of reading learned in the metropolitan academy—was more rewarding. While reading the novel again, my first task was to trace the origin of the title itself. If it did not imply that the Qur'ān was the work of Satan, then what exactly did the term "Satanic Verses" mean? My quest was certainly aided by critical works about the novel, for the Rushdie Affair had quickly become an industry. The first bit of information was made available by the work of American Arabist and neoconservative Daniel Pipes. And though I absolutely disagree with Pipes's take on the book and the ensuing Muslim protests and violence, he did provide a starting point toward an understanding of the title's meaning. Pipes provides an insightful discussion of what he calls the "Satanic Verses incident" as part of the early Islamic historiography of the revelation of the Qur'ān (56). Pipes is also right to suggest that not many Muslims were aware of this particular incident and that in its Arabic or other sources, it was not called the "Satanic Verses incident" but rather the "incident of the birds." The main source for the recording of this particular incident happened to be the history of Al-Tabarī. Naturally I looked for Al-Tabarī's work, one that provides the following account of the verses:

> The Messenger of God was eager for the welfare of his people and wished to effect reconciliation with them in whatever ways he

could. . . . With his love for his tribe and his eagerness for their welfare it would have delighted him if some of the difficulties . . . could have been smoothed out, and he debated with himself and fervently desired such an outcome. Then God revealed:

By the star when it sets, your comrade does not err, nor is he deceived, nor does he speak out of [his own] desire. . . . Have you thought upon al-Lāt and al-'Uzzā, and Manāt, the third, the other? . . .

These are the high-flying cranes; verily their intercession is accepted with approval. (Al-Tabari, vol 6., 108)

In the novel, Rushdie stages this particular encounter as an ultimate test for the future of the Prophet's new religion. The revelation— the so-called Satan-inspired revelation—comes to the Prophet while he is facing his opponents:

The Star. Mahound cries out, and the scribes begin to write.
In the name of Allah, the Compassionate, the Merciful!
By the Pleiades when they set: Your companion is not in error; nei-
    ther is he deviating.
Nor does he speak from his own desires. It is a revelation that has
    been revealed: one mighty in power has taught him . . .
Have you thought upon Lat and Uzza, and Manat, the third, the
    other? . . .
They are the exalted birds, and their intercession is desired indeed.
    (*Satanic* 114)

In this scene, the deluded Prophet puts forth a more inclusive brand of his faith, a faith that would include and accommodate the three pagan goddesses along with the one true God. This, cer- tainly, would change the very monotheistic core of Muhammad's revelation and make it into yet another brand of Arab paganism. But then, in staging the repudiation scene, Rushdie also suggests that it was this particular repudiation that made Islam an idea that would last. The fictional Prophet of the novel repudiates his earlier revelation based on his belief that the earlier verses were inspired by Satan. The new verses are announced as follows:

> He stands in front of the statues of the Three and announces the abrogation of the verses which Shaitan whispered in his ear. These verses are banished from the true recitation, *al*-Qur'an. New verses are thundered in their place.
>
> "Shall we have daughters and you sons?" Mahound recites. "That would be a fine division!"
>
> These are but names you have dreamed of, you and your fathers, Allah vests no authority in them. (*Satanic* 124)

According to the editors of *Alqur'ān Alkarīm*, the particular text of the Qur'ān I am using here, the Sūra An-Najm (the Star), listed as Sūra 53 in all extant copies of the Qur'ān, "is an early Makkan Sūra" (Residency 1635), which means that, in historical terms, it was revealed during the early part of the Prophet's ten years in Makkah. This also means that Rushdie has the time frame correct in the novel, as he presents the revelation of the verses as an early and most important test of the Prophet's career. While explaining the main theme of the Sūra, the editors of *Alqur'ān Alkarīm* provide the following summary:

> The impression received by the Prophet in revelation is neither error on his part nor deception by others, nor does he speak from selfish motives: it comes clearly from Allah, Who is not what the vain imaginations of men conceive. He is all-in-all, First and last, Lord of all, Ample in forgiveness. (1635)

This brief summary implies that the Sūra is meant to assert that whatever the Prophet conveys as truth is not of his own making but rather a product of divine revelation. As such, the Prophet is merely a conduit, a vessel, and associating any personal motives to his pronounced revelation is absolutely unacceptable in Islamic interpretation. More on this later. Here, I cite the first few verses of the actual Sūra:

> By the star when it goes down/your companion is neither astray nor being mislead
> nor does he say (aught) of (his own) desire
> it is no less than inspiration sent down to him. . . .
> Have you seen Lāt, and 'Uzza
> And another, the third (goddess), Manāt? . . .
> These are nothing but names
> Which ye have devised
> Ye and your forefathers
> For which Allah has sent down no authority. (Residency 136–39)

These verses can only be fully understood with the proper application of traditional Muslim textual hermeneutics. In other words, one must first return to what Said terms the "philological-interpretive model," of which Islamic hermeneutics of the text is but one branch (*Democratic*, 34). Such a reading, to use Said's words, "will gradually locate the text in its time as part of a whole network of relationships whose outlines and influences play an informing role *in* the text" (62). There are two such modes of reading developed in Islamic history of Qur'ānic interpretation as well as philosophical inquiry. In fact, Said had briefly touched upon them. In *The World, the Text, and the Critic*, Said explains two modes of reading—that of the Zahirites and that of the Batinist—as follows:

> Batinists held that meaning in language is concealed within the words; meaning is therefore available only as the result of an inward-tending exegesis. The Zahirites—their name derives from the Arabic word for clear, apparent, and phenomenal; *Batin* con-

notes internal—argued that words had only a surface meaning, one that was anchored to a particular usage, circumstance, historical and religious situation. (36)

Within the history of Islamic interpretation, both these views of reading have held sway, and even today they determine the rules for interpreting sacred texts. The Zahirite position, which Said explains in the above-cited work, is more worldly and, in Said's words, forces the reader to acknowledge "that a text has a specific situation, placing restraints upon the interpreter and his interpretation not because the situation is hidden within the text as a mystery, but rather because the situation exists at the same level of surface particularity as the textual object itself" (39). Thus, to sum up a large history of Islamic interpretation, the practice of interpretation in Islam can be broadly divided into two categories: one that deals with the words alone and seeks meaning by tracing their roots to the narrowest possible definition, and another that takes the words as they appear and then traces their meaning by locating as precisely as possible the particular circumstances of their revelation and the occasion of their first appearance. In both cases, the purpose is to reach the specific intentionality behind the text, which means, in Qur'ānic exegesis, to read the mind of God, as it is He who revealed the word to the Prophet in the first place. This is done in two ways. First, a scholar can very easily look at other adjacent verses of the Qur'ān and connect them with the verses in question. Second, a scholar can also trace the meaning by placing and connecting a particular verse within its historical context. In this process, another important distinction must be made: the question of whether a certain verse is interpretable. According to early interpreters of Islam, the Qur'ān has two kinds of verses: the 'amr verses and the mutshabihāt. The 'amr verses are central to the teaching of religion and, therefore, should be understood clearly by the reader. The mutshabihāt are allegorical verses that concern the attributes of God that have no particular need of comprehension for one to be a good Muslim. As James Pavlin suggests:

> The orthodox scholars of Islam, starting with the Companions of the prophet, have maintained a belief in the clarity of the Qur'an based on the seventh verse of the third surah.[4] This verse states that the Qur'an contains clear verses of legislation, which the believers follow, and obscure or allegorical verses, which the believers accept without question. (105)

The verses that Rushdie satirizes in his novel belong to the first category, the clear verses that can be understood and which impart instructions to be followed, though some mutshabihāt are also present in the novel. They can be interpreted both in a Zahirite as well as a Batinite mode. A textual reading of these verses requires attention to detail, especially the words and their usages within the immediate context of the Sūra itself. The second and third verse—"Your companion is neither astray nor being mislead/nor does he say (aught) of (his own) desire"—should be deciphered first to understand, simply, who the addressee of the verses is. In this case, it seems, the Prophet's opponents, the Quraish, are those addressed by these particular verses, for the "companion" refers to the Prophet himself. In other words, God is addressing the Quraish and pointing out to them, through the voice of his vessel, the Prophet is not in error, nor is he being misled by Satan or any other temptation. The second verse also suggests that what he says does not stem from his own desires, including the desire to reconcile with his tribe. Rather, what he says is spoken purely by God, a process in which he has no particular agency of his own. Hence, if he has no agency over the words that he utters, then he achieves an absolute form of detachment and objectivity, a sort of objectivity that eliminates personal desire.

When Rushdie rewrites these verses, he posits the Prophet

as a subject who is creating religion on his own instead of gaining knowledge through divine revelation. That belief, of course, according to the logic of the Islamic modes of meaning-making is absolutely impossible, for the Prophet is a conduit of God's truth and not its creator. To those of us who did read the book, Rushdie's fictionalized account came to represent not something revisionist but something absolutely foreign to our mode of reading the Prophet. Presenting the Prophet as fallible also had its own ramifications. In all accounts of the Prophet's life, there is no doubt left in the Muslim mind that the Prophet is human and not divine, but there is also no possibility to read the Qur'ān as something created by the Prophet himself. Thus, this particular Sūra is less about the goddesses and more about emphasizing the fact that what the Prophet reveals as a revelation passes through him directly in ways beyond his control. And since he has no control, he cannot be accused of tailoring his revelation to appease the people of his tribe.

Another important aspect of Islamic historiography, philosophy, hadīth, and Qur'ānic commentary is the system of *isnad*. The scholar, or philosopher, principally, must attempt to reach the earlier and the most authentic account of a particular verse and particular saying of the Prophet. This tracing of the chain of narration is termed *isnad*, the plural of *sanad*, which literally means "to authenticate." What this particular Hadīth suggests is that any claims to authenticity were also guided by the personal conduct of the narrator. If the chain of narration is found to be weak in a revision of Islamic history, later historians consider the information suspect and exclude it from their own accounts. Similarly, if the claims of a particular saying cannot be authenticated through actions permitted by the Qur'ān, then the information is considered untrustworthy and edited out. This science of narration became the cornerstone of the process of recoding of the Hadīth, and it is because of these stringent rules of authentication that only six major works of Hadīth are considered reliable.[5]

The incident recorded by Tabarī, having been found inauthentic, was excluded from most other Islamic works of history and the works of *surah*.[6] A closer look at the source text used by Rushdie suggests that he either used the Tabarī translation or an English or Orientalist translation of the event. When the novel reached the market, few Muslims were aware of this particular account by Tabarī. For learned Muslims, the issue had already been settled as unreliable by Muslim historians who did not find it authentic enough to include in their histories. While the title foreclosed any possibility of reading the book for a lay audience, the central role of an apocryphal tradition—the event itself—asked serious readers to transcend the boundaries of their own meaning-making system to read the book.

Obviously, I cannot offer a detailed critical reading of the entire book, and the discussion provided above is just an example of what can be done with a small amount of knowledge of the historical and cultural particularities of Islam. This approach, however, must be further complicated by incorporating not only the sacred and historical texts of Islam in a diachronic movement but also by incorporating the regional and cultural aspects of Islam synchronically.

The responses to *The Satanic Verses* offered by metropolitan critics tended to be one-sided. For most Western critics, the Rushdie Affair primarily came to revolve around authorial free expression, and the lines were more harshly drawn in the wake of the fatwa issued by Ayatollah Khomeini of Iran. Between the two extremes of free expression and death, the voices of common Muslims— who would have never really endorsed the fatwa itself—were completely silenced. Said provided the following response about the publication of the book:

> *The Satanic Verses* is an astonishing and prodigiously inventive work of fiction. Yet, it is like its author, in history, the world, the crowd and the storm. It is, in all sorts of ways, a deliberately transgressive work. It mimics the central Islamic narratives with bold,

nose-thumbing, post-modern daring. And in doing so it demonstrates another side of its author's unbroken engagement with the
politics and history of the contemporary scene. Salman Rushdie
is after all the same distinguished writer and intellectual who has
spoken out for immigrants, black and Palestinian rights, against
imperialism and racism, as well as against censorship, and he has
always unhesitantly expressed willingness to take active political
positions whenever his voice has been needed.

Above all, however, there rises the question that people from
the Islamic world ask: Why must a Moslem, who could be defending and sympathetically interpreting us, now represent us so
roughly, so expertly and so disrespectfully to an audience already
primed to excoriate our traditions, reality, history, religion, language, origin? Why, in other worlds, must a member of our culture
join the legions of Orientalists in Orientalizing Islam so radically
and unfairly? (*Rushdie* 165)

Said's response to the Rushdie Affair is exceptionally sophisticated,
for he attempts to reintegrate Rushdie into the Muslim community
as one of their own. In this sense, Said wants his Muslim readers to
read Rushdie within the context of his overall service to the cause
of Islam—Palestine in particular—and issues of other marginalized
groups. Said also gives a compassionate account of Muslim grievances, but they are also couched in the language of an in-group. In
the same statement, Said also clearly condemns the fatwa issued
by the Ayatollah and in his concluding remarks and requests of
all Muslims: "If we have accepted Rushdie's help in the past, we
should now be ensuring his safety and his right to say what he has
to say" (167). This response, I suggest, comes from an ideal place of
enunciation, a place that only a critic privy to at least the basics of
Islamic modes of reading can occupy. Resultantly, Said's response
is more compassionate: he neither outright absolves Rushdie
nor supports the radical Muslim view on the subject—rather, he
responds by being on both sides of the argument simultaneously.

In his statement, Jimmy Carter acknowledges the unacceptability of the Ayatollah's fatwa while reminding readers, "This is the kind of intercultural wound that is difficult to heal. Western leaders should make it clear that in protecting Rushdie's life and civil rights, there is no endorsement of an insult to the sacred beliefs of our Moslem friends" (237). Carter is doing what we always expect our students to do in responding to literary texts: looking at the Other, if possible, from the point of view of the Other; after all, this is what humanistic scholarship, ideally, should be about. Sadly, though, during the Rushdie Affair, this important point of humanistic scholarship was mostly erased and silenced, not the least because of the extreme binarism posed: death for the author or his freedom of speech. Or, to be a bit dramatic, the choice boiled down to either silence or speech.

Said also points out, while explaining the act of close reading of texts, that

> [l]aw, *qanun*, is what, in the public realm, governs or has hegemony over acts of personal initiative even when freedom of expression is decently available. Responsibly, one cannot just say anything one pleases and in whichever way one wishes to say it. (*Humanism* 69)

Similarly, in the realm of literary representation, an author might write what is appropriate in one cultural milieu, but the same principles cannot be applied ipso facto to the reception of the work in another culture.

The responses by Carter and Said are not necessarily perfect responses, but they are, in their very expression, richer and more attuned to a world of differing ideas and sensitivities. What creates such a response? Specifically, what kinds of existential experience makes it possible for a person—scholar or student—to acknowledge both sides of the question? Not knowledge alone, for knowledge alone also creates the kinds of responses that came from the American Right, mostly from Arabist scholars—instead, a liberal humanistic response that acknowledges human differences and which transcends the boundaries of what Said terms one's "affiliative loyalties." Almost all Muslim intellectuals who experience a liberal humanist education system (in the United States or in Europe) master the current discourses and synthesize them with their preexisting worldview. On the other hand, there are few Western scholars in the humanities who can claim to have done the same with Islamic thought.

As my brief discussion of *The Satanic Verses* suggests, Islam is not only a distant reality; it has also become an important source for literary representations. In literature departments, we teach these fictional representations. Can we afford to teach them only from a place of ignorance, without incorporating at least a basic knowledge of Islamic modes of meaning-making and an elementary knowledge of Islam? In the field of the humanities, we expect our students to learn feminist, minority, queer, and so many other theoretical discourses of the marginalized in order to be more nuanced and productive scholars. How can we, then, expect them to read the texts of the Islamic periphery without even a basic knowledge of the rich history of textual interpretation that provides the core principles of an Islamic mode of reading texts? These are some of the questions that we must answer if we are seriously interested in widening the reach and appeal of critical theory.

CHAPTER 6

READING DIFFERENTLY

The Case of the Taliban

To further elaborate what I have discussed in the previous chapter, I will now offer, by way of an example, a kind of critical reading that is informed by the meaning-making processes of the West as well as the Islamic world.[1] The purpose here is to highlight the importance of such cross-cultural efforts, for, as I have already suggested, within the complex array of current global conflicts, monocultural assumptions about texts and concepts are no longer tenable. In this chapter, I will offer my take on the Taliban, probably the most fundamentalist group in the Islamic world, one that needs to be discussed and read with a cosmopolitical understanding. I must also assert clearly here that I have often written against the Taliban and other such militant Islamist groups. I have learned that my writings are more powerful when they argue against the Taliban and other extremist groups from within the Islamic tradition. This chapter, therefore, provides a method that involves both a knowledge of metropolitan theory and an understanding of the Muslim sacred.

There is a tendency in Western scholarship about Islam to capture the figure of the fundamentalist in its presence, as a fully realized subject of its own will without accounting for the material conditions necessary for the creation of such a subjectivity. In such an engagement with the figure of the fundamentalist, the genealogy of fundamentalism is traced directly to the pernicious ideologies that construct such a subjectivity. Such reductive explanations of Islamic fundamentalism, especially in the works of American conservative scholars, presuppose that a subjectivization such as that of the Taliban can somehow take place outside of history and is therefore completely unavoidable. The fundamentalist is thus a subject created without an external cause.

"Fundamentalists," suggests Terry Eagleton, "are basically fetishists," and "a fetish is whatever you use to plug some ominous gap" (*After* 208). Eagleton further suggests that what fundamentalists fear the most is "nonbeing," which they attempt to fill "with dogma" (208). As a cursory reference to Eagleton's discussion of fundamentalists suggests, the gap that the so-called fundamentalist attempts to fill preexists the desire to fill it; it is part of being human in the world, for "nonbeing is what we are made of" (208). Eagleton recuperates this sense of being in the world through an acute reading of David Hume. The basic assumptions of Hume's discussion of human understanding can be gleaned from one interesting passage provided in the beginning of his *An Enquiry Concerning Human Understanding* (1748):

> But though our thought seems to possess this unbounded liberty, we shall find, upon a nearer examination, that it is really confined within very narrow limits, and all this creative power of the mind amounts to no more than the faculty of compounding, transposing, augmenting, or diminishing the materials afforded us by the senses and experience. (11)

It is this particularly empiricist and experiential explanation of thought and ideas by Hume that allows Eagleton to provide an instructive suggestion about the impossibility of a stable self, for, in Eagleton's words, "because we are historical animals we are always in the process of becoming, perpetually out ahead of ourselves" and that is one reason why we "can never achieve the stable identity of a mosquito or a pitchfork" (*After* 208). Resultantly, Eagleton suggests, "we cannot choose to live non-historically: history is quite as much our destiny as death" (209).

The emergence of the figure of a Talib (the Pashto pluralization "Taliban" has now become an established concept in English) can also not be traced and discussed outside of history. Even though some American conservatives suggest that "the Arab and Islamic worlds are not products of Western colonialism and Imperialism" (Palmer 235), instead tracing the problems of Islam to its own sacred texts, the figure of the Talib is not only a production of Islam but also a composite figure created by the power of global capitalism. I suggest that the rise of neoliberalism and neoliberal globalization is the ultimate plane of emergence for the Taliban as well as other global fundamentalist movements.[2] What I am suggesting is that the Talib is a historical figure, and its emergence as a subject cannot be understood without the material and ideological terrain upon which this subject attempts to fill the hole of its non-being with dogma. Furthermore, the rise of the Talib also impacts the larger culture in which it seeks to fill its emptiness.

A brief discussion of neoliberalism as a system but also as conceptual and material ground for the emergence of the figure of the fundamentalist is necessary here. I will then trace the impact of this configuration on the role and space of minorities within the *nomos* of the Pakistani nation-state.

While the "globalization" part of "neoliberal globalization" is fairly transparent and often mobilized in defense of a universalist cultural paradigm to challenge all antiglobalist discourses, it is the "neoliberal" part that has more drastic consequences for the global periphery. According to Saskia Sassen, the restructuring of the global economy constructs a specific kind of global economy that involves "the formation of a global market for capital, a global

trade regime, and the internationalization of manufacturing production" (14). Despite its claims to bring development and progress
to the entire world, Sassen points out, the power dynamics of this
new global economic regime are still lopsided and "the center of
gravity of many transactions . . . lies in the North Atlantic region"
(58). This also means, in other words, that while labor-intensive
manufacturing jobs are exported to the global periphery, the upper
management and flow of profits remain directed toward metropolitan centers. Globalization, despite its claims to a free-market
economy, is still a system of global hierarchies in which the so-
called playing field is not as even, nor is the world as "flat" as certain economists lead us to believe.[3]

The neoliberal aspect of globalization has more pernicious
effects. John Rapley provides an extensive list of attributes that
mark the neoliberal regime:

> In the neoliberal regime, the locus of accumulation shifts more
> unambiguously to the private sector. Via politics of privatization,
> the state renounces its direct role in accumulation, and shifts its
> function from ownership to regulation. . . . But it is not simply
> accumulation that shifts toward the private sector; so too does dis-
> tribution. The welfare state is pared back and streamlined: some
> functions are left to the private sector altogether (private charities
> have taken up much of the work of poor relief in some countries,
> particularly in the Third World). . . . Thus, the government both
> reduces taxes and shifts the burden of taxation from income to
> consumption, with an eye to putting more money in the hands of
> those most likely to invest it. (40)

What becomes obvious through this brief reference to neoliberalism is a drastic shift in the functioning of the nation-state and
its engagement with the people. A neoliberal state, by focusing on
accumulation, must forsake its welfare functions in order to create
efficiencies that ensure a stable consumption-based economy. This

ends up privatizing pretty much all redemptive functions of the state. Rapley's critique of neoliberal globalization is based on this dissonance between two important functions of the state: accumulation and distribution. He theorizes these two functions of the state by presupposing certain legitimizing strategies essential to the creation and sustenance of political regimes. Dominant political regimes, Rapley suggests, "depend on the assent of the mass support bases over which they preside" and, accordingly, "when an elite can consolidate its hegemony over rival elites, a regime comes into being" (33). Thus, the neoliberal regime, with the attributes cited above, is perfect in its accumulative function, for those who have money are likely to make more. However, it fails miserably in its distributive function. This concentration of wealth upward and the failure to distribute wealth downward is what Rapley posits as the ultimate moment of crisis for the current neoliberal state, for a regime enters its moment of crisis due to a "sudden change in the distribution of resources" or a situation that "brings rival elites onto the scene" (32).

Having failed to legitimize itself through good works and the redemptive functions of welfare, the state seeks other modes of legitimation to maintain the balance required to sustain the elite-masses consensus, and it is this moment that becomes the originary moment, so to speak, for the rise of a more Islamized and fundamentalist public sphere in Pakistan. In most developed economies, the state, having lost this mode of legitimizing power, transforms into a security state, so "the defense of the territory—the 'safe home'—becomes the pass-key to all doors which one feels must be locked" in order to safeguard against all perceived threats (Bauman 117). Securing the bodies, and by extension the possessions of citizens, becomes the new form of a mostly biopolitical regime.

In the case of Pakistan, the rise of neoliberalism coincides with two important markers in Pakistani history: the Soviet-Afghan war and the beginning of the illegitimate dictatorship of general

Muhammad Zia-ul-Haq. These two events reconfigure the legitimizing structure of the Pakistani *nomos* both in symbolic and material terms.[4] The symbolic shift in the Pakistani nomos was already evident during the 1977 elections. For the first time in the fraught electoral history of Pakistan, two parties—the Pakistan People's Party and the Islamic Democratic Alliance (Jamhoori Ittehad)— fought for the very definition of what would and could constitute the *Bios* (Muslims) and the *Zoē* (non-Muslims) of Pakistani nomos. The Pakistan People's Party mobilized a sort of politics that was seemingly inclusive despite its actions against the Ahmadies, and would have included the Zoē within the larger nomos of the state. Conversely, the Islamic political parties, through an Islamic perception of the nation, stood for a specific Bios and thus had the capacity to exclude the minorities as Zoē by default.

It is in this symbolic scenario that the postelection coup of Zia-ul-Haq unfolds—through ousting the so-called secular prime minister, he had thus mobilized the symbolic affinities and political alignments of Zulfikar Ali Bhutto's opponents: the *ulama*. Zia-ul-Haq's Islamization project is deeply enmeshed in a zone of indistinction where religion and "qualified life" can no longer be differentiated but rather combine to legitimize his claims to leadership. Let us not forget that the mid-1970s is also the very time in history when the global economy was being restructured and shaped into what we now understand as neoliberal globalization. We must also read the rise of Islamism and attendant fundamentalism within the very specifics of Pakistani history—after all, one person, no matter how charismatic or powerful, cannot reshape the symbolics of an entire nation. As Aijaz Ahmad points out, "the precise developments which are causing this rapid shift within Islamicist movements, from moderate electorally inclined Islamism, to armed extremist movements" must be read within their spatiotemporal specificities (25).

While India has always provided the necessary foil—in the shape of an outside threat—for Pakistani leaders to structure and articulate their messages, Zia-ul-Haq also used the Afghan-Soviet war as another legitimizing narrative. Called the Afghan Jihad in the local parlance, the Afghan-Soviet war, while providing the general with an ideal material condition to foster his rule, also centers Jihad as the main signifier of a purely Muslim identity within Pakistan specifically and also within the Islamic world generally. This combination of material circumstances—a failing distributive regime and a "religious" war next door—provides an ideal basis for Islamizing Pakistan and for the emergence of a subjectivity called the Taliban.

This shift to an Islamized identity is more performative than substantive because the emphasis is on appearances and not necessarily on deeper religious aspects. In this sense, one could say that the attempt to Islamize Pakistan, though enacted through ritual, appearance, performance, and law, is the exact opposite of the importance accorded to the rituals and practices by Al-Gazaali in *Ihya Ulum Al din*. According to some scholars, this work "achieved the reconciliation of Sufism and orthodoxy" (Campanini 264) by emphasizing, besides other things, the role of *muhabbah* (love) in the life of a true Muslim. The daily rituals of Islamic practice, therefore, were just a process to create a sort of human subject who could love God and His creations. The problem with the rise of Islamism during Zia-ul-Haq's regime and its eventual spillover into Afghanistan is that ritual appearances and performative acts are taken to be the end of this process instead of the beginning. Ritual loses its transformative power and becomes the absolute horizon of spiritual desire and quest.

In such a scenario, all those who do not appear to be Muslim, or, worse, who are not Muslim at all, become suspect, become bare life. Such life is excluded from the body politic and, sometimes, worthy of death without legal repercussions or, at the least, any kind of remorse. Furthermore, during the Zia-ul-Haq regime, this bare, controllable life becomes a crucial part of the body and law of the sovereign state. My claim relies heavily on Agamben's theorization of bare life and sovereignty:

The Sovereign sphere is the sphere in which it is permitted to kill without committing homicide and without celebrating a sacrifice and a sacred life—that is, life that may be killed but not sacrificed—is the life that has been captured in this sphere. (*Homo Sacer* 83)

Thus it is, Agamben adds, that "what is captured in the sovereign ban is a human victim who may be killed but not sacrificed: *homo sacer*" and, "the production of bare life *is* the originary activity of sovereignty" (83). In the case of the Islamization of Pakistan during the Zia-ul-Haq regime, the capture and creation of this homo sacer is a natural outcome of the state policies, for, after all, only that which is not Islamic, or that which is Islam's "other"—culturally and judicially defined—is absolutely essential to constructing an "Islamic" public sphere and system of law. The sovereign—in this case the state of Pakistan under Zia-ul-Haq—cannot exist without the presence, capture, and isolation of this elusive figure, the bare life. Minorities, naturally, provide this necessary ingredient for the stabilization of an Islamic sovereign power. That minorities in Pakistan have always had the role of the homo sacer is undeniable. The recent case of the capital punishment of Aasia Bibi (more details later) is a good example. Her punishment in juridical terms is an expression of the full force of law on the body of bare life as a means of forestalling and strengthening the writ of sovereign law. Also, in the popular domain, I have heard that a local maulvi is offering 500,000 Pakistani rupees to anyone who would kill Bibi. This serves as another example of the importance of bare life to the self-legitimizing strategies of powerful "Muslim" private citizens.

There are two other important ways in which the system of power transforms in Pakistan after the Zia-ul-Haq coup: (1) the power structures its system through "constituting power" instead of "constituted power" and (2) the return to Islamic jurisprudence, Sharia, accentuates the differences between active rights and passive rights of citizens. Let me first unpack the four terms that I have used to describe this further shift within the Pakistani public sphere.

Agamben suggests that the most acute aspect of the "paradox of sovereignty" (*Homo Sacer* 39) lies in understanding "the problem of constituting power and its relation to constituted power" (39). Agamben provides the following appraisal of the role of constituting power in contemporary times:

> Today, in the context of general tendency to regulate everything by means of rules, fewer and fewer are willing to claim that constituting power is original and irreducible, that it cannot be conditioned and constrained in any way by a determinate legal system and that it necessarily maintains itself outside every constituted power. The power from which the constitution is born is increasingly dismissed as a prejudice or a merely factual matter, and constituting power is more and more frequently reduced to the power of revision foreseen in the constitution. (39–40)

Of course, Agamben's discussion of the differences between *constituting* and *constituted power* is very specific to his experience as a European. In the case of Pakistan, during the Zia-ul-Haq regime, constituting power becomes transcendental and timeless and comes to haunt constituted power at every turn. A return to Sharia, even if it is a gesture, is the ultimate assertion of an originary constituting power into the very fabric of the constituted power of the Pakistani state. This prominence of an originary and absolute constituting power is posited as an ultimate solution against the symbolics of people's power mobilized by Zulfikar Ali Bhutto. The mere fact that his political party was named Pakistan's People's Party, regardless of whether it truly was a people's party, captured and excluded any Islamic constituting power and replaced it with the will of the people as the ultimate constituting power for the constitution. This gesture (for that is all that it was) had the potential to unleash the most democratic and transformative politics, for if the people were the ultimate force of construction and revision, then they could not be excluded or devolved into bare life through law or through an originary, unchangeable, extrahuman (divine) constitutive power.

Another revolutionary aspect of invoking the people, or the citizens, was that such a politics could not posit an exclusivist view of the people—symbolically, all national subjects were citizens possessing active rights and not divided into those with active rights and those with passive rights. This brings me to a brief explanation of the second pair of terms I used above: *active rights* and *passive rights*. While explaining the development of the discourse of rights in the Western tradition, Agamben suggests that "at the very moment in which native rights were declared to be inalienable and indefeasible, the rights of man in general were divided into active rights and passive rights" (*Homo Sacer* 130). This distinction between holders of active and passive rights is inherently gendered, racialized, and theologized. In such a scenario, those deemed "proper" citizens tend to hold active rights with a right to active participation within the political sphere of a nation, whereas those with passive rights are, in a sense, bare life and can only hold the right to live within the national political sphere without access to any form of political power. Thus there is a constant drive, Agamben argues, in the modern biopolitical sphere of a national space to "redefine the threshold in life that distinguishes and separates what is inside from what is outside" (131).

While this applies to the rise of the Islamized nation of Pakistan, there are specific permutations of the inside and the outside, the active and passive bodies, within the national space. The increased Islamization of the Pakistani public sphere has immediate consequences for women and minorities. Both in juridical terms as well as through social pressures, women and minorities, though native citizens of the Pakistani nation-state, are transformed into passive bodies, bodies discouraged to be active rights holders within the public sphere. And this transition is accomplished by foregrounding the defining power of the constitutive power of the state—the Sharia—as an absolutely unchallengeable body of law as opposed to the constituted power of the Pakistani constitution. Thus, constitutive power, instead of receding and becoming suspect or irrelevant, captures these bodies with full force as the only living power within the political sphere. Pakistan, sadly, has never recovered from this reconstruction of and articulation of constituting power as an absolute, irreducible presence.

Surprisingly, however, the figure of the refugee, posited as the ultimate emblem of crisis in the national space by Agamben, is not seen as an outsider, at least not within the sovereign's attempts to legitimize itself. In fact, the figure of the Afghan refugee becomes the ultimate symbol of masculinity and a legitimizing emblem for Zia-ul-Haq and his followers. Thus, at the very moment that neoliberal globalization begins unfolding, the Pakistani nation's self-legitimation is connected to the most international symbol of the global human crisis. The refugee, however, is not an average displaced figure. This particular refugee is inscribed in the most potent masculinist project in Islam, for he is a mujahid. It is his status as a mujahid that is incorporated in the national paradigm of sovereignty, and, resultantly, Jihad becomes the ultimate point of arrival for a male Muslim subjectivity. This international Jihad supported by the West and fought by the Afghans and their international volunteers becomes the ultimate self-legitimizing concept for sovereign power in Pakistan. It is this confluence of material and symbolic currents that creates the ideal conditions for the rise of the Taliban, not just as a movement but also as a mode of being in the world.

It is no secret that during the Afghan Jihad the Pakistani government actively engaged in supporting the mujahedeen. However, Zia-ul-Haq used Jihad as a symbol to support other Jihadist groups in the world as well. It is this prehistory of modern Jihad that has constructed, both symbolically and materially, Pakistan into an ideal space for Jihadists from across the globe. The concept of Jihad that underwrites Zia-ul-Haq's regime and the current politics of the Taliban is an extreme reading of the concept itself. As I have argued elsewhere, a Talibanistic reading of the term *Jihad* is a limited reading of the concept, just as the Taliban's reading of the Sharia is a limited reading.[5] In this act of reading, the concepts at the limit of their semiotic and semantic force, a Talibanistic imagination focuses only on the most literalist and the most extreme interpretations of the concept. Even though Jihad is made central to their project, what is meant by "Jihad" is actually "Qital," which is the end point of the concept and not its beginning. Similarly, in terms of justice, *Hadd*, the strictest punishments available under Islamic law, become the norm. The system of being in the world and the act of being human become inextricably connected to the power to kill and the power to punish. Sharia is thus reduced to a simple system of speedy justice practiced through harsh punishments.

In traditional anti-Islamic writings in the United States, all these developments are attributed to inherent flaws in the Islamic sacred, thus precluding any room for a materialist explanation of the term. In fact, in one of my earlier projects as a graduate student, I was guilty of making such hasty judgments.[6] But in order to engage fully with the rise of fundamentalism in Pakistan, one must look at this process with an intimate understanding of the *dispositif*, or the apparatus within which a subjectivity such as that of the Taliban finds its expression. Foucault, describes the term *dispositif* in a 1977 interview:

> What I'm trying to pick out with this term is, firstly, a thoroughly heterogeneous ensemble consisting of discourses, institutions, architectural forms, regulatory decisions, laws, administrative measures, scientific statements, philosophical, moral and philanthropic propositions–in short, the said as much as the unsaid. Such are the elements of the apparatus. The apparatus itself is the system of relations that can be established between these elements.

Secondly, what I am trying to identify in this apparatus is precisely the nature of the connection that can exist between these heterogeneous elements. Thus, a particular discourse can figure at one time as the programme of an institution, and at another it can function as a means of justifying or masking a practice which itself remains silent, or as a secondary re-interpretation of this practice, opening out for it a new field of rationality.

In short, between these elements, whether discursive or non-discursive, there is a sort of interplay of shifts of position and modifications of function which can also vary very widely. ("Confession" 194–228)

In a way, one could say that all subjects are articulated within a complex array of material and symbolic expressions of power. Therefore, one cannot attribute the creation of subjects to just one locus or cause. In order to understand the rise of the Taliban, then, one must also attempt to understand the particular dispositif that structures Talibanistic subjectivity. In Agamben's explanation of Foucault's usage of the term, a *dispositif* or apparatus "is a decisive technical term in the strategy of Foucault's thought" and, Agamben suggests, "for Foucault, what is at stake is rather the investigation of concrete modes in which the positivities (or apparatuses) act within the relationships, mechanisms, and 'plays' of power" (*What* 16). The dispositif that structures Talibanistic subjectivity must, therefore, be studied within this complexity. I believe that the rise of neoliberalism, the Afghan-Soviet war, and the rise of Zia-ul-Haq's regime constitute a sort of dispositif that becomes the ultimate ground of expression for Talibanistic subjectivity.

This apparatus, or plane of emergence of the Taliban, also has its peculiar differences from Foucault's and Agamben's discussions of biopolitics. In fact, as the *Bios* and *politics* of this dispositif are mobilized to affect human bodies, the state and the sovereign increasingly come to define themselves through the power to kill and punish and not through, in Foucault's words, "the right to *take life* or *let live*" (*History* 136). The Afghan-Soviet war also provided the necessary conditions and the human capital to be reshaped into the masculinist, Jihadist, and purist model of a so-called Islamic subjectivity. Conceptually, while the culture foregrounded Jihad—in its version with *Qital* (struggle) as the main signifier of its masculinity—materially, the orphans produced by the war became the docile bodies to be shaped into a particular kind of social weapon. According to Ahmad Rashid, the Afghan Jihad provided Jamiat Ulema-e-Pakistan, a religious political party, a unique opportunity to "set up hundreds of madrassas along the Pashtun belt in the NWFP and Baluchistan" (89). These madrassas become crucial in shaping these orphans into what they would eventually become a part of: the Taliban.

Defined through Jihad and a purist idea of a Muslim subjectivity, the Talib is constantly attempting to fill the hole of nonbeing with dogma. If modernity and all its signifiers become contaminants to a pure identity, then reshaping the entire project of modernity becomes the ultimate quest, and any conceptual or material threats to this pursuit become suspect. Increasingly, while these subjects are taking shape, emerging within the current state of international capital, the state, having bought into the myth of progress through neoliberalism, has lost any means of offering more complex and possibly secular modes of experiencing national life.

In such a scenario, the figures of the minority and the women become the ultimate markers of Otherness, which must first be reduced to the role of a passive rights-holder and then mobilized to foreground the power of the state. The case of Aasia Bibi is a prime example of such juridical and extrajuridical mobilization of passive bodies for the project of power. While Bibi, a Christian citizen, was sentenced to death for alleged blasphemy under Pakistani blasphemy laws, the judge deciding her case went beyond his mandate to ban any commutation or pardon of her sentence by the president of Pakistan, a power vested in the president by the

Pakistani constitution. Furthermore, those who have attempted to speak in support of Bibi have also been silenced through private acts of violence: Salman Taseer, the governor of Punjab, was murdered by one of his own security guards for his vocal opposition to the blasphemy laws. Shahbaz Bhatti, the federal minister for minorities, was also murdered for his stance against Bibi's sentence and the blasphemy laws.[7] It seems that in Pakistan, the state and the Taliban may not be able to provide any redemptive material help to citizens, but they will certainly punish those who pose a threat to Islam or insult its sacred symbols.

To sum up this inconclusive argument, the power to punish becomes the ultimate mode of sovereignty in the Pakistani public sphere. Minorities, as passive citizens, become crucial to asserting the juridical power of the state and the power to kill with impunity that has now become the hallmark of the politics of death espoused by the Taliban.

I will conclude with one example from Islamic history, without offering any neat solutions to the troubling questions that I have raised in this chapter. As a scholar, I believe my primary job is to pose questions, not to provide neat, conclusive answers. In his theorization of power, Foucault provides the image of power as a web rather than a hierarchical structure, for power "is everywhere, not because it embraces everything, but because it comes from everywhere" (*History* 93). In this web of power, Foucault also acknowledges the existence of resistance as a pregiven node within the tentacles of power. But to add to this fascinating theory of power, one could say that in its expression within a particular dispositif, power also performs a two-pronged move: it moves upward to seek the body of the sovereign and it courses through the body politic, seeking the weakest and the most vulnerable nodes within its web. Thus, in this two-pronged movement, power latches onto the preexisting powerful nodes and intensifies its force by literally affecting the very bodies and souls of the most vulnerable and the most disenfranchised within a specific sphere. The ideal role of political power in Islam, in Sharia, had been to forestall and redirect this two-pronged movement of power, which is best described in the words of Abu Bak'r, the first caliph of Islam:

> I have been given the authority over you, and I am not the best of you. If I do well, help me; and if I do wrong, set me right. Sincere regard for truth is loyalty and disregard for truth is treachery. The weak amongst you shall be strong with me until I have secured his rights, if God wills; and the strong amongst you shall be weak with me until I have wrested from him the rights of others, if God wills. Obey me so long as I obey God and His Messenger. But if I disobey God and His Messenger, ye owe me no obedience. Arise for your prayer, God have mercy upon you. (Lings 344)

This was the initial revolutionary potential of Islam as one of the most dominant religions of its time: its potential to force power to move against its natural flow, its natural drift. Unfortunately, the Taliban and their sympathizers have only adopted a part of this message; they all believe in the social restructuring of society and the distribution of resources, but they have forgotten that the primary role of the sovereign in Islam is to bend power so that it redeems and enables the weak and does so without making the weak and their bodies the very site of power's self-presentation as absolute.

Thus, while metropolitan critics need to read the Taliban as a sign within its material and contextual complexity, Muslims themselves must also read it differently. The most important problem with the explanation of the concept and the group is that the material conditions that produce the Taliban are accorded a sort of natural causality; as such, when the Taliban kill innocent Pakistanis or Afghans, the ulama and other Muslim scholars want us to see these actions within the broader logic of war. There is nothing wrong with this way of looking at Taliban actions, for unless the material conditions change, the situation cannot improve. But this contextualizing should not become an apologetics. After all, no matter what the material causes of their actions, the Taliban do intentionally target civilians and now, after the Peshawar attack of 16 December 2014, they also murder school children. These acts must be condemned by all Muslims with no rationalizing narratives and without any covert or overt apologetics. And the most successful challenges in the case of Taliban also come from within Islam itself—the Muslim scholars who condemn the actions of the Taliban rely on Islamic traditions to reach their conclusions. As such, their argument is more likely to be appealing to general Muslim populations. While metropolitan critics need to understand the material and symbolic causes of Talibanization in order to understand it as a phenomenon, Muslim scholars and laypersons should make sure that this larger context does not become grounds for justifying the Taliban's actions.

While metropolitan scholars must stop capturing the figure of the mujahid in the moment of its most violent expression and should dig deeper and connect the act to the symbolic and material structures within which the act becomes possible, Muslim scholars, who are aware of the context, must also realize that although context is important for understanding actions, it must not be used as a rationalizing narrative. The act must also be condemned. It is only this nuanced approach to understanding the actions of the Taliban and the Other that would lead us to clearly read the sign and find some way forward in developing cross-cultural and transnational understanding of each other: a truly cosmopolitan approach to understanding cultures.

I have offered in this chapter a different mode of reading: a kind of reading that reads the sign within its own context, with a requisite degree of historical and semiotic understanding. This is not the final word on these kinds of readings, nor the most successful method, but such attempts are absolutely necessary. For to understand the sign in all its material and symbolic manifestations is the beginning of a more acute and attentive criticism.

To deal with Islam and to teach and write about Islamic themes—even subjects as controversial as the Taliban and terrorism—a synthesis of the meaning-making processes of both sides is absolutely necessary. Otherwise, our conclusions will be one-sided and lack the complexity that they need to effect change in the world. I will now move on to discuss the dire need for such complex readings of texts and reading practices for readers in the West and the Islamic world.

CHAPTER 7

READING AND THE PROBLEM OF
RECOGNITION AND REDISTRIBUTION

To this point, I have suggested that in order to enhance the level of cross-cultural understanding between the West (on an abstract generalized level) and the Islamic world (on a similarly abstract level), a more nuanced mode of reading is required. I have, in the previous pages, highlighted and explained the various flaws in our approaches to reading Islamic texts or texts about Islam and then provided a few explanatory chapters on developing a more nuanced mode of approaching the Muslim sacred and thus understanding the varied Muslim responses to what I have termed *the poetics of incitement*. In this chapter, I will focus primarily on seeing cross-cultural differences from a slightly different philosophical angle. I am relying on two important concepts, discussed by Nancy Fraser, to explain why these problems of misrecognition occur and how we as humanists can address this in our research as well as in our pedagogy.

In her book *Justice Interruptus* (1997), Fraser discusses what she calls the "postcolonialist" condition, which is "the general horizon within which political thoughts necessarily moves today" (1). This horizon, or condition, according to Fraser, has three main attributes: (1) "absence of any credible progressive vision of an alternative to the present order," (2) "a shift in the grammar of political claims-making," and (3) presences of a "resurgent economic liberalism." On the whole, according to Fraser, liberatory narratives now compete under two often irreconcilable philosophical registers: redistribution and recognition. These two registers, in another way, reflect the "split between 'the social left' and the 'cultural left'" (3). Meaning that while those invested in redistributive justice tend to see the world from a socialistic perspective, those engaged with questions of cultural and social recognition find themselves engaged in one or the other form of identity politics (3–4). Within this agonistic paradigm, Fraser attempts to theorize a middle ground and suggests the following:

> Critical theorists should rebut the claim that we must take an either/or choice between the politics of redistribution and the politics of recognition. We should aim instead to identify the emancipatory dimensions of both problematics and to integrate them into a single, comprehensive framework. (4)

It is important to note that this mixing of the two registers requires the presence of critical theorists who are aware of this divide. So, in the end, what Fraser suggests and what she attempts to highlight is not only how these two registers could be mobilized in concert and coordination but also that in order to do this, we all must become the kinds of critical theorists who can see beyond the limits of our own chosen or adopted modes of textual engagement.

The problem of reading the poetics of incitement falls under both these registers: redistribution and recognition. In order to be effective scholars and teachers of literary texts about Islam, we must understand the nature of our field under both of these registers. In other words, we will have to assume both a socialist-materialist approach and an identitarian approach, for one single register alone is unlikely to offer a viable way of engaging with the text.

Now, it is evident that one must look at the material conditions that produce the Taliban and Talibanistic imagination and subjectivity, without sounding like an apologist, in order to figure out why certain representations of Islam and the Islamic provoke such a drastic and violent response. This is necessary if we want to understand such responses and hope to understand how the poetics of incitement works. We can do this without making the material causes a rationalizing strategy for the actions of those who murder and kill in the name of religion. We must also posit this material understanding within the history of Muslim colonial experience. In such an understanding, the figure of the Talib or the fundamentalist is grasped with an eye toward history and with a critical view of the global division of labor, and the solution, in the last instance, is to address global inequalities and disparities. But if the reasons for such acts were only material and related to capital, then one would not find well-to-do Saudis or other Muslim citizens of the developed world in sympathy with forces of destruction. This is where a materialist and socialistic understanding of Islamic fundamentalism breaks down. True aspects of it can only be understood if we also understand Islam and the Islamic from the perspective of recognition. Thus both distribution and recognition are the constitutive registers of Islamic fundamentalism.

As attentive readers of texts, we should be able to read and write with a clear understanding of the constitutive register of reader responses without being perceived as apologists. A clear understanding of redistribution is crucial in confronting the rise of fundamentalist radicalism in the Islamic world as well the world as a whole. However, I will primarily focus on the rise of fundamentalism in the Islamic world. In a purely distributional explanation of the problem, the argument follows its own inherent logic.[1]

In explaining the role of the unequal and unjust global economic order, one critic argues that due to the global imperatives of the neoliberal global regime, developing nations increasingly lose their power to legitimize themselves, which in turn gives rise to the privatization of violence. Achille Mbembe captures this impact of colonial history and shifting economic regimes quite brilliantly by explaining the role of salaried compensation in the legitimizing ventures of the postcolonial state:

> Since enjoyment of a salary was almost always of moment to more than the individual who earned it, the salary as an institution was an essential cog in the dynamic relations between state and society: It acted as a resource the state could use to buy obedience and gratitude and to break the population to habits of discipline. The salary was what legitimated not only subjection but also the sanctitution of a type of political exchange based, not on the principle of political equality and equal representation, but on the existence of *claims through which the state created debts on society*. (emphasis in the original, 45)

Based on this, one could argue that salaried work was more than just the exchange and by creating and sustaining a salaried labor force, the state could gain more than just the commodified outcome of labor—it could create a network of symbolic and material dependencies of the populace on the state. Thus, according to Mbembe, "by transforming the salary into a claim, the state granted means of livelihood to all it had put under obligation" (45). In return, it was hoped, all those in obligation to the state would extend their loyalties and allegiances to the state. In this way, salaried compensation, as a distributive function of the state, was not just essential to the material functioning of the state but also, more importantly, crucial to its symbolic reproduction as a legitimate institution.

Under the neoliberal regime, when the state cannot legitimize itself through its distributional function, private players (religious groups included) then take it upon themselves to offer an alternative for the people. It is this legitimacy crisis that gives rise to fundamentalist movements. There is a certain truth in this line of argument, as theorists and critics openly point to such instances of the post-1980s rise of fundamentalism. John Rapley, for example, clearly connects the rise of all forms of fundamentalism to the failure of the distributional function of the state. For Rapley, most political systems are grounded in a certain specific regime and work through a tacit agreement between the elite and the masses (10). According to Rapley, "political elites succeed in consolidating their position when they establish distributional networks that solidify their support bases, and when they construct accumulation regimes" (10). Within this logic, the state within an exigent regime has two functions: it must ensure equitable redistribution of national wealth and it must create conditions for the accumulation of capital. In most cases, if a certain balance is maintained between these two functions of the regime, the elite/masses consensus is not disturbed. A regime, however, experiences crisis when it fails in its distributional functions and relative inequality increases drastically, which, according to Rapley, happens to be the case with the neoliberal regime. As a result of this failure of redistribution, new and alternative elites emerge and vie for the loyalty of the masses. Rapley explains this distributional crisis of the neoliberal state as follows:

> The erosion in the state's ability to distribute resources to its support base has eroded the loyalty of those at the bottom. Excluded altogether from the regime, or increasingly marginal within it, people have begun to look elsewhere in their search for resources. . . . Where political entrepreneurs have filled the gap, offering access to the resources people seek, they have been able to create rival political networks to that of the state. (89)

These rival networks, within the Islamic world, range from nonviolent charity organizations that offer general care to militant fundamentalist networks that offer speedy justice and the promise of revolution. What I am suggesting here is that these radical organizations—for example, the Taliban—do not just offer economic remedies for the inequalities of the neoliberal regime. Rather, they also work on the symbolic register of recognition. In other words, while the distributional crisis provides them their recruits, it is a combination of a fair distributional regime and symbolics of recognition that enable them to support and perpetuate their message. As critics, we must be able to understand this phenomenon in its inherently dual complexity. In Rapley's words, purely in the distributional sense, "if the rebels needed a sea of support in which to swim, the Islamists, as they are also known, have created one through good works among those who have been marginalized by the changes in the global economy" (129).

Along with the distributional problems and the crisis of the neoliberal state, the rise of fundamentalism, as I have already stated, also relies quite heavily on the symbolics of recognition. One aspect of this recognition that is very pertinent to our approach to readings of Islamic texts, or texts about Islam, happens to be the symbolics of the Muslim sacred, which asks, How is the Muslim sacred viewed and treated by non-Muslims? The Rushdie Affair, the murder of Theo van Gogh, and murders of the *Charlie Hebdo* editors can only be understood clearly under the recognitional and not the distributional register.

As such, the question ought to be simply this: What does a Muslim subject *seek in terms of recognition* within the neoliberal regime? The question should *not* be: What does a Muslim subject of neoliberal capital *want in terms of material acquisition*? If the most important aspect of our being in the world is the recognition of our identity, and if we need to acknowledge the importance of identity and the maintenance of it "as a motivating force" (Bracher 3), then looking at the problem from the perspective of recognition is even more urgent and necessary. So, while analyzing the material conditions that produce radical subjectivities is important, it is also crucial to see it as a crisis of recognition.

The killers of the *Charlie Hebdo* editors—all from the disenfranchised margins of French society—walked into the editorial offices and murdered people in cold blood.[2] It has been reported that while performing this act of murder, they were also raising the well-known Muslim slogan *Allah-o-Akbar* (God is great). Naturally, the murderers were abhorrent and the attack on unarmed civilians is morally wrong. But to understand this act in its menacing particularity, one needs to conflate the material conditions that produce these subjects as well as the symbolic register of recognition that prompted them to restore their collective identity with an ultimate act of violence. Bracher convincingly argues that "the most fundamental identity need is the need for recognition, the need to have one's being appreciated and validated" (7) and withholding or effacing this recognition creates "the worst evil that could befall" (8) human subjects, which ends in violence and other problematic social behaviors.

With these insights into recognition, and also bringing to bear the distributional aspects of the *Charlie Hebdo* murderers, I suggest that only through a clear understanding of both registers—the distributive and recognitional—can one truly understand the causes of their actual act. I am not suggesting that this understanding somehow excuses the act itself; I am rather suggesting that we need to understand the various causes of such an act in its full complexity, especially since we must realize a way of cross-cultural communication in which such acts of violence cease becoming the norm. Naturally, killing the perpetrators, declaring public statements, and performing street marches will not solve the problem, especially if the constitutive causes of the act itself are not fully understood. This is where we, the readers of complex material and literary texts, come in. This is one reason we cannot give up our task to represent "with a flourish" (Spivak 104). So, let us assume that the three perpetrators of the *Charlie Hebdo* incident were from a poor and marginalized immigrant group, a group outside the assimilative promise of the French nation-state. Viewed from this perspective, their actions become an automatic outcome of the failure of cultural assimilation. The logic goes like this: had they been truly French, they would have seen the cartoons with the eyes and perceptions of the French people and thus understood the satirical nature of the cartoons. Of course, this assumption relies on a particularly naturalistic, essentialized understanding of Frenchness, as if being French means one is subtle in modes of reading and tolerant in one's views about the world. We know that this does not happen to be the case in France—a large segment of the French population already voted for an extreme-Right, racist, and anti-immigrant party during the last election. Furthermore, if poverty alone were the cause of the murders, then with a population of over five million poor Muslim immigrants, France would have a much larger problem to deal with. Yes, there are material causes, for after all, these cold-blooded murderers had been ideologically indoctrinated by an international terrorist organization; the ideology employed might have been tethered to a material cause. Its ultimate unfolding, though, cannot be understood without the recognitional register.

There must have been something about the actions of the *Charlie Hebdo* editors that became the ultimate cause, in the eyes of the terrorists, to declare them killable, to reduce them to the level of *Zoē* from *Bios*. I suggest that the heart of the issue was the desecration of what the terrorists and their trainers considered a threat to their sense of the sacred and a denial of its recognition by the editors. This denial of recognition thus becomes the ultimate cause for the mobilization and unleashing of the most virulent reactionary responses in the metropolitan as well as the Muslim world, and that is why I call it the poetics of incitement. In the case of *Charlie Hebdo*, the so-called insult, or incitement, was deeply layered. First of all, the paper graphically represented the figure of the Prophet, which in itself is considered taboo in most Islamic societies. In a further layering of the "insult," the figure of the prophet was rendered in various cartoons, sometimes naked, as a terrorist, a stereotypical Arab camel rider, and others. In all these cases, though *Charlie Hebdo* editors deemed themselves to be free to express their opinions, the opinion itself was deeply offensive to about a billion people worldwide. It is perhaps unsurprising that if a billion people are incited and derided, a select few are going to go beyond traditional semiotic responses and resort to violence. We also know, through Bracher and others, that violence is a possible response to the erasure of one's individual or collective identity. One could argue that in its sad logic, the cartoons were not only eliciting a violent response but also, within the logic of identity stabilization, ensuring that such a response would occur.

The *Charlie Hebdo* cartoons were the ultimate expression of the poetics of incitement: a satirical rendition of the Muslim sacred with the most obvious racist undertones. It seems that metropolitan engagement with the Muslim sacred—post-Rushdie, Theo van Gogh, Sherry Jones—has found its ultimate expression: racialized caricatures of the most sacred person in Islam, a person who, in accordance with the taboos and traditions of his own culture, is not even supposed to be represented in any visual form. Thus, the transgression was the ultimate test of the Muslim faith and its adherents. In a way, it was the most semiotically violent attack on Muslims possible, an ultimate act of cultural hubris by one group against another, an act announcing itself as intentionally transgressive. In that announcement, it also expressed its own power to insult, hurt, and incite. Note that any offense taken by the recipients of this act can only be understood under the register of recognition, especially since the transgression targets the core identity of a Muslim subject. In the end, then, as terrible as it is, expressing shock at the murders without understanding the recognitional crisis that caused it leaves us only with superficial explanations of the act itself.

But when this open act of aggression about the individual and collective identities of Muslim subjects produces a violent response, we act as if it had no cause beyond—as the American Right would put it—the fundamental "backwardness" of Islam itself, as if the act of murder were not somehow connected to incitement and negation of identity. I know these are harsh, perhaps unwelcome words. I am also fairly certain my opponents will be "outraged" and will have certain interesting names to toss my way. But I believe my job as a scholar of culture is to think dangerously instead of following the flow and offering nicely polished platitudes in the service of the dominant culture.

One reason metropolitan critics and political leaders get so fixed in their responses to such acts is that they see any form of concession to Muslims as a form of capitulation. The response is never about understanding the causes of the problem but is instead about insisting, sometimes quixotically, that the Western press has the absolute right to free expression, and those who threaten it—physically or semiotically—are uncivilized and unsophisticated. Thus, the very aggressions that lead to such irrational acts of violence are forgotten, and the act of violence itself becomes yet another piece of evidence used to prove to the Muslim world that they are far behind and need to catch up with the West, a place where insulting the most sacred aspects of Islam is not only acceptable but also, very often, laudable.

Now, let us look at the other side of this story—chiefly, at the semiotic and rhetorical strategies employed by al-Qaeda and other terroristic recruiters. After all, there must be worldly causes that enable them to recruit and indoctrinate their followers. Let us forget about the distributional aspects of such mobilizations, for material explanations of radicalization are an oft-traversed territory in metropolitan scholarship. Also prevalent and often invoked in the West are inherently essentialist explanations of the general Muslim response to modernity. This branch of writing has a long list of scholars in the United States like Bernard Lewis, Daniel Pipes, and Michael Palmer, along with popular figures like Sam Harris.

But how would a radical Muslim cleric represent the West on a recognitional register to recruit and indoctrinate new and old followers? *He will use some of the very "freedoms" that one valorizes in the West to make certain claims.* Not because they "hate our freedoms" but because some of these freedoms are used to attack Islam whenever possible. The absolute freedom of the press would become one great example for this would-be recruiter. He would not even have to make a case for economic injustice or offer information about the exploitation of the Islamic world by the West or the evils of colonization. The distributional register can be totally elided and is unnecessary to mobilize new troops for the terroristic machine. All a mullah must do is point to one or two cartoons of the Prophet published in a Western newspaper. Yes, that is all it would take to recruit someone with a certain predisposition toward the West and provide said recruit some training and time. This person would then train to restore their individual as well as collective identity through an act of violence aimed at those who had "attacked" them and derided what they considered "sacred."

I have felt the impact of these cultural battles in my own work in Pakistan. I have noticed quite frequently when I am presenting in Pakistan that the questions asked of me, especially by religious audiences, relate to either the militaristic nature of the United States or to what is said and written about Islam in the West. Generally, the most common question posed concerns the "freedom to insult the holy Prophet." Naturally, I have no answer to these questions, but this one aspect of free expression and its role in creating the necessary conditions to insult the Muslim sacred becomes the ultimate grounds for irreconcilable cultural differences between the West and the Islamic world. This underscores the importance of this issue to average Muslims.

Now, it is also important to know that criticizing power is not an ideological "no-go zone" in the world of Islam. In fact, the right to challenge the figure of the sovereign is often openly expressed and practiced in Islamic-dominant societies. My second chapter on the Islamic sacred already offers a genealogy of a whole tradition built on this important duty in the Islamic world. Criticism of power in general is also strongly encouraged in Islamic texts as well as in praxis. It is only the core of the Islamic sacred that is considered sacrosanct—deriding the Qur'ān, the Prophet, and God, for instance. What the Western press and writers want is for the Islamic world to concede at all levels of their sacred, which, of course, is asking for Muslims to completely capitulate their sacred for the utility and playful activities of the West. Naturally, then, this intrusion into the inner sacred sanctum of Islam becomes the basis for semiotic and material violence.

Furthermore, such acts of semiotic violence enable the very forces of intolerance that works of religious satire challenge. Those acts also weaken progressive Muslims, for whom it becomes increasingly untenable to posit the West as a place and concept that the world of Islam can peacefully coexist with. In the previous chapter on the blasphemy law and its enactment in Pakistan post-Rushdie Affair, I traced the general trajectory of such responses to the poetics of incitement. Here, I am asserting that the cultural crisis that unleashes what happened in France is a problem of recognition at both poles of this global divide: on one end, the French satirists asserted through their work that they had the absolute right to represent, and on the other, the three terrorists, in their own way, enacted the most extreme form of reaction to the received insult. Both parties were wrong, and no amount of sloganeering can make either action acceptable, but only if looked at from a slightly transcendent perspective. For fundamentalist Muslims, some who have valorized the act of murder, the act needs to be viewed as an extreme violation of the rights of the editors to live. On the other hand, for the *Charlie Hebdo* editors and others who practice the poetics of incitement, due care is necessary to understand the limits of their freedom to express, for limits exist even if we refuse to acknowledge them.

On the other side of this debate, of course, are the three perpetrators and their sympathizers. In a court case in Pakistan against a security guard who had murdered the governor of Punjab, the murderer's lawyer (celebrated by a fringe of Pakistani society who sympathize with nonstate violent punishments for blasphemers) used the *Charlie Hebdo* murderers as an example[3] to bolster claims about his client's right to murder the very person he was supposed to protect. Naturally, this line of thinking and legal argumentation also needs to change, especially since the power to dispense justice cannot be posited as an ultimate individual right. The lawyer's line of argument suggests—and he lauds the actions of *Charlie Hebdo* murderers for this very reason—that every Muslim can be a judge of others' actions, and if others are proven to have done wrong, the individual is free to judge and punish others accordingly. This is, of course, against the very essence of the Islamic justice system, but in the heightened zeal of their religiosity, even the lawyers in Pakistan can argue for the kind of street justice that needs to be replaced, in the classical sense, by the systems of justice controlled and organized by the state. Unless the scholars, lawyers, and judges in Pakistan and other Muslim countries start defending the rule of law against the anarchist system of justice practiced by Islamic terrorist groups, the crisis of law and justice will continue to degrade Islamic societies, and they will ultimately become the very societies they are represented as in the metropolitan press.

Going back to my original argument, I once again emphasize the need to recognize the basic identity needs of Muslim subjects while also assuring that at a certain point these needs cannot outweigh the needs and consensus developed by humanity as a whole. While the West needs to recognize that certain aspects of the Muslim sacred are sacrosanct and must not be touched without care, the Muslim world must also recognize the general freedom of expression that has enabled the metropolitan West to create diverse political spheres in which all voices are heard and none are silenced—at least de jure—from speaking about what is important to them as individuals or as collectivities.

Note that new recruitments for the radical causes within the Islamic world are now increasingly underwritten by the recognitional and not the distributional register. Distribution and its failure within capital was usually the mainstay of leftist recruitment and reorientation in the global periphery. While this still makes sense within the leftward turn in South America and elsewhere, in the Islamic world, at least, radicalization is now strongly and inherently connected with issues of recognition. This recognition can be summed up under varied subregisters: for some, simply being treated as equal to other humans is the issue; for others, it is about the recognition of Islam and Muslims as equal global citizens of modernity; for others, it is about respecting some of the particularities of their religion when dealing with social issues.

There is, however, a great degree of *embricature* between the distributional and recognitional register. One often overlooked aspect of it is the functioning of the neoliberal economy, especially the financialization of the globe. Within metropolitan cultures, the existence of an interest-based global economic system is almost axiomatic. One could argue, and many economists indeed do, that due to the financialization of the global economy, interest-based financial instruments have now become crucial to the global economic system. Furthermore, the entire consumer and commercial banking sector depends upon a viable interest-rate system. But when this system is normalized and offered as the only viable and preferable economic system, it causes, within the distributional register, a crisis of recognition for most practicing Muslims.

In the Qur'ānic injunctions as well as in the hadīth tradition, "riba," or usury, is absolutely forbidden (*haram*). So, the Muslim world and its denizens are dually impacted by current global policies: they are at the receiving end of the rapacious drive of global capital and they must also experience an extreme lack of recognition concerning their views of personal and collective interest. Here is one of the most convincing and clear injunctions about usury in the Qur'ān:

Those who consume interest cannot stand [on the Day of Resurrection] except as one stands who is being beaten by Satan into insanity. That is because they say, "Trade is [just] like interest." But Allah has permitted trade and has forbidden interest. So, whoever has received an admonition from his Lord and desists may have what is past, and his affair rests with Allah. But whoever returns to [dealing in interest or usury]—those are the companions of the Fire; they will abide eternally therein. (Al-Qur'ān 2:275)

The translation I used above tends to conflate interest and usury, but in most cases, it is only riba, excessive rates of interest, that is forbidden, which would include all forms of compound interest. As the verse above also clarifies, there is no injunction against trade. In fact, in Islam, the exchange of goods and trade are considered crucial and important functions of human life. But crude profiteering by itself is absolutely forbidden.

By far, the most important question that rises out of this injunction in the Qur'ān is that the term *riba* is not clearly defined in the Qur'ān. Most Islamic scholars, therefore, rely on the tradition of the hadīth to define what constitutes riba. In a juridical opinion, the Federal Sharia Court of Pakistan, for example, defined *riba* as follows:

As regards the interpretation and nature of the word riba, the Court, keeping in view the texts of the Holy Qur'an and the Sunnah, examined and analysed in detail the relevant writings of jurists, scholars and economists and concluded that riba includes both 'usury and interest' as known in English terminology (Para: 71). In other words, wherever there is money from the one part andthere is only grace period or deferment of the repayment of loan on the other, and for that a return is stipulated, it is riba. (qtd. in Ayub 17)

Based on this, a general understanding of riba involves all activities in which a general exchange of goods does not happen. I am not suggesting here that all Muslim cultures are, somehow, entrapped in an unchanging essential mode of being, but like any other faith, most actions of Muslims are also governed by a sense of what is forbidden and permissible in their religion. In the case of riba, for all practical purposes, it is not only forbidden but is also considered a sinful act. The global economic system, however, is oblivious to this aspect of Islam. There is no room, other than a few noninterest initiatives in the mortgage market, for an average practicing Muslim to move through this financial system without feeling at least a bit under duress, a bit contaminated. This denial of recognition through countless unacknowledged transactions within the modern economy is also one of the important blind spots of the modern world and creates yet more identity threats through lack of recognition. Thus, recognition and its withholding become the most important register for interactions between the Islamic world and the West.

In this chapter I have dealt with the very sensitive and arguably controversial issue of free expression versus the right of the Muslim subject to receive and respond to texts produced under the rubric of the poetics of incitement. But I work on the borders of cultures in a liminal, undefined space where my loyalties are always in question and under threat. And as a critic and worker of culture, this liminal space, for me, is also the ultimate space of creation, compassion, and possibility. At the risk of overstating my case, I have suggested in this chapter that we must learn to read the sign—both the transgressive acts of the writers and artists who make Islam an object of their artistic renderings and the actions of Muslim readers and even murderers—with due attention to their own particularities and from a transcendent place. Truly democratic criticism, I have suggested in this book, will never offer neat universalist solutions and will certainly see beyond the sign itself to give readers a more nuanced and compassionate reading of our cultural others and their actions. Furthermore, truly democratic criticism must, in my humble opinion, be informed, inclusive, and compassionate. In the next chapter, I hope to focus primarily on my Muslim readers (loosely defined) in order to initiate a serious discussion for positive change in the reception of literary texts within general Islamic cultures.

CHAPTER 8

IQBAL AND MAWDUDI

The Need for Critical Reading and Thinking

On 13 April 2017, a mob of students at Wali Khan University in Mardan, Pakistan, publicly and brutally murdered a student, Mashal Khan, on the suspicion of blasphemy. After Khan's body was taken to his family, the village *maulvi* refused to lead the funeral prayers and instructed others not to attend the funeral. Not only was a young man murdered by his peers for an unproven crime, a crime not punishable by death, at least within the Hanafi school of Islamic jurisprudence,[1] but the so-called religious scholars were also fine with denying him his last rites. This denial abrogated the right of the victim in a dual act of injustice: the maulvi deemed it absolutely Islamic for the mob to kill their fellow Muslim in a brutal act of popular justice, and then having been so "punished," it seemed as if the victim had still not paid the price for the alleged sin. If the punishment was just and right, then the victim had, according to the Islamic rules of jurisprudence, paid for his crime and deserved a decent Islamic burial, for he had, through this "punishment," been cleansed of his "sin." But the mullahs found it apt to punish the victim through a gross act of violence and then punish his soul by denying him rightful passage into the next life.

Their actions, therefore, were un-Islamic at both ends, for collective punishments of such sort, without the due process of the law, are un-Islamic, and the last rites of passage cannot be denied to anyone who has "apparently" paid for the sins that were attributed to them.

Eventually, it took the courage of a few fellow Muslims to finally arrange for the funeral and burial of the murder victim. If such acts are permissible and laudable in twenty-first century Islam, then the entire Islamic world needs to think deeply about its own practices. If such acts are not permissible in Islam, and I believe they are not, then dissenting voices need to be heard and recorded at all levels of the Muslim public sphere: pulpits, places of leadership, mosques, universities, and streets. For unless scholars and laypersons within the Islamic world offer some form of semiotic and material resistance to those who have reduced Islam to an ideology of death and punishment, Islam as a great religion will become totally irrelevant in the contemporary world. I believe that the ultimate core of Islam is based in love, and unless this love is made supreme, instances of semiotic and material violence will continue to increase, and Islamic societies will become societies of fear, intimidation, and death.

This chapter, albeit brief, is primarily addressed to Muslim readers in the hope that I can, at the least, encourage some of my fellow Muslims to think about what is happening in the Islamic world and remind Muslims that we all need to work tirelessly to make our societies more compassionate, more tolerant of differences, and above all more peaceful and loving. I believe much of what has come to pass in the Muslim world is because its citizens have acceded the right to read and interpret the sacred to a select few. Thus, a religion that traditionally had no official clerical class has now been reduced to the masses blindly following clerics. These clerics have the power not only to define the truth but also to pit us against each other through the cynical and motivated use of religion. It is time that the Muslim youth and laypersons take it upon themselves to read differently and to read the sacred to find and popularize instances of love and compassion instead of normalizing practices of hate and violence, to find a peaceful way of living and thriving within modernity.

That Western modernity entered the Islamic hinterlands as a handmaiden to colonialism is a fact. That it unleashed a crisis of confidence and faith in Islamic lands is also a fact acknowledged by Muslim scholars. In this chapter, I will discuss some of the intellectual responses to Western modernity by a few major Muslim scholars and then proceed to discuss ways of changing the general perception of modernity as a temporal and spatial structure for my Muslim readers.

My purpose here is to encourage Muslim readers to, at the least, acknowledge that new understandings have armed us with better tools to read texts both sacred and mundane, and that there must be a transformation in the way texts, sacred and mundane, are received, discussed, and taught generally in the Muslim world. The main crisis of thought in Islam, in my humble opinion, is that reading and critical processes have been tethered to a system of critical analysis that is deeply conservative and mostly outdated. In these reading practices, while varied interpretations are permissible at the reception end, no speculation or critical thinking is permitted about the recording end of the texts. Because of this straightjacketing, while critics, scholars, and *ulama* continue creating new interpretations of the sacred, the questioning of the origins of the sacred texts are almost sacrosanct. The sacred texts, therefore, become fixed and immutable and are deemed void of any impact in terms of human agency. But these texts, one must admit, even when revealed by the Almighty, were recorded and reproduced through human agency, and earlier Muslim scholars were willing to consider that non-Qur'ānic sacred texts should not always be taken as stable and immutable. Unfortunately, that trend no longer exists in the general Islamic world. I will, however, not discuss any sacred texts here, for I neither have the expertise nor the necessary training to undertake such an enterprise. I will, however, dwell a little on some modern texts and some modern scholars whose works have taken on a certain aura of universality and immutability.

I hope to encourage readers from dominantly Muslim cultures, in all their diversity, to acknowledge that reading differently also means to read literary and public texts with an eye toward current reading practices in the world—in other words, to use, adopt, and transform the interpretive tools developed and articulated in the West. There will be, I am sure, challenges to my alleged "Western bias." But my counterargument is simply that the most radical in the Islamic world are already using the most destructive modes of destroying life made available by the technologies of warfare developed in the West. The Taliban, for example, kill and maim with guns and ammunition developed in the West. Similarly, ISIS and other such terroristic organizations have no qualms about using the technologies of destruction acquired from the West. So, if they are willing to borrow and use these technologies of destruction, then why not use some of the liberating and progressive ideas also developed in the West and make those useful within the specific locales of Muslim nations?

There is yet another phenomenon that needs attention and that figures prominently in the works of the two scholars I will be discussing, one that also thrives in the contemporary literary and popular writing in the Islamic world: the essentialized, binaristic view of East/West. In this worldview, the West and the world of Islam are discussed and articulated as two binary entities with diametrically opposed value systems: the West as materialistic and faithless and the East as spiritualistic and holder of ancient wisdoms. The crisis of the East, then, is offered as a loss of this spirituality for the sake of advancing within the inherent logic of Western materialism. These are not necessarily native-constructed tropes. In my view, such established views of East/West also enter the native Muslim (and otherwise colonized) imaginary through the discourses developed by Orientalists, who, as is obvious after Edward Said's magisterial work, romanticized and exoticized the East. This exoticized East, in so many ways, is the East that some native poets and scholars take as real and as lost due to the Western colonial encroachment into Islamic lands.

Modernity in the colonized Muslim world was never an unmotivated idea—rather, it was experienced in a sort of chronotopic way with its originary location (both temporal and spatial) in Europe. Thus, according to Mikhail Bakhtin, the general Muslim view of Western modernity is chronotopic, and this view is further complicated by the connection of the rise of modernity to the fall of Islamic political power.

Historians and cultural critics have already opined quite often about this crisis within the Islamic world. While I cannot claim to cover the entire Islamic world and its responses to the loss of its political power, I will focus here, in a symptomatic manner, on the responses offered by a couple of Indian Muslim scholars and religious leaders against the British ascendency and the resultant rise of Western modernity.

In this chapter, I will focus on the works of and Muhammad Iqbal (a poet philosopher) and Abul A'ala Mawdudi (a religious scholar). I must admit that the responses were many and varied, and my sampling of these two figures is in no way suggesting that these two can somehow carry an explanation of the reactions and responses of an entire culture. I am choosing these two also because by the time they became prominent within British India, India had already transitioned into a colonized space with its own local intelligentsia, political parties, and vibrant freedom movements. These two scholars, therefore, not only offer us some insights into Muslim aspirations but also offer a certain worldview about the West and its political and symbolic systems. Furthermore, these two also attempt to retrieve and rearticulate a newer kind of Muslim identity as a response to modernity within and beyond modern India. After discussing these two scholars, I will also opine about the current state of thinking about the West in Pakistan in particular and the Islamic world in general. I will then conclude this chapter with some suggestions precisely addressed to people from the Islamic world, especially in terms of their responses to modernity.

ALLAMA SIR MUHAMMAD IQBAL (1877–1938)

Born in 1886, Muhammad Iqbal was a deeply religious but humanistic poet and a scholar. Much has been written about his life and works in Urdu, and in Pakistan, it would not be untrue to say that Iqbal is an industry. His works are read and taught at all levels of the Pakistani educational system; he is considered one of the spiritual founders of the idea of Pakistan, and scholars and pundits alike mobilize Iqbal's writings to various ends. The problem in Iqbal studies, in my opinion, is that it tends to be mostly hagiographic. Most Pakistani scholars of Iqbal read him as a trance-historical figure whose teachings remain valid and worthy of emulation despite the changing times. This reliance on a certain universality and timelessness when discussing Iqbal's work is deeply problematic. In fact, Iqbal himself admits the possibility of change in one's views and opinions in one of his most philosophical, last major, works:

> It must, however, be remembered that there is no such thing as finality in philosophical thinking. As knowledge advances and fresh avenues of thought are opened, other views, and probably sounder views than those set forth in these lectures, are possible. Our duty is to carefully watch the progress of human thought, and to maintain an independent critical attitude towards it. (*Reconstruction* 8)

Despite Iqbal's own views about the provisionality and temporality of all philosophical thought, most Muslim scholars of the subcontinent, especially those from Pakistan, offer Iqbal as the font of eternal and, to some extent, unsurpassable wisdom. In one such account, for example, one scholar, while discussing the lack of understanding of Iqbal's "doctrine of *Khudi* or self" (1) by most scholars and laypersons, attributes it to the following causes:

> One principal cause [of lack of understanding of Iqbal's concept of *Khudi*] is the general superficialities of the Eastern mind. Asia has been torn away from her own ancient springs of inspiration and looks to the West for light and guidance, and the West has nothing but a materialistic view of life to offer. (Durrani 1)

Thus, it seems, according to F. K. Khan Durrani, while Iqbal himself was a product of both Western and Eastern systems of education, he can transcend the very givens of his culture; his countrymen and women cannot rise to a level where they can, at the least, attempt to understand Iqbal's work. Maybe there is some truth to this, for to really understand Iqbal, one would require a thorough grounding in Islamic philosophy, Western philosophy, and Islamic teachings. Such scholars are relatively rare. But nowhere in this engagement with Iqbal's work itself is there even a suggestion that Iqbal himself never develops a cogent and coherent explicatory narrative of his own philosophy. Nonetheless, my point is that Iqbal is offered by scholars, politicians, and opportunist cultural pundits as an ultimate answer to affirm and confirm their own prejudices and preferences. About Iqbal, Israr Ahmed, another religious scholar, suggests that "Iqbal is a true interpreter of the Qur'an and the Qur'an happens to be the main source of his poetry" (26). In his reading, then, all that corresponds to his view of Iqbal's poetry is privileged, but all of Iqbal's humanistic and suprareligious ideas are either neglected or offered as irrelevant. Similarly, in yet another hagiographic newspaper article, a famous Urdu journalist, while taking Iqbal's own poetic reverie as "real," declares that, as per Iqbal's dream (composed by Iqbal himself in which he meets the Prophet Muhammad), Iqbal's work is "laden with the fragrances of Hijaz" (Jan) and is, therefore, truly Islamic and sanctioned by the Prophet himself.

Here I will focus on just a few major themes from Iqbal's vast corpus, as it is not possible to provide an exhaustive and comprehensive account of his work. I am also choosing themes that recur frequently in Iqbal's work. The very same themes are recycled and regurgitated by scholars, pundits, and laypersons alike within the Pakistani public sphere. Most of the time, Iqbal posits the East and West in a binaristic vein. Also, Iqbal's views of the West are guided and shaped by the experience of an Eastern writer who is not just in awe of the West but who also believes that Western modernity was built around the basic foundations provided by Islam and its contributions to the sciences, philosophy, and general global culture. There is for Iqbal a strange fascination with the West but also a deep sense of loss as a Muslim subject experiencing the material West and the philosophical West.

Furthermore, the Orientalist training of Iqbal's readers, translators, and critics also plays an important role in retrieving the kind of Iqbal that suits their purposes or corresponds with their narrative frames. For example, in the preface to his translation of Iqbal's *Mathnavi pes che bayad kard au aqwame mashriq* (What should be done to people of the East), B. A. Dar provides, by way of explaining Iqbal, the reason/spirit duality that Iqbal, in Dar's opinion, seems to inhabit as a poet:

> By reason's revolt, Iqbal seems to emphasise the secular trends of thought that characterize the life of the Western people, severing the individual's social, economic and political life the operation of moral and spiritual principles. The remedy for this, therefore, lies, according to Iqbal in raising recruits from the Kingdom of Love . . . It is the translating power of faith that is to be awakened which transforms heartless people into noble and gentle spirits. (vii)

This binaristic view of East and West, in which the former inhabits the spiritual realm and the latter the world of materialism, secularism, and reason, is one of the most potent tropes used by native Muslim scholars of the past and present. The West as a large monolithic place was never truly all about materialism, just as the Islamic East was never really outside the exigencies of material life. But this oversimplification enables native Muslim scholars, during colonial times, to argue that adopting Western ways is always at the cost of Islamic spiritualism and a journey from the realm of the heart to the domain of heartless and often destructive secular reason. But during the colonial contact phase, the loss of political power centered this crisis of identity for colonized Muslims. Conservative Muslim scholars, therefore, attempted to retrieve the cause of this great failure, and while most attributed Muslim defeats to stagnation and the loss of Muslim access to new knowledge, quite a few also blamed Muslims for losing touch with their own value systems. It is this strain of Islamic thought, with emphasis on revitalizing the religious and spiritual realms, that has won out over time as any attempts at "Westernizing" the Muslim world, in all its diversity, are posited as contaminating and suspect. It is important to note here that Iqbal does not have such a simplistic view of East and West. In his entire corpus, especially his later works, there is an attempt at fusing the East and the West, but by and large, the way Iqbal is interpreted, coupled with his own often self-contradictory writing, leads one to have a rather distorted view of the complexity of his message. But if this surface message of East/West is read as eternal and transhistorical then no possibility of an East/West fusion or cooperation can be offered. East and West, in such a scenario, are locked into irresolvable, perpetual conflict.

Iqbal's views of the West, however, are influenced by his own experience as a colonized intellectual and as a human subject aware of the symbolics of his own cultural history. Iqbal, therefore, while being very critical of the Muslim elite of his time, places much trust in a specific kind of action-oriented Islamic renewal. His retrieval of a particular Muslim male subjectivity, I have argued elsewhere, can be deeply problematic for our own present if we read Iqbal's works as immutable and transhistorical.[2]

The kind of Islam that Iqbal prefers is certainly clarified in one of his last series of lectures, though he offers this with caution and with due regard for the possible pernicious effects of this new brand of Islamic revivalist movement. He writes,

> But the spirit of Ibn-i-Taimiyyah's teaching found a fuller expression in a movement of immense potentialities which arose in the eighteenth century, from the sands of Nejd.[3] . . . It is really the first throb of life in modern Islam. To the inspiration of this movement are traceable, directly or indirectly, nearly all the great modern movements of Muslim Asia and Africa. . . . The great puritan reformer, Mohamamd ibn-i-Abdal-Wahab . . . finally succeeded spreading the fire of his restless soul throughout the whole world of Islam. (*Reconstruction* 134)

In the very next passage, though, Iqbal does consider this movement "conservative" and "uncritical" but, nevertheless, while suggesting that it is imbued with a certain "spirit of freedom" (134). Thus the possible reformative history of Islam that Iqbal retrieves as the seminal modern movement in Islam, a movement that brings the revolutionary and the martial potential back to decadent Islam, is the very movement that now, in its various permutations, is producing the kinds of Muslim subjectivities that happen to be responsible for some of the worst atrocities against Muslims and non-Muslims.[4] There are reasons, of course, as to why Iqbal chose this movement and its potentialities as the ideal for a Muslim renaissance: such movements were against the established, corrupt hierarchies of the Muslim political system, and they encouraged a kind of individualistic spirit focused on struggle, piety, and Jihad against the West as well as the heretical and decadent Muslim rulers of their time. This Wahabi movement was, and is, also transnational and Pan-Islamic, providing an ideal organizational ideology for Islam, a religion that, in Iqbal's view, is the ultimate point of arrival for all great religions.

If this Wahabi movement is Iqbal's inspiration, then one must also at least attempt to tease out its reasons to see what kind of human subjectivity this forces Iqbal to imagine, think, and perpetuate. For Iqbal, as a colonized subject, any interpretation of Islam that offers a muscular and militant potential for uprising and revolution is likely to be enticing. That precisely, in my opinion, is the reason Iqbal finds this movement and its surrogates the most useful for the Islamic world, for every liberatory movement needs an active ideology to see its project through. Reading Iqbal's sympathetic attitude toward this militant Muslim movement as transhistorical erases the vast complexities of Iqbal's work, reducing him to the level of a poet for contemporary reactionaries and Islamic fundamentalist movements.

We should, instead, find in Iqbal instances where he offers more universalist and cosmopolitan ideas of being in the world, as such instances are plentiful. But such attempts at discussing Iqbal, I must admit, often go against the usual terrain of Iqbal scholarship in Pakistan. In Pakistani academic circles, most scholars are more concerned with the sources of Iqbal's "wisdom" or with the validity of his work relative to Islamic thought; as a result, most such works tend to be hagiographic. Iqbal is cherry-picked and quoted by most constituencies in Pakistan—from Marxists, to Islamists, to capitalists.

It is in one of his last works, *Javid Nama*, a work addressed to his son, that Iqbal, in a way, gives us his final word on his views on East and West. It is, therefore, necessary to read this message alongside his other assertions about East and West. The concluding verses of *Javid Nama* are translated as follows:

> Be not enchanted by the West
> Nor on the East thou needest dote,
> For both this ancient and this new
> Together are but not worth an oat. (*Javad* 186)

The young Muslim subject addressed, according to Iqbal, must transcend the pulls of his own ancient culture while avoiding the uncritical adoption of the West. The Muslim subject can neither be a pure nativist nor a pure convert to the "ways of the West." Instead, Iqbal proposes an extreme form of individual will, a will informed by both these strains of the human enterprise. Thus, his parting advice is as follows:

> Full jealously life guards itself
> Although it doth in company dwell;
> And ever in a caravan
> Alone live thou, with all tread well. (187)

Iqbal's Muslim subject must be shaped by the combined knowledges of East and West, and he or she must also be a communal subject, a subject who is part of a "caravan" while still maintaining an individual subjectivity that others may find of value. Sadly, though, this message of Iqbal's regarding a complex human subjectivity that can negotiate the pressures and pulls of various cultures and social identities is lost when conservative religious scholars retrieve the kind of human subjectivity that they think Iqbal is proposing in his works. There is, therefore, a clear need in the literary and critical practices of the Islamic world to be aware of the reading practices available in the West, for only then will Muslims be able to read their own seminal and originary texts with the kind of complexity and nuance that is absolutely necessary to live fruitfully in the modern world.

However, in most of his other poetic works, Iqbal constantly laments the loss of Muslim vigor and power, though he does not blame it solely on the West. In fact, I would argue that Iqbal sees the rise of the West against the East, specifically against Islam, as a result of the internal weaknesses of the Islamic world and Muslims' loss of contact with the original message of Islam. It is in retrieving this purist strain of Islam that Iqbal's work enters the kind of retrieval that can be mobilized for the most reactionary form of male subjectivity by his readers and by the scholars who find Iqbal's work useful for such retrievals. It is, however, important to note that Iqbal articulates a more expansive and complicated account of the decline of Muslims and Islam; this account is often contradictory. For example, the same Iqbal who derides Muslims for having lost their active vigor also exhorts them for not embracing modern ways of life. The retrieval of what Iqbal means by the "decline of Islam" is always motivated by the politics and preferences of any given individual's act of retrieval.

For example, here is how Iqbal defines the figure of a *Momin*.[5] Momin, for Iqbal, is a man of action but also someone aware of the fine balance between war and peace, friend and foe:

> Ho halqa-e-Yaraan to bresham ke tareh narm
> Razm-e-Haqo baatil ho to faulad hey Momin. (*Zarb-e-Kaleem* 45)

> A Momin is Like silk amongst the company of friends
> And like steel in the battle of good against evil.

Similarly:

> Jis se jigare lalal mein thandak ho wo shabnam
> Daryaoon key dill jist sey dehl jain wo toofan. (60)

> One who brings softness to the heart of a tulip
> But drives fear into the hearts of mighty rivers.[6]

Iqbal's Momin is a balanced human subject capable of differentiating peacetime conduct from wartime actions. Furthermore, this subject is also supposed to model his life on that of the Prophet and be imbued with kindness and compassion. But even this balanced representation in Iqbal's own work is further undermined by Iqbal's own words, for within the same collection of poems, Iqbal also expresses a searing critique of blind Westernization and the loss of Muslim martial vigor:

Tera wajood sarapa tajalli-e-Afrang
Ke too wahan ke amarat garoon ki hay ta'meer
Magar ye paiker-e-Khaki Khdui se khali hay
Faqat niyam hay tu, zar nigaro bay shamsir (*Zarb-e-Kaleem* 33)

You are a creation of the West
For it is the architects of the West that built you
But within this body, there is no pride
Only a sword-less, bejeweled, scabbard[7]

This is not necessarily an uncomplicated critique of Westernization but rather a critique of the loss of one's own culture as one's self is shaped by colonial, ideological, and material imperatives. One could see nothing wrong with such a critique of colonized, Europeanized subjects. In fact, Iqbal himself was a product of this East/West encounter. But to many readers of Iqbal, this becomes a rallying cry for the elimination of all Western influences in a fruitless search to recuperate a pure Islamic identity. Any such move, then, becomes a journey to the past at the cost of the present, a denial of a more nuanced and cosmopolitan future. It is this Iqbal, the Iqbal who defends the East against the ideological and material onslaught of the West, who lives on and is retrieved, recycled, and privileged over the Iqbal who might have been useful to develop a more compassionate, open human subjectivity. There is nothing wrong with retrieving the kind of strident Iqbal who enables the Muslims of India or Pakistan to remember and recuperate the glorious history of Islam, for we all need such retrievals to challenge the sensitivities and values created and enforced during the colonial experience. But taking this Iqbal as the ultimate sage for all times also locks Pakistani political thought to the colonial paradigm within which Iqbal wrote and normalizes the conflictual politics of the contact phase of colonialism even within the contemporary politics of Pakistan and, on a broader scale, the rest of the Islamic world. This makes Islamic politics, political movements, and systems of governance perpetually reactionary in nature, as they are always defining themselves in an ossified mold of perpetual conflict. I am not denying that much of the old colonialism has now been recycled in the shape of the current global economic system—in a previous chapter I discussed the impact of this system on Muslim politics—but by reading our writers in the same vein as they were read during their own times, instead of reading them differently in the light of the present, we are forced to abandon the possibilities of the present. This perpetually locks the Islamic world to a conflictual past. It is also important to note that the retrieval of Iqbal is achieved through a total erasure of what people like Iqbal and others find useful and useable in terms of the East/West encounter. Iqbal, let us not forget, becomes Iqbal because of his experiences in both the East and the West.

There is yet another strategy of native response to the colonial imperatives, or colonial claims to cultural superiority, that develops in Iqbal's work and that still defines both popular and academic responses to the West. In many of his poems, Iqbal refutes European claims to cultural and civilizational superiority by highlighting the very hypocrisy of the colonial "civilizing" mission and the hypocrisy of Europe more generally. Thus, Iqbal compares stereotypes mobilized against the natives with the incongruities within Western modernity itself, suggesting that while the natives may not be as "civilized" as the colonizers, the latter themselves are "savage" in their own way. Of course, such critique was and is necessary and served the purpose of rallying native thought and action against claims of colonial moral superiority upon which the entire edifice of the colonial enterprise was built. Furthermore, such an intervention was necessary because so many of the early native intellectuals had absorbed these ideas as true and had developed a sort of self-loathing attitude toward their own history and cultures.[8] This critique is offered under several registers and is interspersed throughout the entire body of Iqbal's work. It is sometimes offered from an Eastern vantage point, other times from the point of view of Western figures demonized in the West. Before I provide some examples, I must clarify why it is necessary to dwell on this point. It has become a norm for some within the Islamic world, specifically in Pakistan, to compare tragedies. For example, when ISIS or another Islamist organization commits an atrocity in Europe or the North Atlantic regions, journalists and laypersons within the Islamic world, instead of outright condemning such atrocities, point to the atrocities suffered by their own people. The purpose is to rightfully highlight the dual standards of the Western media that do not give the same degree of recognition and importance to loss of life and tragedy within the global periphery as they do to attacks and incidents in the West. I find such comparisons troubling, as instead of developing a common global vocabulary for condemning all acts of terror and aggression, it trivializes certain acts with references to other such acts.[9]

Thus, for the world to develop a more comprehensive global response to acts of terror and aggression, both the so-called West and the so-called Islamic East must develop the intellectual capacities and political will to condemn all loss of life at the hands of terrorists and invaders. This practice of comparing tragedies and, in a way, erasing the East's own cultural ills by suggesting that others are equally terrible, if not worse, creates a destructive logic within which no universal condemnation of violent acts of terror is possible. And this sort of convoluted argument develops during the colonial contact phase, and Iqbal's work displays its most articulate and deft version. My hope is that by pointing to this binary structure of Iqbal's thought and its usage by those who quote Iqbal, I can encourage a more humanistic and global way of looking at and dealing with each other. I provide below a discussion of some instances in Iqbal's work where this strategy is at play.

In one of his long poems published in 1936, *Iblees Ki Majlas-*

e-Shura (Satan's parliament), Iqbal offers general views of Western civilization. The poem is staged as a sort of executive meeting between Satan and his advisers. Satan begins the meeting with the following declaration, which I offer in truncated form:

Satan:

Main ney dkhlaya Fragangi ko malukiyyat ka khawab
Mein neyb tora masjido dir o kalisa ka fasoon
Main ney nadaroon ko sikhlaya sbaq taqdeer ka
Mein ney man'am ko diya srmayadari ka janoon
Kaun ker sakta hey is Aatish-e-Sozan ko sard?
Jis key hangamon mein ho Iblees ka sauz-e-daroon
Jis ki shakhain hon hamari Aabyari se buland
Kaun ker sakta hey is nakhl-e-kuhun ko sernigoon? (*Armughan-e-Hijaz* 5–6)

It was I who showed the Europeans the dream of Kingship
And I who broke the "magic" of mosques, temples, and churches
I taught the poor the lesson of predestination
And gave the rich the madness of capitalism
Who can smother this raging fire
That is imbued by [my] Satanic spirit
And who can uproot this tree
That is tended by someone such as Me?[10]

Note again the staging as a kind of executive meeting of the devil's cabinet or parliament. Before they discuss what is happening in the world, Satan offers his opening statement. According to Satan, the system in place is deeply connected to his own grand design, and he is sure that by weakening the role of religion, by introducing the division of labor, by giving the poor a belief in fate, and by making the moneyed capitalists proud of their greed, he has created a self-sustaining "satanic" system, a system so robust that

Satan is not worried about any threat to its perpetual existence. One can, of course, learn much from this single stanza. For Satan, the stanza's narrator, the world at the time of the publication of the poem is shaped according to satanic design. A trained reader would not read these as Iqbal's own views but rather as the views of the speaking subject of the stanza, Satan. But most Iqbal scholars find no problem in reading these words as Iqbal's own views about the global order, taking this as Iqbal's indictment of the current global system. Iqbal, of course, employs a specific strategy in this poem. The poem starts with the absolutist certitude of Satan about his own system, but his advisers introduce various doubts about his project, which he refutes until they reach the last possible threat. Satan has no solution for this threat, and he sees the particular threat as the ultimate undoing of his system. But I get ahead of myself. Let us parse the rest of the poem first.

Hearing Satan's opening pronouncement, the first adviser provides the following supporting assertion:

First Adviser:

Is mein kiya shak hey key muhkam hey yeh Ibleesi nizam
Pukhta ter is sey huhay khouey ghulami mein awwam
Yeh hamari sa'i-e-peiahm ki kramat hey key aaj
Suif o mullah malukiyyat key bnady hein tamam
Hey tawaaf o haj ka hangama agar baqi to kiya
Kund ho ker reh gaye momin ki taigh-e-beniyyam
Kis ki nomidi peh hujjat hey yeh farman-e-Jadeed?
Hey Jahad is daur mein mard-e-muslaman per haram! (*Armughan-e-Hijaz* 6–7)

No doubt, this Satanic system is strong
For people have become accustomed to habits of slavery
It is because of our perpetual work that
Sufis and Mullahs are all subjects of kings

Even if the rituals of Islam still remain
The sword of Momins is dull and useless
In this system build of such hopelessness
Jihad is forbidden [haram] for Muslims[11]

So, keeping in view that this is a plenary meeting of Satan's parliament, one can glean from this exchange that, according to Iqbal, the system in place has been normalized by Satan's minions, and as it applies to the Muslim's world, it has dulled the "martial" vigor of Muslims to a point where they have been rendered inert and useless. However, one could argue that the entire project of Satan is to keep Muslims away from their "natural" tendencies. These natural tendencies, at this point in the poem, are all related to questions of faith and martial vigor, for the Mullahs and Sufis, who must be the bearers of the intellectual traditions of Islam, are caught in a web of mental slavery to powerful monarchs and other such systems, and, on the other hand, the common Muslim's martial drive has been stymied and their "swords" have been dulled. One learns, imperceptibly, that this entire satanic system is meant to keep the material and intellectual prowess of Muslims at bay. And within this system, promulgated by Satan, Jihad is seen as an unwelcome practice. This mention of Jihad and the sword then offers the duty to Jihad as not just an exception or an aberration to the Muslim way of life but as its very life force. One could argue that by "Jihad," Iqbal means "struggle" and not necessarily armed conflict, for the literal meaning of Jihad, as explained in one of the preceding chapters, is "to struggle." But that interpretation is foreclosed because of the symbolics of swords, for swords are, after all, used to wage war.

As the meeting proceeds, Satan's advisers point out various threats to the satanic system, including democracy and communism. But Satan does not see these as potent dangers, for he sees only one major future threat to his system:

Hey agar mujh ko khatar koi to is ummat se hey
Jis ki khakaster mein hey ab tak sharer-e-Aarzoo
Janata hey, jis pe roshan baatin-e-ayyam hey
Muzdkiyat fitna-e-farda najin Islam hey (*Armughan-e-Hijaz* 12)

If I see any danger, it is from this Ummah
For a spark still lingers in its ashes
You know, to me secrets of tomorrow are known
Workers struggle is not my worry, Islam is!

So, in this poem, Islam in its true spirit (whatever that means) is the ultimate threat to Satan's system. Satan's system, let us remember, is the world system as it exists, or existed when Iqbal composed the poem; it includes all monarchical, democratic, and socialist systems. The only system outside of this satanic realm that can be a possible threat to Satan's world order is, according to Iqbal, Islam. It is in Satan's best interest to keep the "true" Islamic spirit from rising again. Since it is a return of the Islamic system, we know already that the true Islamic system for Iqbal, as discussed above, is from eighth-century Hijaz. Thus, the return of Islam will only be truly disruptive to the satanic system if eighth-century Islam were to be revived, a goal that the Wahabi movement strived for and still does. But within the logic of the poem, Muslims must be kept away from their true religion through specific means. These include capitalism, materialism, and entrapment in "shrine worship" (15).

"Shrine worship" is the derogatory term that Abdul-Wahab and his followers used, and still use, to describe all Muslims who believed in a more mystical tradition of Islam in which visiting the shrines of venerable Sufi saints was considered, and is still considered, a rewarding spiritual experience. Iqbal, however, is deeply critical of this form of Islamic Sufism, even though in so many ways his own practice of religion and his views on spirituality draw heavily on the Islamic Sufi tradition. He, however, is skeptical of all forms of Sufism that encourage the renunciation of the material world, for struggling in this material world, for Iqbal, is truly Islamic. Another reason for his distrust of the mystical tradition is highly contextual: within India, most of the mystical traditions were deemed to be highly influenced by Hinduism, and these practices detached humans from their material realities and transformed them into people lacking care for the world around them. Within a colonial struggle, such detached subjectivities are utterly useless to any liberatory struggle. Within the binary logic of Islam against the West, such impractical political subjects would be totally useless to the cause of Islam in general and the cause of Muslims of India in particular. That is why, in this long poem, Satan wants to keep Muslims embroiled in discussions of doctrine and ritual and away from their action-oriented martial history. Thus, the subject most threatening to the satanic, and the colonial system, is the very Muslim subject who truly believes in pure Islamic doctrines, is not afraid of Jihad, and is deeply imbued with the "original" striving spirit of Islam. As such, Iqbal's retrieval of "true" Islam is, despite his critiques of Wahabism, the very form of Islam that is literalist, militant, and uncompromising in its attitudes to interpretive or practical differences.

This privileging of the action-oriented Muslim fighter is not just an isolated act in this particular poem. In fact, as I have argued elsewhere,[12] this strident Muslim subject *is* the ideal Muslim of Iqbal's vision, but while he balances this subject with its gracious and compassionate qualities (man of action only when needed), the radical politics of militant Islam transform this particular subject into the ideal male subject. Of course now, post-Taliban and ISIS, this very subject—uncompromising, literalist, and brutal— has become the most potent incarnation of the Muslim *mujahid*. Reading Iqbal uncritically can make Iqbal's work, unjustly I suggest, into a war song for the Taliban and the brutal soldiers of ISIS.

By and large, Pakistani Muslim scholars only rely on retrieving the very reductive aspects of Iqbal's poetry, especially when it comes to recuperating and arguing for a more militant and action-oriented Muslim subjectivity. The compassionate Muslim as represented by Iqbal is sidelined and substituted with the mujahid, the fighter, and the Jihadist Muslim as a privileged male subjectivity. It is clearly easy to understand that within the logic of his anticolonial thought that a Muslim subjectivity capable of resisting colonial power was essential. That is why he retrieves the early Muslim fighter as a sort of iconic figure to exhort Muslims to rise against the British. But in his own life, Iqbal lived as a law-abiding British subject, even accepting knighthood, a knighthood that he did not surrender during the Quit India Movement[13] when pretty much all other major Indian figures did so as a form of resistance.

So, by and large, Iqbal is a much more complex figure than the poet of resistance that he is made out to be through reductive readings of his work, and his last series of lectures is a testament to his global and humanistic understanding of the world. We need to recuperate, read, and discuss the Iqbal who believes in peaceful coexistence between East and West, who asserts that the old must change as new knowledge becomes available. If only his militaristic views are selected and offered as a transhistorical norm, then they end up underwriting the destructive subjectivities that are operative within Pakistan and the rest of the Islamic world.

Before I go any further, I must reiterate my reasons for reading differently within Islamic cultures so that my argument is not simply dismissed as Western-centric. It is very easy to dismiss and trivialize the efforts of people like me: *What do you know of our struggles, for you live in America.* But since part of me also, as Walter Mignolo asserts, "dwells" in my primary culture, I must, despite the possible opposition, continue to speak and my words must be fair—fair to both sides of the global cultural divide for I am, after all, asking my Western readers to be fair in their assumptions about Islamic cultures and about the textual representations of those cultures. So, what is at stake?

Iqbal is the most highly regarded and anthologized poet in Pakistani school curricula. Furthermore, he is also considered one of the founding fathers of the Pakistan Movement, and selected references to his poetry and political statements find their way into all aspects of Pakistani cultural and political life. Words and ideas attributed to him are not only simple linguistic signs—they become mythic speech. Which means, according to Roland Barthes, that linguistic signs used by Iqbal become more than just the combination of the "signifier" and the "signified."[14] Barthes explains:

> In myth, we find again the tri-dimensional . . . the signifier, the signified and the sign. But myth is a peculiar system, in that it is constructed from a semiological chain which existed before it: it is a *second-order semiological system*. That which is a sign (namely the associative total of a concept and an image) in the first system, becomes a mere signifier in the second. We must here recall that the   materials of mythical speech (the language itself, photography, painting, posters, rituals, objects, etc.), however different at the start, are reduced to a pure signifying function as soon as they are caught by myth. (113)

Let me unpack. We know that a sign is a combination of a signifier and a signified.[15] For example, the term *Muslim* signifies the figure or concept of a Muslim who, simply understood, is a person who practices a religion called Islam. But in its mythic usage, this whole process of signification (the signifier plus the signified) become a signifier and thus offer another signified: the Muslim as retrieved, represented, and articulated by Iqbal. This mythologizing of the sign renders a Muslim as a strident, aggressive, martial hero. Iqbal's poetry, therefore, through its mythic usage ends up highlighting a very literalist and warrior-like Muslim male subjectivity, a subjectivity that was probably essential during the anticolonial struggles, but a subjectivity that now finds itself at war with all those who are either non-Muslims or are not considered "good" Muslims. The simplistic readings of the mythic speech in Iqbal's writings, therefore, have the potential of normalizing the very subjectivities that are wreaking havoc all over the Islamic world. What makes it even more dangerous and seductive is that these ideas are offered in the words of a poet who is considered, without a doubt, a philosopher and a sage who "truly" understood the spirit of Islam. It is then imperative for Pakistani readers to read and interpret texts like Iqbal's differently. Learning interpretive skills developed in the Western academy, of course with some modifications, will go a long way in performing more sophisticated readings of figures like Iqbal.

ABUL A'LA MAWDUDI (1903–1979)

Born in 1903 and educated in more traditional religious and philosophical ways, Mawdudi can be considered the most prominent scholar of Islamization and Islamic revivalism in not only India but also the rest of the Islamic world.[16] In his works, Mawdudi not only offers an Islamist way of resisting the West but also theorizes the nature and functioning of a modern Muslim state. Mawdudi's legacy lives on in the shape of his huge scholarly corpus as well as the political party, Jamaat-e-Islami, that he founded in 1930. The party is not a political powerhouse in Pakistan but is the most organized political party and a major presence on university campuses. The party still follows some of the basic ideas about an Islamic state as envisioned and elaborated by Mawdudi, but, sadly, its current leadership has moved far away from the gradualist approach of Mawdudi and aligned itself with more radical and extreme strains of Islamist political activism in Pakistan. During his lifetime, Mawdudi became extremely prominent because of his accessible writing style and because of his publication of one of the major commentaries on the Qur'ān. His early career was that of a journalist, and his writing, because of its journalistic style, tends to be accessible to average Muslims. His writings, therefore, are easily understood and widely circulated even after his death.

There is a need in Pakistan to reread Mawdudi—partially to build upon his legacy but also to challenge points where his own followers have abandoned his moderate and gradualist stance on the Islamic system within Pakistan. Furthermore, Mawdudi also needs to be read and understood with an eye toward his own spatiotemporal conditions and their determinisms. Reading his works as transhistorical and immutable fixes his thought to the specific colonial moment and tethers Pakistani national and international politics to the binaristic Islam/West structure.

In one of his early writings, published in a popular Islamic magazine, Mawdudi provides an account of the fall of Muslim empire in India in particular, as well as in the rest of the world. In his view, there are two connotations of civilizational defeat: intellectual and material. In his view, it is the intellectual defeat of the Muslims of India at the hands of the British that is more dangerous, as it sunders Muslims from their own sources of inspiration and knowledge. Mawdudi opines about the general reasons for the fall of nations and empires as follows:

> Rulership, governance, and dominance is of two types: intellectual and moral dominance, and political and material dominance. In the former case, one nation becomes so advanced in its intellectual and moral prowess that other nations follow them to a point that their thoughts, ideas, and practices are shaped in the image of the ascendant power. In case of material and political dominance, the vanquished nations can no longer sustain their own sovereign political or administrative systems. In the same sense defeat is also of two kinds; intellectual and political.
>
> Now these two kinds of defeat (intellectual and political) are of two different types and may not exist simultaneously at one place. But ii is a law of nature that a nation that uses intellect thought, and research it also gains material success as a natural outcome of its intellectual success. (*Tanqihat* 5; my translation)

This collection of essays is entitled *Tanqihat: Islam aur Maghrabi tehzeeb ka Tasadum aur us se Paida Shudah Masaail* (Discussions: The confrontation between Islam and Western civilization and the problems caused by it). Within the logic of the text, Mawdudi offers not only a history of this conflict but what this defeat does to the Muslims of India in particular and to Muslims of the world in general. His solution often relies on the removal of the intellectual dominance of the West and the retrieval of "true" Islamic teachings. In these essays, however, Mawdudi clearly believes that for a civilization to be free and dominant, both its thought as well as its actions must constantly be renewed and sustained. While he challenges the dominant Westernization of the Islamic world, he also exhorts his Muslim readers to learn new knowledges and then use Islam as a criterion to measure whether certain knowledges can be adapted into Islam. There is never a blanket condemnation of all things Western in Mawdudi's corpus. In fact, Mawdudi would have no objection to adopting any Western ideas or practices that do not directly abrogate the Sharia. Overall, counter to what the current followers of Mawdudi believe and practice (an absolute denial of Western practices), Mawdudi would have been quite comfortable with democracy and human rights so long as they had been rearticulated and theorized within the true teachings and spirit of Islam.

I have also discussed Mawdudi's political thought in the earlier parts of this book, especially his theorization of the Islamic state. I am suggesting here that this mode of thinking of the imperial West and its ascendency over Islam and the intellectual and material causes provided for this Muslim downfall, even though offered during colonial times, still form the core of the East/West binary structure that the Islamist political parties still use in Pakistan and other Muslim countries.

Bear in mind that these assertions were made at the height of British rule, and Mawdudi, like so many other Muslims scholars, was attempting to ascertain the causes of the fall of Islam. Maybe such power dynamics still exist, for we still live in a Eurocentric world. There is nothing wrong with a global politics in which the leaders and writers of the Islamic world challenge any essentialized and ossified views of Islam by those in the West; there is also nothing wrong with offering a constant and persistent critique of the often-rapacious global economic system fostered and at times enforced by the West. Such critiques are necessary in order to forge a different and more compassionate global order for all inhabitants of the globe, and Muslims and Muslims scholars can become part of the global resistance to the imperatives of neoliberal capitalism. But essentializing the West as a monolithic and unchanging place is unjust and unfair, for just as not everything about Islam is wrong and dangerous, the West similarly has much to offer the Islamic world. Seeing the world in these conflictual terms is no longer the only way of experiencing the world. If we keep reading these scholars as transhistorical and immutable, then the worldviews that they offer, within the material realities of their own time, become fixed and remain conflictual, and there is no possibility to forge ahead and have a conversation with our cultural others, even our former oppressors. Unless that conversation happens at both ends of the global divide, the reactionary forces that thrive in interreligious and intercivilizational conflicts will continue to hold sway over our imaginations and actions.

This oversimplification of the Other happens at both ends of the global divide. We have watched the Trump administration openly conflate Islam and Islamism, and its recent anti–Islam policies rely on this fear of the global Other. I have, in the preceding chapters, imagined a humanistic approach that eliminates any ill-informed, blanket assertions about the literatures and texts of the Islamic world. I have also attempted to introduce a method of critical engagement that comes from an informed place and performs the act of reading with an understanding of Muslim meaning-making processes.

In this chapter, albeit briefly, I have suggested that the Muslim readers—intellectual and popular—also need to develop the same kind of intellectual generosity when dealing with Western literary texts and accept the practices that are useful and liberating, for there is no harm in borrowing from each other in a reciprocal manner. Maybe such intellectual commerce, such borrowing and lending of ideas as equal shareholders within the imaginative economy of the world, could be the beginning of a transformed worldview at both ends of the global divide. Those who thrive in cleavages and in building walls already have too much power to destroy and commit violence. Under such conditions of hate and violence, the least we can do is practice more compassionate, liberating, and cosmopolitan acts of reading. Reading our own Muslim scholars and literati with an eye on the present and with a hope for a more accepting and prosperous global future would be, in my humble opinion, a good start.

AFTERWORD

Writing this book has been a deeply personal and enlightening journey. Throughout the research and writing phases of the book, I have struggled to find the right balance between the freedom of expression, a principle I hold dear, and the rights of readers to have their own responses to texts, especially those texts that play with the sacred. In the end, the poetics of incitement is the ultimate test of this tension. At stake for me as a scholar of cross-cultural encounters has been the issue of representation and its limits. I am also acutely aware of my own privileged location within the metropolitan academy and the role of the humanities in it. I have tried as best as possible not to adopt what Bruce Robbins so aptly calls the "view from above" or the "bombsight perspective" (2), a perspective that places the Western (or West-based) intellectual in a spatial and symbolic verticality with a right to view the rest of the world from a privileged and powerful perspective. Instead, I have tried to wade into the most contested intellectual terrain and have offered, in a tentative and inconclusive way, the returning gaze and the silenced echo of the object of observation: the postcolonial Muslim subject. I have, however, done this from my privileged place in the Western academy. That I am aware of this privilege and try my best to undermine it is also a continuous process, one also started by another book coedited by Bruce Robbins, which, it seems, I had read and internalized in another lifetime (Chea and Robbins).

Of all the things that we do as scholars under so many different registers and legitimations, there is one thing that we must not do: dismiss the reader. For it is in the hands of a reader that texts come to life, find their value, and gain their cultural weight. Poetics of incitement, for me, privileges one form of readerly reception over another; it also attempts to silence the rights of Muslim readers to think and feel differently about their own representation by others. I find this to be troubling and unjust. Thus, this book has been an interrogation of my own thoughts and feelings.

In the Muslim world there is often a tendency to reduce the complexities of metropolitan representation to certain established stereotypes. I have provided a catalogue of such stereotypes in my discussion. It is also time for those of us from the Muslim world and those much better qualified than myself in the field of Islamic studies to dare a little, to stop relying on empty and outdated stereotypes, and to open the discursive framework of thinking our present and hence the future. There is no dearth of ideological and material conflicts in the world, and there is a long list of mutual wrongs and global injustices. Our existence cannot just be agonistic and conflictual. There is a lot wrong with this world. Much of it can be attributed to the evils of an unresponsive and dictatorial capitalistic system, but the answer is not reliance on an unsullied, pure past. There is no pure past: the past is just an amalgamation of texts and textual traces made linear and palatable through the agential hands of those who have the power to arrange things as such. The ultimate possibilities of our world lie in love and understanding: understanding differences and loving even those we disagree with, for loving only those who match our cultural matrix is not really love but an expectation of sameness, and sameness is achieved only through gross acts of aggression and silencing.

There is an anecdote immortalized in the work of Rumi. It is about Moses and his close relationship and understanding of God, for he, in all traditions, is one of the very few prophets who had witnessed the Absolute Spirit. Rumi writes that, while on his way to meet God, Moses overhears a shepherd praying to God:

> Where art Thou, That I that I may become Thy servant and sew
> Thy shoes and comb Thy head?
> That I may wash Thy clothes and kill Thy lice and bring
> milk to thee, O worshipful One;
> That I may kiss Thy little hand and rub Thy little foot (and
> when bedtime comes I may sweep Thy little room). (150)

Moses, hearing this rendering of God by the shepherd, admonishes the shepherd for his base thoughts about the absolute spirit and, as he approaches the being of beings, the thing of all things, he hears God admonishing him upon deriding one of God's ardent lovers:

> A revelation came to Moses from God—Thou hast parted
> My servant from me.
> Didst thou come (as a prophet) to unite, or didst thou come
> to sever?
> So far as thou canst, do not set foot in separation: of (all)
> things the most hateful to Me is divorce.
> I have bestowed on every one a (special) way of acting: I
> have given to every one a (peculiar) form of expression. (Rumi 150)

Thus, in Rumi's parable, we learn that love can take many forms, and expression is never really universal: understanding the particularities of any expression is the key to greater understanding. In the end, love of the other should guide our writings and readings. While metropolitan critics must train themselves to understand the deeper meaning-making processes of the Islamic world, Muslims in general should also develop a more nuanced and compassionate approach to issues of cultural difference, for not every offense is intended and not all offenses deserve the same punishment.

Unfortunately, the poetics of incitement has now become an established genre within metropolitan culture. It is partially attributable to the immigration pressures from North African Muslim countries to Europe and partially because of the new norm created by post-9/11 media in the United States. Note that these armies of Islam bashers preexisted that awful tragedy, but the attack on the World Trade Center provided these scholars and media talking heads their ultimate legitimizing moment. Now, sadly, despite the amount of knowledge available about all cultures in all possible media, bashing Islam is not only acceptable but also good for ratings. On the other hand, defending Islam, in so many circles, wins one the label of apologist for ISIS, the Taliban, or al-Qaeda.

There is a dire need within the Islamic world to develop a different and more complex understanding of modernity. Yes, it is salutary to seek a kind of altmodernity[1] or embrace decolonial thinking,[2] but it cannot be done only through extreme reliance on the past. The past, as we know it, exists only in texts and texts are always mobilized through motivated subjectivities. There is no pure history, nor are there any unmotivated objective readings or mobilizations of texts. In our zeal to protect the Muslim sacred, we should not make this into a punitive venture that addresses all wrongs with the same punishment. Furthermore, Muslim scholars and lay citizens alike need to nourish, sustain, and perpetuate a politics of love, for without love, especially of those with whom we disagree, all we will end up creating and sustaining is a kind of ruthless thanatopolitics, a politics of death in constant embrace with the past, wary of the present and terrified of the future.

I have suggested here that changing something as normal and everyday as our reading and reception practices can create space for larger and grander changes. This radical expansion of reading practices will have to be accomplished at both ends of the global divide. Only if we venture into this liminal and ambiguous territory shall we be able to transform this world into one defined by love.

APPENDIX: THE CONTROVERSY ABOUT
THE CREATEDNESS OF THE QUR'ĀN

In simple terms, the main controversy[1] divided the medieval Muslim community into two large groups: those who believed that the Qur'ān is a creation of God and those who believed that the Qur'ān is coeternal with God. Both sides refuted counterclaims to their argument, and the issue came to head when al-Mamun, the eighth Abbasid caliph, declared the createdness of the Qur'ān a state doctrine and declared a *mihana* "an inquisition, that was designed to ensure acquiescence in this doctrine" (Nawas 615). Further, "The *mihana*, an unprecedented event in the history of Islam, was begun by al-Mamun just four months before his death in 833 and continued by his two successors" (615). The mihana was not only questioning but also involved torturing scholars or imprisoning them in order to force them to acknowledge the sovereign policy on the issue of createdness of the Qur'ān.

The controversy of the "createdness of the Qur'ān" can only be fully understood with a clear understanding of different strains of Muslim philosophy and the orthodox reactions to the medieval Muslim philosophers. According to most scholarly sources on Islam, the controversy about the createdness of the Qur'ān is placed within the debates involving the conflict between orthodox scholars and the *kalām* philosophers (*Mutakallimūn*). "In orthodox sources" Jahm ibn Safwan (d. 127/745) "is seen as the actual founder of *kalām*" (Pavlin 106). Eventually, the "terms *kalām* and *mutakallimūn* came to refer to those who engaged in any form of speculation concerning the attributes of God" (106). In other words, it could be said that, due to their reliance on reason and logic, the *kalām* philosophers were considered to be in error by the orthodox scholars who relied on explanation of the Qur'ān through an emphasis on hadīth, or sayings of the Prophet. The conflict was then one of methodologies and the limits of reason. Within this context, the declaration by the Mutazilla[2] and other speculative theologians that the Qur'ān was a creation of God became a highly controversial issue, for it brought to the fore questions about the nature of God and his attributes. But first, we must understand how this became an issue.

According to some sources, the infusion of Greek philosophy and increasing contact with other religions and cultures forced the traditional scholars of Islam to develop a different method of explaining the sacred (kalām) to the Muslims as well as people from other religions. But most of all, kalām became a necessity when debating scholars from other major religions prevalent within the Muslim empire. Most Muslim scholars invoke a hypothetical conversation between Muslim scholars and their Christian counterparts, a conversation that needed kalām to answer some basic questions. This is how this conversation is often staged:

> Christian: What is the Arabic word for Jesus Christ?
> Muslim: Kalimatullah.
> Christian: What does that mean?
> Muslim: The word of God.
> Christian: Is Qur'ān the word of God?
> Muslim: Yes, absolutely!
> Christian: Well, if both Jesus and the Qur'ān are the word of God, then don't they   share the same essence as both are coextensive with God and thus eternal?

Naturally, this conclusion—that there are three eternal entities—was in direct contrast to the Islamic concept of Tauheed, the absolute oneness of God.

So, simply stated, when the Mutazilla argue about the createdness of the Qur'ān, what they are attempting to articulate is that by becoming a creation, the Qur'ān ceases to be coeternal with God and thus the argument about coeternity with Jesus is also refuted. But declaring the Qur'ān a creation also has its own ramifications, the least of which being yet another debate about there being pairs of all creations of God.

Notes

INTRODUCTION

1. I use the term *metropolitan* to denote the centers of former and current imperial power. In postcolonial studies, the term is used to name the capitals of former European colonial powers and the term is now extended to include other capitals, as well as nations, of the North Atlantic region.

2. Beyond the writings, the general approach to political Islam, especially by the mainstream conservative media, has also become openly hostile and reliant on simplistic Muslim stereotypes.

3. I am intentionally including just the descriptive meanings of the two terms, for a philosophical discussion of them is beyond the scope of this book.

4. I am using the term *primordial* here as it is defined and discussed by Clifford Geertz, for whom primordialism is usually tribal and constructed through blood and kin ties.

5. Said here refers to a specific work by Ricouer, "What Is a Text?" Said's explanation of worldliness is a response to the following passage from Ricoeur: "A text . . . is not without reference; it will be precisely the task of reading, as interpretation, to actualize the reference. At least, in this suspension wherein reference is deferred, in the sense that it is postponed, a text is somehow 'in the air.' Outside of the world or without a world; by means of this obliteration of all relation the world, every text is free to enter into relation with all other texts which come to take the place of the circumstantial reality shown by living speech" (qtd. in Said, *World* 34).

6. Since the reading experience and response of the reader is so crucial to my argument, I have spent the last few paragraphs laying down a provisional framework for my privileging of the reader.

CHAPTER 1

1. For details, please see Bracher, *Radical*.
2. Note that in this passage, Bracher is citing from the work of Haslam.
3. This didactics of reading is further clarified in my discussion of Rushdie's essay about how to read his novel in chapter 3.
4. Propositional beliefs, according to Bracher, are based in semantic memory, thus related to language and facts offered on the surface. Nonpropositional beliefs, according to my understanding, are the deeply internalized structures, or schemas, that often overdetermine when a sign is proffered to us. In other words, we could say that facts and signs alone are not sufficient to alter our views of the other, and to change the larger structures within which the sign is posited would, thus, be crucial to altering one's views about a group or an entity. Note that Bracher uses the perceptions of Africans in the West to elaborate his point. One could very easily substitute "Muslim" for "African" in his discussion and reach the same results.
5. By "overlap-obscuring schemas" Bracher means any preestablished views that might deny that one could share some form of human and cultural elements with our local and global others.

CHAPTER 2

1. I have intentionally kept the Shi'a schools of interpretation out of this discussion, as their inclusion would prolong this discussion beyond the scope of this chapter. For an introduction to Shi'a Islam, I recommend Noojan Momen's work on the subject.
2. By far the most interesting modern work of tajdīdi scholarship can be found in Fazlur Rahman's book on the subject. Similarly, a vast corpus of work about Islam and Islamic philosophy does exist in English; it just has not found an honorable mention in major anthologies of literary criticism or in the works of major theorists except, of course, the works of Edward Said.
3. Some parts of this chapter were published, with some modifications, in one of my earlier articles and reproduced here with the permission of the publishers. For details see Raja, "Democratic" 449–69. © South Asian Studies Association of Australia, reprinted by permission of Taylor & Francis Ltd., www.tandfonline.com on behalf of South Asian Studies Association of Australia. Permission must be sought for any further use.
4. A brief discussion of the debate about the createdness of the Qur'ān is provided in the appendix.

5. For a detailed discussion of Abdul Wahab's impact on Islam please see Raja, "Textual" 95–106.

6. All citations from Ahmad's biography of the Mujaddad in Urdu are my translation.

7. Iqbal's verses are my translation from the original Urdu poem.

CHAPTER 3

1. Here, I cannot bring myself to quote the actual passages, so this paraphrased reference should suffice.

2. I have already provided my own response to this in my published work, which has been reproduced, with some modifications, in the next chapter.

3. This discussion is important for reading audiences on both ends of the global divide and is a sort of extension of my earlier work on the subject. See Raja, "Democratic" 449–64.

4. In summary, according to Muslim historians, Aisha was blamed by some to have had an affair, and as it becomes a huge issue for her and for the Prophet, a direct revelation from God absolves Aisha of all accusations.

5. For details of Aisha's narration see Al-Tabarī, *History*, vol. 8, 57–67.

6. The term *hypocrites* has specific meaning within the history of early Islam. Called *Munaafiqeen* in Arabic, the Hypocrites were those who had apparently converted to Islam but were still sympathetic to the old order.

7. All citations from the Urdu text of *Haqooq-e-Niswan* are my translation.

8. For details, please see Raja, *Constructing*.

9. All references to the reader's questions and Mawdudi's answers are my translation.

10. The discussion of Mikhail Bakhtin's explanation of the novel and novelistic mode of representation has been adapted from an article previously published on my blog *The Pakistan Forum*, accessed 22 Nov. 2014. The blog entry is no longer available.

11. For details, see Qureshi.

CHAPTER 4

1. The discussion of Jauss up to this point has been cited, with some slight modifications, from a previously published article. For details see Raja, "Pakistani" 81–89.

CHAPTER 5

1. I am relying on Gayatri Spivak's discussion of *sous rature* in her translator's preface to *Of Grammatology*. Writing *sous rature* implies that one uses a certain word/term but crosses it out in the text with an X, thus suggesting that "since the word is inaccurate, it is crossed out. Since it is necessary, it remains legible" (xiv).

2. All my references to this article are to the one included in Spivak's book.

3. Interestingly, this choice of translation, when read within the reading and meaning-making process of Pakistan, makes the term perfectly acceptable, as it suggests that the book itself is satanic because the term *compositions* presupposes an author (Rushdie) as a creator of these satanic compositions.

4. The entire verse reads as follows:

   He it is Who has sent down
   To thee the Book:
   In it are verses
   Basic or fundamental
   Clear (in meaning);
   They are the foundation
   Of the Book: others
   Are not entirely clear. But those
   In whose heart is perversity follow
   The part thereof that is not entirely clear. (Qur'ān 3:7)

5. The six authentic collections of hadith, *Al-Sihah al-Sittah,* include the collections of Bukhāri, Muslim, Tirmidhi, Abu Da'ūd, Ibn Māja, and al-Nasā'i. Almost all these collections were put together about two hundred years after the Prophet's death. The first two collections referred to are considered the most authentic by most Sunni Muslims.

6. According to footnote provided by the translators, the particular volume of Tabarī to which I refer, Ibn Hisham, one of the earliest sources on the Prophet's life, omitted this information from his account of the Prophet's life. Similarly, Shibli Naumāni, also quoted, does not mention the incident.

CHAPTER 6

1. This chapter is a revised version of an essay published in 2011. For details, please see Raja, "Neoliberal" 21–31.

2. I have consistently suggested this in some of my previously published work as well. For details see Raja, "King" and *Constructing*.

3. I am referring here to Friedman.

4. I am relying here on Georgio Agamben's discussion of the Greek terms *Bios* and *Zoē*, according to which Zoē "expressed the simple fact of living common to all living beings" and Bios "which indicated the form or way of living proper to an individual or a group" (*Homo Sacer* 1). Within the symbolic terrain of the 1971 election, both the parties would have treated the minorities as Zoē, as bare life, but the chances of their inclusion as Bios, as qualified life, were higher within the class-associated politics of the Pakistan People's Party, especially since the party was not mobilizing Islam as the leading signifier of national identity.

5. See Raja, "Jihad."

6. See Raja, "Death."

7. The murderer was received as a hero by the fundamentalist groups and individuals, which points to the degree of decay of the Pakistani public sphere.

CHAPTER 7

1. I have offered this materialistic understanding of fundamentalism in quite a few of my other publications. For details, see Raja, "Neoliberal" 21–31 and "Jihad" 47–71.

2. On 7 January 2015, at about 11:30 a.m. CET local time, two French Muslim brothers, Saïd and Chérif Kouachi, forced their way into the offices of the French satirical weekly newspaper *Charlie Hebdo* in Paris. Armed with rifles and other weapons, they killed twelve people and injured eleven others.

3. For details, please see Bhatti.

CHAPTER 8

1. For thoroughly researched discussion of the blasphemy law in Pakistan, please see Mazhar.

2. For details of my earlier assertions about Iqbal, please see Raja, "Allama" 107–26.

3. The central region of present-day Saudi Arabia.

4. The Wahabi Islam, based in the teachings of Abdul-Wahab, is the Islamic faction that becomes a sort of slippery slope ideology for Alqeda, ISIS, and other such Jihadist organizations. Currently, this version of Islam is the main source of jurisprudence and governance in the Kingdom of Saudi Arabia.

5. In Iqbal's and in many other Muslim scholarly and creative works, the term

Muslim is used for all generic Muslims, whereas *Momin* is a specific term reserved for those who truly practice and follow the Prophetic tradition. Since this designation relies on subjective definitions of what constitutes a Momin, the resultant specific definitions vary according to the sect attempting to define the term.

6. My translation.

7. My translation.

8. This defeatist way of thinking about one's own culture was caused by the literal defeats of native cultures but was also developed and perpetuated ideologically through the colonial educational system. As the native youth moved through the colonial educational system, they also internalized the power of the colonial language and culture and then looked at their own culture from the point of view of their colonial masters. This construction of native colonized subjectivities is discussed at length by writers as diverse as Franz Fanon, Ngugi Wa Thiong'o, Gauri Viswanathan, and many others. For the role of colonial education in creating disdain for one's native culture, please see Thiong'o's *Decolonizing*.

9. Furthermore, this tendency of false comparisons often underwrites the most reactionary and paternalistic cultural practices. For example, in my conversations with some Pakistani scholars, when I invoke the questions about rights of minorities or those of women, I am often told that these rights are not so perfect in America either. Of course, I am aware of the racial and gender inequalities in America, but does this somehow absolve the Pakistani scholars and politicians from creating better conditions for minorities and women?

10. My translation.

11. My translation.

12. For more details on this please see Raja, "Allama" 107–26.

13. The Quit India Movement was launched by the Indian National Congress (led by Gandhi) on 8 August 1942. The Indian Muslim League, however, boycotted the movement, as their leadership needed British support to carve out a separate nation-state for the Muslims. Thus Iqbal's decision to not surrender his knighthood is more in line with his allegiance to the Muslim League and less about his allegiance to the British.

14. This is the basic structure of a sign, as discussed by Ferdinand Saussure.

15. This comes from Ferdinand de Saussure's work on language. For details, see Saussure.

16. Until the Saudis discovered Mawdudi's writings against the hereditary kingship, he was very popular in the Kingdom, and most of his works were trans-

lated into Arabic. His works are also widely read by other Wahabi practitioners of Islam all over the Muslim world.

AFTERWORD

1. A concept theorized and discussed by Michael Hardt and Antonio Negri.
2. As theorized by Walter Mignolo.

APPENDIX

1. For further reading, see Martin.
2. Mutazilla were the rational Muslim philosophers from the eight to the tenth centuries, whose basic belief was that the Qur'ān and Islamic teachings can be accessed and understood through reason. This emphasis on reason brought them into conflict with orthodox theologians, who claimed that God or his intentions could not be understood through reason alone and that to truly understand the intentions of God, Muslims only needed to rely on the Qur'ān itself and the sayings of the prophet.

Works Cited

Abdallah, Anouar, ed. *For Rushdie: Essays by Arab and Muslim Writers in Defense of Free Speech*. George Braziller, 1994.

Adams, Lorraine. "Thinly Veiled." *The New York Times*, 12 Dec. 2008.

Agamben, Georgio. *Homo Sacer: Sovereign Power and Bare Life*. Translated by Daniel Heller-Roazen, Stanford UP, 1998.

Ahmad, Aijaz. "Islam, Islamisms and the West." *Socialist Register*, 2008, pp. 1–37, socialistregister.com/index.php/srv/article/view/5873.

Ahmad, Muhammad Masood. *Seerat Mujaddad Alif Sani*. Imam Rabbani Foundation, 2005.

Ahmed, Israr. *Allama Iqbal aur Ham*. Markazi Anjuman-e-Khuddam Al-Qur'an, 1977.

Al-Ghazali. *Al-Munqid min Al-Dalal* [Deliverance from Error]. Translated by R. J. McCarthy, Fons Vitae, 1980.

Ali, Mumtaz Maulana. *Haqooq-e-Niswan* [Rights of women]. Darul Asha'at Punjab, 1898.

Al-Khattab, Huda. "Brief Biography of Imam Ahmad bin Hanbal." *Musnad Imam Ahmad bin Hanbal*, translated by Nasiruddin Al-Khattab, vol. 1, Riyadh Darussalam Publishers, 2012.

Al-Tabarī, Abū Ja'far Muhammad. *The History of Tabarī*. Translated by W. Montgomery Watt and M. V. McDonald, vol. 6, SUNY Press, 1988.

———. *The History of Tabarī*. Translated by W. Montgomery Watt and M. V. McDonald, vol. 8, SUNY Press, 1988.

Ammitzbøll, Pernille, and Lorenzo Vidino. "After the Danish Cartoon Controversy." *The Middle East Quarterly*, vol. 14, no. 1, 2007, pp. 3–11.

Appiah, Anthony Kwame. *Cosmopolitanism*. W. W. Norton, 2006.

Archibugi, Daniele. *Debating Cosmopolitics*. Verso, 2003.

Ayub, Muhammad. "Qur'an, Hadith and Riba Connotation." *Journal of Islamic Business and Management*, vol. 2, no. 2, 2012, pp. 1–40.

Bakhtin, Mikhail. "Epic and Novel: Toward a Methodology for the Study of the Novel." *The Dialogic Imagination: Four Essays*, translated by Caryl Emerson and Michael Holquist, U of Texas P, 1981.

Barthes, Roland. *Mythologies*. Translated by Annette Lavers, Noonday Press, 1972.

Bauman, Zygmunt. *Globalization: The Human Consequences*. Columbia UP, 1998.

Bhabha, Homi. *The Location of Culture*. Routledge, 1994.

Bhatti, Haseeb. "Mumtaz Qadri Lawyer Hails Charlie Hebdo Attackers as 'Heroes.'" *The Dawn Daily*, 4 Feb. 2015.

Bone, James. "Salman Rushdie Attacks 'Censorship by Fear' over The Jewel of Medina." *The Times Online* (UK), 16 Aug. 2008, entertainment.timesonline.co.uk/tol/arts_and_entertainment/books/article4543243.ece.

Bracher, Mark. "Educating for Cosmopolitanism: Lessons from Cognitive Science." *Critical Pedagogy and Global Literature: Worldly Teaching*, edited by Masood Ashraf Raja, Hillary Stringer, and Zach VandeZande, Palgrave-Macmillan, 2013, pp. 25–46.

———. *Radical Pedagogy*. Palgrave, 2006.

Bukhari, Abu Abdullah Muhammad ibn Isma'īl. *Bukhari Sharīf*. Translated from Arabic to Urdu by Muhammad Abdullah, vol. 1, Lahore: Idāra-e-Islamiat, 2003.

Campanini, Masemo. "Alghazzālī." *History of Islamic Philosophy*, edited by Seyyed Hossein Nasr and Oliver Leaman, Routledge, 1996.

Carter, Jimmy. "Rushdie's Book Is an Insult." *The Rushdie File*, edited by Lisa Appignanesi and Sara Maitland, Syracuse UP, 1990, pp. 236–38.

Cowan, J. M., ed. *Arabic English Dictionary*. Spoken Language Services Inc., 1976.

Culler, Jonathan. *The Pursuit of Signs*. Cornell UP, 1981.

Dar, B. A. "Introduction." *Mathnavi pes che bayad kard au aqwame mashriq* (What should be done to the people of the East), 26 June 2022, http://www.allamai-qbal.com/works/poetry/persian/pas/translation/index.html.

Durrani, F. K. Khan. "Iqbal's Doctrine of the Self." *Aspects of Iqbal: Iqbal Day Lectures*, Qaumi Kutub Khana, 1938, pp. 1–40.

Eagleton, Terry. *After Theory*. Basic Books, 2003.

———. *Literary Theory: An Introduction*. Anniversary ed., U of Minnesota P, 2008.

Farah, Caesar E. *Islam*. Barron's Educational Series, 1970.

Fanon, Frantz. *Black Skin, White Masks*. Translated by Charles Markmann, Grove Press, 1967.

Fish, Stanley. "Interpreting the Variorum." *Reader Response Criticism*, edited by Jane P. Tompkins, Johns Hopkins UP, 1980, pp. 164–84.

Foucault, Michel. "The Confession of the Flesh." 1977. *Power/Knowledge Selected*

Interviews and Other Writings, edited by Colin Gordon, Vintage, 1980, pp. 194–228.

———. *History of Sexuality: Volume 1*. Translated by Robert Hurley, Vintage, 1990.

Fraser, Nancy. *Justice Interruptus*. London/New York: Routledge, 2014.

Freire, Paulo. *Pedagogy of the Oppressed*. Translated by Myra Bergman Ramos, Continuum, 2004.

Friedman, Thomas L. *The World Is Flat*. Picador, 2007.

Geertz, Clifford. "Primordial and Civic Ties." *Nationalism*, edited by John Hutchinson and Anthony D. Smith, Oxford UP, 1994, pp. 29–33.

Habermas, Jurgen. "Modernity Versus Postmodernity." *New German Critique*, vol. 22, 1981.

Hardt, Michael, and Antonio Negri. *Empire*. Harvard UP, 2001.

Haslam, Nick. "Dehumanization: An Integrative Review." *Personality and Social Psychology Review*, vol. 10, 2006, pp. 252–64.

Hume, David. *An Enquiry Concerning Human Understanding*. 1748. Hackett Publishing, 1977.

Hunter, W. W. *The Indian Musalmans*. 1871. 3rd ed., Comrade Publishers, 1945.

Hutcheon, Linda. *A Poetics of Postmodernism*. Routledge, 1998.

Iqbal, Muhammad. *Armughan-e-Hijaz*. 1936. Mahmud Siddiqullah Publishers, 1972.

———. *Baal-e-Jibreel*. 1935. Mahmud Siddiqullah Publishers, 1972.

———. *Javid Nama*. 1932. Translated by Shaikh Mahmud Ahmad, Institute of Islamic Culture, 1961.

———. *The Reconstruction of Religious Thought in Islam*. 1930. Sang-e-Meel, 1996.

———. *Zarb-e-Kaleem*. 1936. Mahmud Siddiqullah Publishers, 1972.

"Irrationalism." *Encyclopedia of Philosophy*, 31 May 2022, www.encyclopedia.com/article-1G2-3446800954/irrationalism.html

Iser, Wolfgang. *The Fictive and the Imaginative*. Johns Hopkins UP, 1993.

Jalabi, Raya. "A History of Bill Maher's 'Not Bigoted' Remarks on Islam." *The Guardian*, 7 Oct. 2014.

Jan, Orya Maqbool. "Andaleeb-e-Baghe-Hijaz." *Dunya Daily*, 9 Nov. 2013.

Jauss, Hans Robert. *Toward an Aesthetic of Reception*. Translated by Timothy Bahti, U of Minnesota P, 1982.

Jussawalla, Feroza. "Rushdie's 'Dastan-e-Dilruba': *The Satanic Verses* as Rushdie's Love Letter to Islam." *Diacritics*, vol. 26, no. 1, 1996, pp. 50–73.

Jones, Sherry. *The Jewel of Medina*. Beaufort Books, 2008.

Khaldun, Ibn. *The Muqaddimah*. 3rd vol., translated by Franz Rosenthal, Princeton UP, 1958.

Lings, Martin. *Muhammad: His Life Based on the Earliest Sources.* Islamic Texts Society, 1983.

Martin, Richard C. *Defenders of Reason in Islam: Mu'tazililism from Medieval School to Modern Symbol.* OneWorld Publications, 1997

Mawdudi, Abu'l-A'la. *Islami Riasat.* 19th ed., Islamic Publications, 1998.

———. *Tanqihat: Islam aur Maghrabi tehzeeb ka Tasadum aur us se Paida Shudah Masaail.* Maktaba Jam'at-i-Islami, 1939.

Mazhar, Arafat. "The Untold Story of Pakistan's Blasphemy Law." *Dawn*, 15 Jan. 2015.

Mazrui, Ali A. "Satanic Verses or a Satanic Novel: Moral Dilemmas of the Rushdie Affair." *Third World Quarterly*, vol. 12, no. 1, 1990, pp. 116–39.

Mbembe, Achille. *On the Postcolony.* U of California P, 2001.

Mernissi, Fatima. *Women and Islam.* 1987. Translated by Mary Jo Lakeland, Blackwell, 1991.

Metcalf, Barbara. *Islamic Revival in British India.* Princeton UP, 1982.

Miall, David S. *Literary Readings: Empirical and Theoretical Studies.* Peter Lang, 2006.

Mignolo, Walter. *The Darker Side of Western Modernity: Global Futures, Decolonial Options.* Duke UP, 2011.

Minault, Gail. "Sayyid Mumtaz Ali and 'Huquq un-Niswan': An Advocate of Women's Rights in Islam in the Late Nineteenth Century." *Modern Asian Studies*, vol. 24, no. 1, 1990, pp. 147–72.

Momen, Moojan. *An Introduction to Shi'i Islam: The History and Doctrines of Twelver Shi'ism.* Yale UP, 1987.

Mufti, Amir. "Reading the Rushdie Affair: An Essay on Islam and Politics." *Social Text*, no. 29, 1991, pp. 95–116.

Nasr, Seyyed Hossein. "The Meaning and Concept of Philosophy in Islam." 1996. *History of Islamic Philosophy*, edited by Oliver Leaman and Seyyed Hossein Nasr, Routledge, 2003, pp. 21–26.

———. "The Qur'ān and Hadīth as Source and Inspiration of Islamic Philosophy." *History of Islamic Philosophy*, Routledge, 1996, pp. 27–39.

Nawas, John A. "A Reexamination of Three Current Explanations for al-Ma'mun's Introduction of the Mihna." *International Journal of Middle East Studies*, vol. 26, no. 4, 1994, pp. 615–29.

Ngugi wa Thiong'o. "Creating a Space for a Hundred Flowers to Bloom." *The Bedford Anthology of World Literature*, edited by Paul Davis et al., vol. 6, Bedford/St. Martin's, 2003.

———. *Decolonizing the Mind.* Heinemann, 1986.

Palmer, Michael A. *The Last Crusade: Americanism and the Islamic Reformation*. Potomac Books, 2007.

Pavlin, James. "Sunni Kalām and Theological Controversies." *History of Islamic Philosophy*, edited by Oliver Leaman and Seyyed Hossein Nasr, Routledge, 2003, pp. 105-18.

Pipes, Daniel. *The Rushdie Affair: The Novel, the Ayatollah, and the West*. Carol Publishing Group, 1990.

Pollock, Sheldon. "Cosmopolitanisms." *Cosmopolitanism*, edited by Carol Breckenridge et al., Duke UP, 2002, pp. 1-14.

Qureshi, Muhammad Ismail. *Muhammad: The Messenger of God and the Law of Blasphemy in Islam and the West*. Nuqoosh Publishers, 2008.

Rabinowitz, Peter. *Before Reading*. Ohio UP, 1987.

Raja, Masood Asraf. "Allama Muhammad Iqbal: Poet Philosopher and the Dangers of Appropriation." *Decolonizing the Body of Christ: Theology and Theory after Empire*, edited by Joseph Duggan and David Joy, Palgrave, 2012, pp. 107-26.

———. *Constructing Pakistan*. Oxford UP, 2010.

———. "Death as a Form of Becoming: The Muslim Imagery of Death and Necropolitics." *igest of Middle East Studies*, vol. 14, no. 2, 2005, pp. 8-26.

———. "Democratic Criticism and the Importance of Islamic Hermeneutics of Reading in the Twenty-First Century." *South Asia: Journal of South Asian Studies*, vol. 36, no. 3, 2013, pp. 449-64.

———. "Jihad in Islam: Colonial Encounter, the Neoliberal Order, and the Muslim Subject of Resistance." *The American Journal of Islamic Social Sciences*, vol. 26, no. 4, 2009, pp. 47-71.

———. "The King Buzzard: Bano Qudsia's Postnational Allegory and the Nation-State." *Mosaic: A Journal for the Interdisciplinary Study of Literature*, vol. 40, no. 1, 2007, pp. 95-110.

———. "Neoliberal Dispositif and the Rise of Fundamentalism: The Case of Pakistan." *Journal of International and Global Studies*, vol. 3, no. 1, 2011, pp. 21-31.

———. "Pakistani English Novel and the Burden of Representation: Mohsin Hamid's How to Get Filthy Rich in Rising Asia." *The Ravi*, vol. 150, 2014, pp. 81-89.

———. "Textual Acts of Translation: Kitab At-Tawhid and the Politics of Muslim Identity in British India." *Decentering Translation Studies: India and Beyond*, edited by Judy Wakabayashi and Rita Kothari, John Benjamins, 2009, pp. 95-106.

Rahman, Fazlur. *Islam and Modernity: Transformation of an Intellectual Tradition*. U of Chicago P, 1982.

Rapley, John. *Globalization and Inequality: Neoliberalism's Downward Spiral*. Lynne Rienner, 2004.

Rashid, Ahmed. *Taliban*. Yale UP, 1989.

Rehman, I. A. "The Blasphemy Law." *Dawn*, 25 Nov. 2010, www.dawn.com/news/585332/theblasphemy-law-by-i-a-rehman.

Residency of Islamic Researchers, IFTA, Call and Guidance, eds. *Alqur'ān Alkarīm: English Translation of the Meanings and Commentary*. Ministry of Hajj and Endowments, 1993.

Ricoeur, Paul. *Interpretation Theory: Discourse and the Surplus of Meaning*. Texas Christian UP, 1976.

Robbins, Bruce and Pheng Chea, and, eds. *Cosmopolitics: Thinking and Feeling Beyond the Nation*. U of Minnesota P, 1998.

Robbins, Bruce. *Feeling Global: Internationalism in Distress*. New York UP, 1999.

Rorty, Richard. "Justice as a Larger Loyalty." *Cosmopolitcs: Thinking and Feeling Beyond the Nation*, edited by Pheng Chea and Bruce Robbins, U of Minnesota P, 1998.

Rosenblatt, Louise M. *Literature as Exploration*. 1933. Modern Language Association, 1995.

Rumi, Jalaluddin. *The Mathnawi*. Translated by Reynold A. Nicolson, vol. 2, Konya Metropolitan Municipality.

Rushdie, Salman. "In Good Faith." *Imaginary Homelands*, Granta, 1991, pp. 393–414.

———. *The Satanic Verses*. Viking, 1988.

Said, Edward W. *Culture and Imperialism*. Vintage, 1993.

———. "Edward Said." *The Rushdie File*, edited by Lisa Appignanesi and Sara Maitland, Syracuse UP, 1990, 164–66.

———. *Humanism and Democratic Criticism*. Palgrave, 2004.

———. *Orientalism*. Vintage, 1978.

———. *The World, The Text, and the Critic*. Harvard UP, 1983.

Sardar, Ziauddin, and Merryl Wyn Davies. *Distorted Imagination: Lessons from the Rushdie Affair*. Grey Seal Books, 1990.

Sassen, Saskia. *A Sociology of Globalization*. Columbia UP, 2007.

Saussure, Ferdinand de. *Course in General Linguistics*. 1972. Translated by Roy Harris, Open Court, 1986.

Shannon, Vaughn P. "Why Who Hates Us?" *Harvard International Review*, 2 May 2007.

Siddiqui, Sabrin. "Americans' Attitudes toward Muslims and Arabs Are Getting Worse, Poll Finds." *The Huffington Post*, 29 July 2014, www.huffingtonpost.com/2014/07/29/arab-muslim-poll_n_5628919.html.

Slatoff, Walter J. *With Respect to Readers*. Cornell UP, 1970.

Spellberg, Denise A. "1 Didn't Kill 'The Jewel of Medina.'" *The Wall Street Journal*, 9 Aug. 2008, online.wsj.com/articles/SB121824366910026293.

Spivak, Gayatri C. "Can the Subaltern Speak?" *Colonial Discourse and Postcolonial Theory*, edited by Patrick Williams and Laura Chrishman, Columbia UP, 1994, pp. 66–111.

———. *Outside in the Teaching Machine*. Routledge, 1993.

———. "Translator's Preface." *Of Grammatology* by Jacques Derrida, Johns Hopkins P, 1974.

Submission. Directed by Theo van Gogh, 2004.

Tan, Kok-Chor. *Justice without Borders: Cosmopolitanism, Nationalism and Patriotism*. U of Cambridge P, 2004.

www.ingramcontent.com/pod-product-compliance
Lightning Source LLC
Chambersburg PA
CBHW070028100426
42740CB00013B/2625